THEOLOGY TODAY

VOLUME ONE:
Theologians of Our Time

VOLUME TWO:
Modern Theologians, Christians and Jews

MODERN THEOLOGIAN,

EDITOR

THOMAS E. BIRD

INTRODUCTION TO THE WORKS OF

MARTIN BUBER

JOHN COURTNEY MURRAY

JOSEF HROMADKA

CHRISTIANS AND JEWS

BERNARD HÄRING

EDWARD SCHILLEBEECKX

JOHN A. T. ROBINSON

BERNARD LONERGAN

JOHN HARWOOD HICK

ABRAHAM JOSHUA HESCHEL

HENRI DE LUBAC

THE UNIVERSITY OF NOTRE DAME PRESS

NOTRE DAME — LONDON

ASSOCIATION PRESS

NEW YORK

Foreword

The guiding principles in selecting the theologians discussed in
this volume have been two. The first is to remedy the obvious
omissions of some major contemporary thinkers from volume
one; and beyond that to consider several figures who are, in
Tillich's phrase, "on the boundary" of the new insights which
will be constitutive of the theology of tomorrow.

There are many kinds of theologians. The rich variety which
characterizes present-day thinking in this discipline has been
recognized in the structure of this second volume. This has
led us to supply some approximate *differentiae*.

Five categories have been suggested in the table of contents
with no implication thereby that the rubric into which a man
has been fitted exhausts his interests or competence. Buber, for
example, who has been dubbed *pro hac vice* a theologian of
dialogue, has done as much as any living theologian to call
renewed attention to the values and validity of mysticism.

Today a systematic theologian who is not simultaneously a

moral theologian is a rare animal. The demands of the modern world make it difficult to be a speculative theologian without drawing upon one's resources as a practical theologian. The practical theologian, on the other hand, may be doomed to failure if his skill does not include a mastery of theory. The man who tries in practical fashion to implement theological change without carefully considering his theoretical presuppositions begins in shallowness and will end in emptiness.

This collection of twelve studies was undertaken to provide an introduction to some of the significant religious thinkers of our time. It is not meant to substitute in any way for careful study of their works. An essay of some six thousand words can only sketch a few of the main features of each author's writing. It has been suggested that a man's ability to integrate his peripheral interests into his central insights determines his creative greatness. In order to observe this *geistliche* brooding upon the surface of diverse intellectual waters, it is necessary to consider a given writer through the tides of his productive life.

The inclusion of certain of the men in this volume suggests that serious attention should be paid to those who are making fresh chartings of the theological seas. Hopefully some of the adventure of reading these pages will lie in the discovery of such possibilities. There remain several obvious lacunae which demand attention if an essay is to be made at representing the chiaroscuro of today's theological spectrum. A subsequent volume will have to deal with such titans as Teilhard de Chardin, Dietrich Bonhoeffer, and Leo Shestov, all of immense influence today. Conspicuous by their absence are such provocative American scholars as Joseph Fletcher and James Gustafson.

Since we are exploring new waters, it is time to investigate the rest of the religiously committed world. The growing recognition of Eastern religions as entities with which the churches can and should enter into dialogue demands the consideration of major Hindu, Buddhist, and Zen representatives at a later date. After all, in the words of the Fathers of Vatican Council II, "Men look to the various religions for answers to those profound mysteries of the human condition which, today even as in olden times, deeply stir the human heart: What is a man? What is the meaning and purpose of our life?"

In addition the time is fully come for the Church to discern the challenge of irreligious movements which her own failures, inconsistencies, and misdirection have spawned. What is envisaged, then, is the widest kind of dialogue with no sense of compulsion. The failure to present ourselves for such dialogue is not merely regrettable, it is gravely sinful. Such failure of dialogic courage will not be excused by those who follow us. As serious as the failure of dialogue could be in a world bruised by racial strife, desensitized by mass killings, and huddled under a nuclear cloud, a superficial pragmatism must not be allowed to dissolve the concrete manifestations of theological, religious, and cultural diversity which give the world of man the fullness of its humanity.

Thomas E. Bird

New York
January 1967

Contents

v   FOREWORD

xi   THE CONTRIBUTORS

Theologians of Dialogue

1   MARTIN BUBER   *by Lowell D. Streiker*
18   JOHN COURTNEY MURRAY   *by Thomas T. Love*
40   JOSEF HROMADKA   *by Charles C. West*

Theologians of the Life of the Church

64   BERNARD HÄRING   *by Stanley O. Weselowsky*
84   EDWARD SCHILLEBEECKX   *by Marinus J. Houdijk*
108 JOHN A. T. ROBINSON   *by Lowell D. Streiker*

Theologians of Intellectual Renewal

126 BERNARD LONERGAN   *by Frederick E. Crowe*
152 JOHN HICK   *by Lowell D. Streiker*

Theologians of Mystical Experience

169 ABRAHAM JOSHUA HESCHEL   *by Fritz A. Rothschild*
183 HENRI DE LUBAC   *by William C. Russell*

201 BIBLIOGRAPHY

ix

Contributors

THOMAS E. BIRD (Editor)

    Member of the faculty of Queens College of the City University of New York.

    Author of *Patriarch Maximos IV* (1964).

    Editor of the Orthodox-Roman Catholic ecumenical quarterly, *Diakonia*.

FREDERICK E. CROWE, S.J.

    Member of the faculty of Regis College, Willowdale, Ontario, Canada.

    Editor of *Spirit as Inquiry: Studies in Honor of Bernard Lonergan* (1964).

MARINUS J. HOUDIJK

    Member of the faculty of Leeuwenhorst Seminary, Noordwijkerhout, The Netherlands.

    Priest of the Diocese of Rotterdam.

THOMAS T. LOVE

Member of the faculty of Cornell College.
Author of *John Courtney Murray: Contemporary Church-State Theory* (1965).

FRITZ A. ROTHSCHILD

Member of the faculty of the Jewish Theological Seminary of America.
Co-Author of *The Goals of Jewish Education*.
Editor of *Between God and Man: An Interpretation of Judaism* (1959).

WILLIAM C. RUSSELL, S.J.

Doctoral candidate in the Department of Romance Languages and Literatures at Harvard University.

LOWELL D. STREIKER

Member of the faculty of Temple University.
American Secretary of the Paul Tillich Society.

STANLEY O. WESELOWSKY

Doctoral candidate in the Department of Religion at Princeton University.

CHARLES C. WEST

Member of the faculty of Princeton Theological Seminary.
Author of *Communism and the Theologians* (1958), and *Outside the Camp: The Christian and the World* (1959).
Editor (with Robert C. Mackie) of *The Sufficiency of God: Essays on the Ecumenical Hope in Honour of W. A. Visser 't Hooft* (1963).

MARTIN BUBER

BY

Lowell D. Streiker

The most influential religious thinker of the twentieth century
has been Martin Buber. This distinguished representative of
Judaism gave classical form to the primary human relationships
I-Thou and *I-It*. There is scarcely a single contemporary theological writer who has not been enriched by Buber. As a leading commentator on Buber notes

> Largely through the influence of Buber on such key Prot-
> estant theologians as Emil Brunner, Karl Barth, Reinhold
> Niebuhr, H. Richard Niebuhr, Paul Tillich, John Macmur-
> ray, John Baillie, Herbert H. Farmer, Friedrich Gogarten,
> Karl Heim, and J. H. Oldham, the "I-Thou" philosophy has
> become, in Paul Tillich's words, "a common good of the
> Protestant world." It has also penetrated deeply into the
> thought of such Catholic thinkers as Erich Przywara, Ernst
> Michel, Romano Guardini, Theodore Steinbüchel, and M.
> C. D'Arcy, as well as Ebner and Marcel, and into that
> of the Russian Orthodox existentialist, Nicholas Berdyaev.

Born in Vienna in 1878, Martin Buber lived with his grandfather in Lemberg, Galicia, in an atmosphere of religious and scholary "enlightenment" until his fourteenth birthday. At this time Buber came into contact with Hasidism, a profound part of his development. He studied philosophy and the history of art at the universities of Vienna and Berlin, during which time he began his career as a spokesman for cultural Zionism. At the age of 38 Buber founded *Der Jude*, which soon became the leading periodical of German-speaking Jewry. He spent the ten years following 1923 teaching philosophy of religion and history of religions at the University of Frankfurt; in 1938 he left Germany to establish permanent residence in Palestine. He was professor of social philosophy at Hebrew University in Jerusalem, where he lived in retirement during the final years of his life.

Buber traveled frequently. He visited the United States three times between 1951 and 1958—from 1951 to 1952 as guest of the Jewish Theological Seminary, in 1957 as William Alanson White Memorial lecturer at the Washington School of Psychiatry, and in 1958 as a fellow at Princeton. In 1951 he was awarded the Goethe Prize of the University of Hamburg and in 1953 he received the Peace Prize of the German Book Trade.

In his late twenties Buber withdrew from Zionist activities and devoted himself to an intensive study of Hasidic materials. Hasidism (derived from the Hebrew word *hasid,* which means holy or pious person), a rather unusual form of Judaism, arose in the eighteenth century in the isolated Jewish communities of Poland. Hasidism lay stress on warm, exuberant manifestations of personal piety (*hasidut*). It was his contemplation of Hasidic texts that led him to believe the essence of Judaism was contained in the quest for inner renewal and religious ecstasy.

In a key passage, Buber tells of his "conversion" from the quest for religious enthusiasm:

> In my earlier years the "religious" was for me the exception. There were hours that were taken out of the course of things. From somewhere or other the firm crust of everyday was pierced. Then the reliable permanence of appearances

2

broke down; the attack which took place burst its law asunder. "Religious experience" was the experience of an otherness which did not fit into the context of life. It could begin with something customary, with consideration of some familiar object, but which then became unexpectedly mysterious and uncanny, finally lighting a way into the lightning-pierced darkness of the mystery itself. But also, without any intermediate stage, time could be torn apart—first the firm world's structure then the still firmer self-assurance flew apart and you were delivered to fulness. The "religious" lifted out of you. Over there now lay the accustomed existence with its affairs, but here illumination and ecstasy and rapture held without time or sequence. Thus your own being encompassed a life here and a life beyond, and there was no bond but the actual moment of the transition.

The illegitimacy of such a division of the temporal life, which is streaming to death and eternity and which only in fulfilling its temporality can be fulfilled in face of these, was brought home to me by an everyday event, an event of judgment, judging with that sentence from closed lips and an unmoved glance such as the ongoing course of things loves to pronounce.

What happened was no more than that one forenoon, after a morning of "religious" enthusiasm, I had a visit from an unknown young man, without being there in spirit. I certainly did not fail to let the meeting be friendly, I did not treat him any more remissly than all his contemporaries who were in the habit of seeking me out about this time of day as an oracle that is ready to listen to reason. I conversed attentively and openly with him—only I omitted to guess the questions which he did not put. Later, not long after, I learned from one of his friends—he himself was no longer alive—the essential content of these questions; I learned that he had come to me not casually, but borne by destiny, not for a chat but for a decision. He had come to me, he had come in this hour. What do we expect when we are in despair and yet go to a man? Surely a presence by means of which we are told that nevertheless there is meaning.

Since then I have given up the "religious" which is nothing but the exception, extraction, exaltation, ecstasy; or it has given me up. I possess nothing but the everyday out of which I am never taken. The mystery is no longer disclosed, it has escaped or it has made its dwelling here where everything happens as it happens. I know no fulness but each mortal hour's fulness of claim and responsibility. Though far from being equal to it, yet I know that in the claim I am claimed and may respond in responsibility, and know who speaks and demands a response.

I do not know much more. If that is religion then it is just *everything,* simply all that is lived in its possibility of dialogue. Here is space also for religion's highest forms. As when you pray you do not thereby remove yourself from this life of yours but in your praying refer your thought to it, even though it may be in order to yield it; so too in the unprecedented and surprising, when you are called upon from above, required, chosen, empowered, sent, you with this your mortal bit of life are referred to, this moment is not extracted from it, it rests on what has been and beckons to the remainder which has still to be lived, you are not swallowed up in a fulness without obligation, you are willed for the life of communion.

Religion becomes a life of dialogue. Men are capable of two basic attitudes or "primary words," "I-Thou" and "I-It." The primary word *I-Thou* designates a relation of reciprocity and mutuality of subject to subject, person to person. Such a meeting or encounter involves one's whole being. The primary word *I-It* designates the relation of subject to object, individual to thing, involving some form of utilization, domination or control.

The life of human beings is not passed in the sphere of transitive verbs alone. It does not exist in virtue of activities alone which have some *thing* for their object.

I perceive something. I am sensible of something. I imagine something. I will something. I feel something. I think something. The life of human beings does not consist of all this and the like alone.

This and the like together establish the realm of *It.*

But the realm of *Thou* has a different basis.

When *Thou* is spoken, the speaker has no thing for his object. For where there is a thing there is another thing. Every *It* is bounded by others; *It* exists only through being bounded by others. But when *Thou* is spoken, there is no thing. *Thou* has no bounds.

When *Thou* is spoken, the speaker has no *thing;* he has indeed nothing. But he takes his stand in relation.

It is through the *I-Thou* relationship that authentic personality emerges.

Through the *Thou* a man becomes *I.* That which confronts him comes and disappears, relational events condense, then are scattered, and in the change consciousness of the unchanging partner, of the *I,* grows clear, and each time stronger. To be sure, it is still seen caught in the web of the relation with the *Thou,* as the increasingly distinguishable feature of that which reaches out to and yet is not the *Thou.* But it continually breaks through with more power, till a time comes when it bursts its bonds, and the *I* confronts itself for a moment, separated as though it were a *Thou;* as quickly to take possession of itself and from then on to enter into relations in consciousness of itself.

The relation to the *Thou* is direct and unmediated. "No system of ideas, no foreknowledge, and no fancy intervene between *I* and *Thou.*" "What, then," asks Buber, "do we experience of *Thou?*" Since the *Thou* is not an object, "we do not experience it." Rather we are met by the *Thou.* "The *Thou* meets me through grace—it is not found by seeking."

In *Between Man and Man,* Buber presents many concrete illustrations of such "dialogical" relations. The relationship of teacher and student is a particularly clear example. "In order to help the realization of the best potentialities in the pupil's life, the teacher must really *mean* him as the definite person he is in his potentiality and his actuality; more precisely, he must not know him as a mere sum of qualities, strivings, and inhibitions; he must be aware of him as a whole being and affirm him again and again as his partner in a bipolar situation." The true teacher is as much educated by his students as they are by him.

It is "the exalted melancholy of our fate that every Thou in our world must become an It."

It does not matter how exclusively present the *Thou* was

in the direct relation. As soon as the relation has been worked out or has been permeated with a means, the *Thou* becomes as object among objects—perhaps the chief, but still one of them, fixed in its size and its limits. . . . The human being who was even now single and unconditioned, not something lying to hand, only present, not able to be experienced, only able to be fulfilled, has now become again a *He* or a *She,* a sum of qualities, a given quantity with a certain shape. Now I may take out from him again the colour of his hair or of his speech or of his goodness. But so long as I can do this he has no more my *Thou* and cannot yet be my *Thou* again.

Every *Thou* in the world is by its nature fated to become a thing, or continually to re-enter into the condition of things. . . .

The *It* is the eternal chrysalis, the *Thou* the eternal butterfly—except that situations do not always follow one another in clear succession, but often there is a happening profoundly twofold, confusedly entangled.

Thus dialogue gives way to monologue. The life of monologue is not due to a turning away from the *Thou* but to reflection. Buber illustrates this with a lovely anecdote drawn from his youth.

When I was eleven years of age, spending the summer on my grandparents' estate, I used, as often as I could do it unobserved, to steal into the stable and gently stroke the neck of my darling, a broad dapple-grey horse. It was not a casual delight but a great, certainly friendly, but also deeply stirring happening. If I am to explain it now, beginning from the still very fresh memory of my hand, I must say that what I experienced in touch with the animal was the Other, the immense otherness of the Other, which, however, did not remain strange like the otherness of the ox and the ram, but rather let me draw near and touch it. When I stroked the mighty mane, sometimes marvellously smooth-combed, at other times just as astonishingly wild, and felt the life beneath my hand, it was as though the element of vitality itself bordered on my skin, something that was not I, was certainly not akin to me, palpably the other, not just another, really the Other itself; and yet it let me approach, confided itself to me, placed itself elementally in the relation of *Thou* and

Thou with me. The horse, even when I had not begun by pouring oats for him into the manger, very gently raised his massive head, ears flicking, then snorted quietly, as a conspirator gives a signal meant to be recognizable only by his fellow-conspirator; and I was approved. But once—I do not know what came over the child, at any rate it was childlike enough—it struck me about the stroking, what fun it gave me, and suddenly I became conscious of my hand. The game went on as before, but something had changed, it was no longer the same thing. And, the next day, after giving him a rich feed, when I stroked my friend's head he did not raise his head. A few years later, when I thought back to the incident, I no longer supposed that the animal had noticed my defection. But at the same time I considered myself judged.

Further, "there are some I-Thou relationships which in their nature may not unfold to full mutuality if they are to persist in that nature." In the teacher-student relationship which we have examined, the teacher must practice what Buber terms "inclusion" (*Umfassung*), living his situation "in all its moments not merely from his own end but also from that of his partner." However, "the special educative relation could not persist if the pupil for his part practiced 'inclusion,' that is, if he lived the teacher's part in the common situation." The I-Thou relationship may assume a new character as a friendship, but "it is plain that the specifically educative relation as such is denied full mutuality."

There is one relationship that can never degenerate in this manner. There is one Thou that by its very nature remains Thou to us and cannot become an It. This is the Eternal Thou, God. God is always present to us in every relationship.

In every sphere in its own way, through each process of becoming that is present to us we look out toward the fringe of the eternal *Thou;* in each we are aware of a breath from the eternal *Thou;* in each *Thou* we address the eternal *Thou*.

In the meeting of person with person, there is a possible self-realization and satisfaction which other experiences lack. In such relationships, e.g., marriage and friendship, there is not

7

only a union of two individuals but also a relationship that absorbs the potentialities of both so that each partner transcends the limits of individual realization. As two persons come to know each other intimately, to react to each other, and to find in each other the opportunity for creative love, something more than a union of their separate natures is discovered. The same is true of any real human relationship, wherever life touches life deeply in all the complex relationships of society. In all these relationships there is available a potential dimension revealing higher levels of mutual self-realization and satisfaction. This is the eternal *Thou*.

In the signs of life which happens to us we are addressed. Who speaks?

It would not avail us to give for reply the word "God" if we do not give it out of that decisive hour of personal existence when we had to forget everything we imagined we knew of God, when we dared to keep nothing handed down or learned or self-contrived, no shred of knowledge, and were plunged into the night.

When we rise out of it into the new life and there begin to receive the signs, what can we know of that which—of him who gives them to us? Only what we experience from time to time from the signs themselves. If we name the speaker of this speech God, then it is always the God of a moment, a moment God.

I will now use a *gauche* comparison, since I know no right one.

When we really understand a poem, all we know of the poet is what we learn of him in the poem—no biographical wisdom is of value for the pure understanding of what is to be understood: the *I* which approaches us is the subject of this single poem. But when we read other poems by the poet in the same true way their subjects combine in all their multiplicity, completing and confirming one another, to form the one polyphony of the person's existence.

In such a way, out of the givers of the signs, the speakers of the words in lived life, out of the moment Gods there arises for us with a single identity the Lord of the voice, the One.

The relationships of the *I* with a finite, human *Thou* and of the *I* with the eternal *Thou* are so inextricably woven that ". . . when he . . . , who abhors the name [of God], and believes himself to be godless, gives his whole being to addressing the *Thou* of his life, as a *Thou* that cannot be limited by another, he addresses God."

"Above the below," Buber insists, "are bound to one another."

> The word of him who wishes to speak with men without speaking with God is not fulfilled; but the word of him who wishes to speak with God without speaking with men goes astray.
>
> There is a tale that a man inspired by God once went out from the creaturely realms into the vast waste. There he wandered till he came to the gates of the mystery. He knocked. From within came the cry: "What do you want here?" He said, "I have proclaimed your praise in the ears of mortals, but they were deaf to me. So I come to you that you yourself may hear me and reply." "Turn back," came the cry from within. "Here is no ear for you. I have sunk my hearing in the deafness of mortals."
>
> True address from God directs man into the place of lived speech, where the voices of the creatures grope past one another, and in their very missing of one another succeed in reaching the eternal partner.

For Buber, much of what is called religion is a subjectivism that exists in alienation from nature and society. Buber agrees with Sören Kierkegaard, the father of modern religious existentialism, that in encounters between man and man, the I-Thou relation is exclusive; but he strenuously denies that this is the case between man and God. For Kierkegaard, faithfulness to God led to the destruction of normal relations—marriage, vocation, politics, etc., thus "the central event of Kierkegaard's life and the core of the crystallization of his thought was the renunciation of Regina Olsen as representing woman and the world." In order to love God, Kierkegaard felt it necessary to renounce all earthly loves. "That," comments Buber, "is sublimely to misunderstand God." Buber insists that one's relationship with God is inclusive of all other relationships. The reader of a poem is unable to meet the whole of the poet in a given poem but must gradually draw a picture of his general personality from several poems. Likewise, while we do not meet God entirely in any given encounter, the Eternal Thou is present to us in each I-Thou meeting. Buber rejects the kind of religion that takes our attention away from the ordinary. One is as likely to meet God at the workbench as at the altar.

Community is essential. "Man's being is contained only in community, in the unity of man with man." It is in community that God is known and realized. For true community is the *locus* of divine activity in the world. The presence of the eternal Thou as a dimension of human potentiality revealing higher levels of mutual self-realization demands an exemplary community for the development of personal relationships of depth. The whole purpose of a religious community is to provide the conceptual material for the construction of truly human experience. The responsibility of a religious society is to discover where *I-Thou* relationships have become shallow or have disappeared altogether.

This description is given not as a tangential addition. No significant aspect of human life can be understood without reference to man's communal or social situation. Man's religious nature is no exception. "The act of faith," says Tillich, "is dependent on language and therefore on community." Religion can have no definite content without a social demension. Although the paradigms of the *I-Thou* are such relationships as marriage and friendship, Buber's concern is for the meaning of religion in all interpersonal relations. He begins with the basic, most intimate of such relationships as our starting point in order to explore the relevancy of what is available in such cases for larger groups: family, system, nation, etc.

In any community it is not the *I-It* relationship that is evil but its predominance. All social structures may be directed by

10

either of the primary relationships. But only when the *I-Thou* guides these structures are they spiritually alive.

The communal life of man can no more than man himself dispense with the world of *It,* over which the presence of the *Thou* moves like the spirit upon the face of the waters. Man's will to profit and to be powerful have their natural and proper effect so long as they are linked with, and upheld by, his will to enter into relation. There is no evil impulse till the impulse has been separated from the being; the impulse which is bound up with, and defined by, the being is the living stuff of communal life, that which is detached is its disintegration. Economics, the abode of the will to profit, and State, the abode of the will to be powerful, share in life as long as they share in the spirit. If they abjure spirit they abjure life.

Only in and through these structures can man meet God. ". . . if you hallow this life you meet the living God."

In this way Buber develops the basic insight of Hasidism. There is no absolute distinction between sacred and profane, the holy and the unholy. Every event of life is a sacrament. "Profane" designates that which is not yet sanctified, the potentially sacred. Everything is waiting to be hallowed.

The Holy strives to include within itself the whole of life. The Law differentiates between the holy and the profane, but the Law desires to lead the way toward the Messianic removal of the differentiation, to the all-sanctification. Hasidic piety no longer recognizes anything as simply and irreparably profane: "the profane" is for Hasidism only a designation for the not yet sanctified, for that which is to be sanctified. Everything physical, all drives and urges and desires, everything creaturely, is material for sanctification. From the very same passionate powers which, undirected, give rise to evil, when they are turned toward God, the good arises. One does not serve God with the spirit only, but with the whole of his nature, without any subtractions. There is not one realm of the spirit and another of nature; there is only the growing realm of God. God is not spirit, but what we call spirit and what we call nature hail equally

11

from the God who is beyond and equally conditioned by both, and whose kingdom reaches its fulness in the complete unity of spirit and nature.

The establishment of such a community is the central demand and challenge of Judaism. "The yearning of Judaism for God is the yearning to prepare a resting place for him in genuine community. Judaism's understanding of Israel is the understanding that from that people genuine community is to spring. Its Messianic expectation is the expectation of genuine community fully realized."

It is Buber's keen awareness that he lives in a yet unredeemed world which evokes strong reaction to Christianity.

> The Jew *feels* unredeemedness physically and in his flesh. He carries the burden of an unredeemed world. He *cannot* concede that redemption is an accomplished fact, for he knows that it is not so. We know of no redeemer who has appeared at one point in history in order to inaugurate a new and redeemed history. Nothing which has already happened can give us rest; hence we are directed with all our being toward that which is yet to come.

The Church's knowledge of Israel and Israel's knowledge of itself differ almost radically.

> The Church sees Israel as an entity *rejected* by God. This rejection follows necessarily from the Church's claim to be the true Israel: the members of Israel, accordingly, have surrendered their claim because they did not recognize Jesus as the Messiah. Christians believe they have received from God this "being-Israel," this office, the honor of Israel, its election; here is an assurance, grounded in faith, which is unassailable. We have no possibility of opposing anything to this, the Church's knowledge about Israel; anything so put forward would have only argumentative effectiveness. But we, as Israel, know Israel from within, in the darkness of knowledge from within, in the light of knowledge from within. We know Israel differently, we know (at this point I can no longer even say "see," for we know it from within, not even with the "eye of the spirit," but only as we live it) that we who have sinned a thousandfold against God, who

12

have apostasized from God a thousandfold, who, throughout these centuries, have experienced God's providence over us —which it is too easy to call punishment; it is something greater than punishment—we know that we are, nevertheless, not rejected. We know that this is an event which does not take place within the limited perspective of this world, but in the reality of the space between God and us. We know that there, within that reality, we are not rejected by God, that in this discipline and punishment, God's hand holds us and does not let us go, holds us within this fire and does not let us fall.

The devisive question is: Has the Messiah come?

If we want to express in a simple formula the difference between Jews and Christians, between Israel and the Church, we can say: The Church is grounded upon the belief that Christ has already come, redemption has been granted to men through God. We, as Israel, are unable to accept this belief.

The Church views our position either as unwillingness to believe, a hardness of heart in a very dubious sense, or a constraint, a fundamental limitation of ability to perceive vis-à-vis reality, as the blinding of Israel which prevents it from seeing the light.

We, as Israel, understand our inability to accept this proclamation in another fashion. We understand the Christology of Christianity throughout as an important event which has taken place between the world above and the world below. We see Christianity as something the mystery of whose coming into the world we are unable to penetrate. But just as we know there is an air which we breathe into our lungs, we know also that there is a space in which we move; more deeply, more genuinely, we know that the history of the world has not yet been shattered to its very core, that the world is not yet redeemed. We feel the unredemption of the world.

The Church can or must understand this feeling as a conviction of *our* unredemption. But we understand it differently.

For us, the redemption of the world is dissolubly one with the perfecting of creation, with the establishment of a unity no longer limited in any respect, no longer suffering contradiction, realized in all the multiplicity of the world, one with the fulfilled kingdom of God. An anticipation of the completed redemption of the world to some partial extent, such as the redeemed state of the soul, we are unable to comprehend, no matter how redemption and the redemption process are proclaimed to us in our mortal hours.

We do not perceive any caesura in the course of history. We know of no mid-point in it, but only a goal, the goal of the way of God, who does not pause upon his way.

Buber allows for the possibility that God may have revealed himself in the person of Jesus of Nazareth.

We cannot define God under any aspect of his revelation. That statement from the burning bush: "I shall be present as he, as whom I shall be present" (*i.e.,* as whom I shall be present at any given time), makes it impossible for us to take anything unique as the ultimate revelation of God. Not as though we could say anything of God's ability to reveal himself or not, as he may choose; I say only that we are unable to draw any absolute conclusions from all the revelations which we know. We do not say that God cannot reveal himself in this manner. We only say that we cannot ascribe finality to any one of his revelations, nor to any one the character of the Incarnation. Unconditionally, that futuristic word of the Lord points to the beyond at every moment of passing time; God transcends absolutely all of his manifestations.

There is no necessity for Christians to convert to Judaism. Buber has expressed this in a moving manner during a debate with the Lutheran theologian Karl Ludwig Schmidt at Stuttgart in 1933.

I live not far from the city of Worms, to which I am bound by a tradition of my forefathers; and, from time to time, I go there. When I go there, I go first to the cathedral. It is a visible harmony of members, a totality in which no part deviates from perfection. With consummate joy I walk about the cathedral, gazing at it. Then I go over to the Jewish cemetery. It consists of crooked, cracked, shapeless, random stones. I station myself there, gaze upward from the jumble of a cemetery to that glorious harmony, and it is as though I were looking up from Israel to the Church. Below, there's not a jot of form; there are only the stones and the ashes under the stones. The ashes are there, no matter how thinly they are scattered. There is the corporeality of men, which has turned to this. There it is. There it is for me. There it is for me, not as corporeality in the space of this planet, but as corporeality in my own memory, far into the depths of history, as far back as Sinai.

I have stood there, have been united with the ashes, and through them with the patriarchs. That is a memory of the transaction with God which is given to all Jews. From this the perfection of the Christian house of God cannot separate me, nothing can separate me from the sacred history of Israel.

I have stood there and have experienced everything myself; all this death has confronted me: all the ashes, all the ruin, all the wordless misery is mine; but the covenant has not been withdrawn from me. I lie on the ground, fallen like these stones. But it has not been withdrawn from me.

The cathedral is as it is. The cemetery is as it is. But nothing has been withdrawn from us.

Were the Church more Christian, were the Christians more sanctified, did they not have to remonstrate with themselves, then, says Karl Ludwig Schmidt, there would ensue a bitter argument between them and us.

Were Judaism once more to become Israel, were sacred countenance to appear once more behind the mask, then I would reply, the separation would indeed continue unabated; but there would not be a more bitter argument between us and the Church, but, rather, something wholly different, which today is still ineffable.

I ask, finally, that you hear two statements which appear to contradict each other, but do not contradict each other.

The Talmud (Yebamot 47a) teaches: If in this age a proselyte comes in order to be received into Judaism, let him be told: "What have you seen among us, that you should want to be converted to it? Do you know that the people of Israel in this age are tortured, battered, buffeted, driven about, that miseries have come upon them?" If he says, "I know, and I am not worthy," then let him at once be received.

It might appear that this is Jewish arrogance. It is not. It is nothing else than the proclamation that cannot be dismissed. The misery is real misery, and the disgrace is real disgrace. But in it there is a purpose of God, which he promises to us that, as God has promised to us (Isa. 54:10), he will never let us fall from his hand.

The Midrash (Shemot Rabbah XIX, Sifra on Lev. 18:5) says: "The Holy One (blessed be he) declares no creature unworthy, but he receives them all. Every moment the gates are open, and whoever seeks to gain entrance, gains entrance. And thus he says (Isa. 26:2): 'Open ye the gates, that the righteous nation [goy ṣaddík] that keepeth faithfulness may enter in.' It is not said that priests shall come, that Levites shall come, that Israelites shall come; but it is said that a goy saddík shall come."

The first statement spoke concerning proselytes; the second does not; it speaks concerning the race of men. *The gates of God stand open to all. The Christian need not go through Judaism, the Jew need not go through Christianity, in order to come to God.*

Despite his refusal to accept Christianity, Buber was always prepared to enter into dialogue with individual Christians. But, such "dialogue" was not the serial delivery of monologues by Jewish and Christian opponents that usually bears this name. "All real living is meeting," the "genuine change from communication to communion." Buber chose a personal experience to explain this concept, an experience which illumines his entire life and work.

> But I can really show what I have in mind only by events which open into a genuine change from communication to communion, that is, in an embodiment of the word of dialogue.
> What I am here concerned with cannot be conveyed in ideas to the reader. But we may represent it by examples—provided that, where the matter is important, we do not eschew taking examples from the inmost recesses of the personal life. For where else should the like be found?
> My friendship with one now dead arose in an incident that may be described, if you will, as a broken-off conversation. The date is Easter 1914. Some men from different European peoples had met in an undefined presentiment of the catastrophe, in order to make preparations for an attempt to establish a supra-national authority. The conversations were marked by that unreserve, whose substance and fruitfulness I have scarcely ever experienced so strongly. It had such an effect on all who took part that the fictitious fell

away and every word was an actuality. Then as we discussed the composition of the larger circle from which public initiative should proceed (it was decided that it should meet in August of the same year) one of us, a man of passionate concentration and judicial power of love, raised the consideration that too many Jews had been nominated, so that several countries would be represented in unseemly proportion by their Jews. Though similar reflections were not foreign to my own mind, since I hold that Jewry can gain an effective and more than merely stimulating share in the building of a steadfast world of peace only in its own community and not in scattered members, they seemed to me, expressed in this way, to be tainted in their justice. Obstinate Jew that I am, I protested against the protest. I no longer know how from that I came to speak of Jesus and to say that we Jews knew him from within, in the impulses and stirrings of his Jewish being, in a way that remains inaccessible to the peoples submissive to him. "In a way that remains inaccessible to you"—so I directly addressed the former clergyman. He stood up, I too stood, we looked into the heart of one another's eyes. "It is gone," he said, and before everyone we gave one another the kiss of brotherhood.

The discussion of the situation between Jews and Christians had been transformed into a bond between the Christian and the Jew. In this transformation dialogue was fulfilled. Opinions were gone, in a bodily way the factual took place.

JOHN COURTNEY
MURRAY, S.J.

BY

Thomas T. Love

The renewal of Roman Catholicism in the contemporary world is an astonishing reality that compels admiration. At the forefront of this renewal stands a theological colossus—John Courtney Murray, S.J.—whose painstaking scholarship, careful and thorough argumentation, and intoxication with the truth of the gospel received and transmitted by Catholicism have placed him in the vanguard of the current renaissance of Catholic thought. This contemporary Catholic scholar is an American—born in 1904 to Roman Catholic parents, Michael John and Margaret Courtney Murray—and symbolizes a new stage in the emergence of the Catholic Church in the United States.

Murray, who grew up mainly in Queens, attended a Jesuit high school in Manhattan and decided upon the priestly vocation at sixteen. Attending Weston College and Boston College, he received the B.A. in 1926 and the M.A. in 1927. After a three-year interval of teaching Latin and English Literature in the Philippines, he completed four years of theological studies at Woodstock College, a Jesuit school of theology. In 1936 Murray earned his doctorate in theology from the Pontifical Gregorian University in Rome. He returned to Woodstock in 1937 as professor of sacred theology, a position he holds at present. Murray's theological specialty is the Trinity, and substantial essays on the subject of the triune God are expected to appear within a few years. Of Murray's published works, only one small volume and a few essays directly address the problem of God.

Murray has held many distinguished posts and has been honored by diverse institutions. He is a consultant to the Center for the Study of Democratic Institutions (formerly the Fund for the Republic, Inc.); director of the John LaFarge Institute; and a member of The Catholic Theological Society of America, the Catholic Association for International Peace, and the Catholic Commission on Intellectual and Cultural Affairs. He was the first editor of *Theological Studies,* and for two years he was an associate editor of *America.* He has been visiting professor of medieval philosophy and culture at Yale University and has received honorary degrees from Harvard, Notre Dame, St. Louis, and Georgetown.

Murray is an expert on the problem of church-state relations and the recognized theological spokesman in America for what may be termed a restatement of Catholic church-state theory. With profundity and clarity, he has set forth a constructive viewpoint of the relation between church and state in the modern world, newly exhibiting the rich historical depth and complexity of the Roman Catholic tradition. In his many works on constitutional matters, political theory, and philosophical problems Murray probes and analyzes not only the immediate issues under investigation but the presuppositions, implications, and consequences involved.

Murray's contribution to the final approval of the Declaration on Religious Liberty (*Dignitatis Humanae*) by Vatican Council II was of singular significance. Although Murray was "dis-invited" to attend the first session of the Council, he was

19

a *peritus* (expert) during the final three sessions, and his influence was pivotal in the redrafting and final acceptance of the schema on religious liberty. Murray was the chief architect of the document; he wrote a profound background paper for the Council Fathers on the problem of religious freedom; he carried on correspondence with some of those who opposed the revised texts; he appeared on the panel sponsored by the bishops of the United States for the press in Rome; he spoke on the problem of religious freedom to a great crowd of international press representatives and bishops in Rome; he lectured to and answered the questions of the Protestant observers. His comprehensive knowledge of the central problem was persuasive; his manner and humor in verbal articulation were unmatched. Consequently, by ability and manner he made a unique contribution to the process and passage of the Declaration.

The purpose of the present essay is to set forth in summary fashion what is basic to the structure of Murray's contribution to contemporary theological thinking in relation to church-state theory and the problem of religious freedom. Two aspects are pivotal: first, his view of the theologian's task and, second, his restatement of the church-state problematic. We will consider only cardinal elements in our brief anatomization of Murray's intricate thought.

THE THEOLOGIAN'S TASK

Murray states clearly what he understands to be the task of the theologian in relation to the church-state problem:

> His [the theologian's] task is the formulation of principles in such terms that they may be asserted as constantly valid, and their organization into a coherent system that will cover all contingencies because it is dependent on none.

First, the theologian must discern and formulate the general principles which are involved in any particular form of church-

20

state relationship. Second, he must systematize these principles and demonstrate their applicability to actual sets of historical circumstances. Hence, for Murray, while "the premises and principles" of the Church's "political theology," as the matter is termed in one place, "are indeed firm and unchanging," still

> there will always remain the task of purifying the developed, practically operative structure of this theology from the contingent elements that necessarily accrue to it in the course of the Church's living through, and wrestling with, the political ideas and institutions of particular ages; there will remain, too, the task of organizing afresh this theology, to insure its exactness, its vitality, and its relevance to new contexts and its solidity against new attacks.

Here, then, we see a central theological concern for Murray. He wishes to emphasize the changelessness of the principles of the Church's sociopolitical doctrine and yet to adapt these to actual historical orders. The task is to work out a theory of church-state relations that will be relevant to all historical conditions.

The principles of Catholic doctrine on church and state are known, however, only in historical interchanges. It is this fact, says Murray, which "makes exploration of Catholic tradition so difficult," for

> All the theories of Church-state relationships cast up in the past were influenced by the facts of the problem as those facts existed at the time. In this matter fact has always had the primacy over theory.

Historically speaking, "principles" and "facts" have always been conjoined. An investigation of the tradition of the Church, which includes past theories, is required in order to determine, formulate, and organize systematically the "constantly valid" and "unchanging" doctrinal principles. But since past theories always reflect the unique relativities of former times, because of the inevitable historical intermixture of doctrinal principles and transitory conditions, it follows that theories must be un-

derstood in relation to the context in which they were framed
and that deductive conclusions may not be drawn from such
theories for radically different circumstances.

In accord with genuine "historical consciousness," then, the
proper theological task is: (1) "to trace the stages in the
growth of the tradition as it makes its way through history";
(2) "to discern the elements of the tradition that are embedded
in some historically conditioned synthesis that, as a synthesis,
has become archaistic"; (3) "to discern the 'growing end' of
the tradition" ("it is normally indicated by the new question
that is taking shape under the impact of the historical movement of events and ideas"); (4) to construct a "synthesis that
will be at once new and also traditional." A consciousness of
historical relativities enables one to judge sociopolitical institutions—such as establishment of religion and civil tolerance—in
their own *Sitz im Leben.* If, for example, historical institutions
were "useful to the people" in their "condition of personal and
political consciousness," then such institutions need not be condemned *in situ,* though they would be anachronisms for subsequent times.

Murray's brilliant analysis of Leo XIII's church-state teachings is illustrative. Here he dissects texts in their historical setting and separates the doctrinal elements out from the contex-
tual accretions of nineteenth-century polemic. According to
Murray, the doctrinal dimension in the Leonine church-state
corpus develops the Gelasian formula of two societies and the
primacy of the spiritual. To summarize some of the "cardinal
emphases" Murray finds in Leo XIII's doctrinal teaching: first,
two societies with respective authorities must be distinguished;
second, the Church must be free from and transcendent "to
civil society and all manner of political forms"; third, the
Church must be free to exert influence on civil society by
means of her purely spiritual power; fourth, there must be an
orderly relationship (*ordinata colligatio*) between the two societies and their powers. Leo XIII did refine Catholic doctrine
on church-state relationships; however, Murray argues, doctri-

nal elements in Leo's pronouncements were intermixed with polemic, and one must be aware of the inevitably unfortunate effect of polemic. If the argumentative element is not taken into account, then one easily misinterprets Leo's teaching and tends to derive erroneous conclusions from it. To the extent that the "stamp of polemic" is found on Leo XIII's teaching, his utterances are dated in terms of the historical context. The precise point may be clarified by considering the issue of "development of doctrine" in relation to the utterances of Leo XIII and Pius XII.

Stating that it seems to be obvious that a development of Catholic sociopolitical doctrine has occurred between the time of Leo XIII and the present day (e.g., compare *Rerum novarum* with *Mater et magistra*, or compare *Immortale Dei* and *Libertas* with *Pacem in terris* and Pius XII's Christmas discourses of 1941, 1942, and 1944), Murray lists several aspects of the development. First, Leo XIII's view of government was paternalistic, whereas Pius XII's conception was political. The conception of Pius, says Murray, is "a clarification of the tradition." Second, Leo XIII's view reflected the historical reality of the "illiterate masses," whereas Pius XII's conception is a "progress in the understanding of the tradition" because it reflects the historical and political realities of "the people" and "the citizen's" responsibility in self-government. Third, Leo XIII failed adequately to distinguish the society and the state, whereas Pius XII distinguishes the political society from the juridical state. Murray argues that Leo XIII's erroneous identification of the broad civil society with the limited juridical state led to a notion of civil tolerance by the state of religious error, a notion that is both misleading and juridically irrelevant in the modern day. Hence, according to Murray, "the Leonine conception of the state has been transcended today by the progress of Catholic doctrine." Furthermore, says Murray, Vatican Council II's schema on religious liberty, "whose premise is this progress, transcends the Leonine theory of civil tolerance by its doctrine

23

of religious freedom." While not wishing to condemn Leo XIII's confused view in its own context, Murray says:

> It is not that the Leonine theory was in any sense false. Today, however, one must say of it, quite gently, that it is archaistic.

New historical consciousness pronounces Leo XIII's theory of tolerance outdated. Since the contours of Leo's theory were shaped by the peculiar circumstances of his time and context, the theory is incongruous with the different concrete political realities of the present day. Thus it is that Murray declares Leo XIII's notions of paternalistic government, illiterate subjects, an undifferentiated society-state, and civil tolerance of religion outmoded. Such notions may have been meaningful in the curious conditions of the nineteenth century, but they are, so to speak, artifacts today.

In order to construct a church-state theory that is relevant to contemporary conditions, the theologian must clarify his use of terminology. It is important to understand in their contexts the meaning of certain terms for Murray. The term "state," for example, is employed in different fashions. Sometimes it is used as a synonym for the entire sociopolitical society. At other times —e.g., in Murray's constructive restatement—the term "state" denotes an instrumental and functional agency of the political society. Murray rejects the former definition of the state as an inclusive political society and criticizes its use by contemporary Catholic scholars, in spite of the long tradition of such usage.

In his restatement of Catholic church-state thought, Murray delineates what he means by civil society, political society, state, and government. "Civil society" designates "the total complex of organized human relationships on the temporal plane." By its very nature it involves pluralism and the principle of subsidiary function. "Political society" is "civil society politically organized, i.e., organized for the common good, constituted a *corpus politicum* by effective ordination toward the political good, the good of the body as such." "The people," the politi-

24

cal society, and the body politic are synonyms.

Since the body politic requires an effective *means* for striving toward its end, the common good, "the body politic . . . connotes a state." It is Murray's definition of the "state" that is salient. He sharply distinguishes the state from the body politic:

> The state is not the body politic but that particular subsidiary functional organization of the body politic, whose special function regards the good of the whole. The state is not the person of the ruler; in fact, it is not personal at all. It belongs to the order of action rather than the order of substance. It is a rational force employed by the body politic in the service of itself as a body. It is "the power," ordained of God, the author of nature, but deriving from the people.

Pivotal here is the fact that the state is conceived *functionally*. Its functions change and hence it changes. The state is limited, though its limitations vary from one political society to another and within any given society. Murray takes the proper and immediate end of the state to be the "public order," not the "common good." In order that the state may carry out its task, it must include the "notion of government."

Primarily Murray wishes to emphasize the "relational" aspect in his interpretation of the term government, even when the relational aspect is institutionalized: "Government is the ruler-in-relation-to-the-ruled; it is likewise the ruled-in-relation-to-the-ruler." It is government that "gives concrete embodiment to the political relationship implied in the state." Government is conceived functionally and is of the order of action. Like the state, it too is a "natural necessity; but its forms, and actual content and implications of the political relationship, are contingent upon reason and the practical judgments it makes in circumstances."

Contrary to traditional Catholic church-state thought, in Murray's view the "state" by definition is not a "perfect society"; it is not a "creature of God"; and it is not in any sense obliged to worship God. The clarification of the conception of "state" enables Murray to set aside as irrelevant many issues

25

that plague much Catholic church-state theory and to undercut many arguments of his opponents. The new notion of state, as separated out from the society, makes possible a new church-state problematic that is relevant to democratic political processes of the modern world.

THE CONTEMPORARY CHURCH-STATE PROBLEMATIC

Murray's constructive restatement of church-state theory emerged after a torturous time of confusion and a prolonged period of meticulous study, exacting argumentation, and remarkable synthesis. It was provoked by what he took to be the inadequacy of the view of church-state relations commonly advocated by Catholics—a view expressed often in Catholic history, codified in modern texts of public ecclesiastical law, and present in papal utterances and the writings of many Catholic theologians and philosophers. In the face of harsh criticism by Catholic scholars in America, he slowly articulated a new understanding of Catholic church-state doctrine, shifting preoccupation away from abstract theological claims and emphasizing, instead, the ethical and political aspects of the church-state problem. In his first attempts to set forth a theory of religious freedom, he failed to perceive clearly the issues involved, partially because he was overly dependent upon past formulations of the problem which were no longer relevant to the conditions of the modern day. Impelled by his failure, he immersed himself in studies of his own religious heritage in order to determine what the doctrinal foundations were for the relationships between the Catholic Church and diverse historical societies. With a deepened understanding of the Catholic tradition, and informed by his own experience in the American political situation, Murray constructed a profound view of the relation between church and state in the modern world which now has gained increasing support. Two elements in his constructive restatement are pivotal. First, Murray outlines the new church-state "problematic," the uniquely contemporary shape of the problem. Second, he defends his restatement in a twofold manner: on the basis of reason and on the basis of Catholic tradition as represented by an interpretation of papal teaching. Primary in our consideration will be the problematic.

The Purpose of the Church

Murray states concisely the basic schema of his church-state theory in terms of the proper purpose of the Church in the temporal order:

> The permanent purpose of the Church in her relations with the state is to maintain her doctrine of juridical and social dualism under the primacy of the spiritual, against the tendency to juridical and social monism under the primacy of the political which is inherent in the state, to a greater or lesser degree. . . . Moreover, the traditional effort has been not only to maintain this doctrine as a doctrine but also to give it such institutional embodiment within every particular historical context as will make it operative within that context.

This is a lucid résumé of the theoretical church-state problem in the *corpus* of Murray's works. He understands his viewpoint to be a modern restatement of the ancient Gelasian teaching which he takes to be "the first classic statement of the Church's fundamental thesis"—"Two there are" and the primacy of the spiritual authority. Two societies exist, one directed toward the eternal end of man, the other directed toward the temporal end of man. The nonpolitical society—the Church—is not to be absorbed into the political order. Neither are the political order and its power to be usurped by the Church. In Murray's view, the Church has no claim over the civil power, even indirectly. She claims, and properly can claim, a direct power over man's sacred life only—that is, she claims the right to direct man to his eternal end. The temporal power is in no sense, even on rare occasions, an instrument of the Church (either as a power or as a Christian people). The sociopolitical society has its own proper and limited end—a strictly temporal, natural, and secular end—and it may not be employed as an instrument

27

for an end which is not its own. Murray argues that the temporal order and its power are thoroughly and authentically secular, not sanctified. Hence, the Catholic Church's claim of primacy over man's sacred life in all its forms is a claim of purely spiritual authority.

It is because the primacy of the spiritual has no meaning, no actuality, to resist the tendency to "social monism" that the Church, an actual society, must be free; and man must belong to *two* Cities and not one. Murray here clarifies Catholic doctrine: primacy (involving *social dualism,* two Cities, "Two there are") is not derived from the hypothetical situation of any historical political society. Hence the notion of primacy of the spiritual must provide a society *beside* the political society, if the primacy of the material or the political is to be avoided. Furthermore, the primacy of the spiritual leaves intact the full autonomy and freedom of the temporal to pursue its properly secular end of the society's well-being.

Murray's résumé, we note, involves both (1) "permanent purpose"—general principles, doctrine—and (2) concrete "institutional embodiment" or the "application," "adaptation," or "realization" of principles in historical contexts. He insists that these are the two inseparable aspects of an "incarnational" theological theory of politics that are "united" concretely but that may be distinguished theoretically.

Basic Principles and Their Adaptation

The purpose of the Church requires three basic principles— freedom of the Church, harmony of laws, cooperation—each of which presumes the primacy of the spiritual authority and the distinction of societies or Cities, i.e., church and state. The first principle is properly theological and asserts the freedom of the Church to teach and of her members to respond; the second principle pertains to the ethical dimension, conceived abstractly in terms of the conscience of man who has the twofold obligation to obey both divine positive law and civil law; the third principle refers to the political level of analysis and declares that there is to be cooperation between the Church and civil society in the manifold dimensions of institutional existence.

Since the purpose of the Church is to be fulfilled in the temporal order, Murray declares that the three "immutable" principles—freedom, harmony or *concordia,* and cooperation—controlling the relations between church and state must be "summoned from the sphere of abstraction and made effectively regulative of Church-state relationships in the actual world of human affairs"; that is, they must be concretely applied and "receive embodiment in law or custom or modes of organized action—in a word, in institutions." This is what Murray meant when he argued that the basic principles "must undergo a vital adaptation to the realities of the moment."

It is important to be aware of Murray's language and intention at this point. Catholic scholars often have spoken of a "thesis" or an "ideal" arrangement between church and state, frequently referred to as a "union of church and state" or a "confessional state"; they also have spoken of a "hypothesis" or a less-than-ideal-yet-tolerable situation which it is "expedient" to allow to exist when pure Catholic principles cannot be applied. In contrast to such a view, Murray speaks of "vital adaptation" of principles to actual conditions as they emerge in history; that is, factual conditions determine to an extent the proper application of the principles. Furthermore, inasmuch as historical processes are not static, the adaptation of principles must be dynamic, i.e., made relevant to whatever circumstances arise. Hence, while principles are held to be "immutable," they are "temporalized" by being adapted to the historical constellation of factors of any given situation. Since historical situations fluctuate, continual adaptation of principles is required. No concretization of principles, so to speak, may be taken as a principle or a "thesis," or an "ideal" political arrangement. The terms "expedient," "opportune," and "toleration" are neither used nor implied in Murray's formulation. This fact accounts

29

for the immediate attractiveness of Murray's restatement to many Catholics and non-Catholics.

The "State-Church"

"The legal institution known as the state-church" and "the concept of Catholicism as 'the religion of the state,' " Murray argues, were simply temporary adaptations of Catholic principles to highly peculiar political situations. It follows, then, that the state-church and the correlative notion of the religion of the state must not be regarded as the Catholic norm or "ideal." On these grounds Murray rejects the view of those Catholics who assert that there is an "ideal" church-state arrangement, a "thesis" involving the "union of Church and state" in contrast to a "hypothesis" involving a relation other than the union of church and state. Murray's fundamental objection to the thesis-hypothesis view is that it is illegitimate to allow a peculiar set of circumstances to be labeled "ideal" and given the status of an eternal principle of Catholic doctrine. A transitory application of principle resulting in a "state-church" may be legitimately defended, perhaps, in the highly exceptional set of conditions of a given time; it would be illegitimate, however, to identify the *application* of principles with a principle thereby elevating, as it were, a contingent condition (i.e., the state-church) to the level of a "thesis" or "ideal."

In an attempt to clarify "the exact status in Catholic doctrine possessed by the concept of the confessional state," Murray scrutinizes the writings of Leo XIII. Here Murray maintains that one must distinguish "three aspects—a doctrinal, a polemic, and what I shall call an historical aspect."

> On the doctrinal level his [Leo XIII's] work was the restatement of the Gelasian thesis . . . this was his fundamental contribution. On the polemic level his work was the refutation of the naturalistic and rationalistic bases of Liberalism. . . . Thirdly, there was his approval of the concept of the confessional state, contained in his treatment of the relations between the "Catholic state" and the various religions within its boundaries.

30

Having distinguished these three elements in Leo's utterances, Murray poses a question: ". . . to which of the two other aspects of his thought is this approval of the confessional state related?" Catholics often have presumed that Leo's acceptance and praise of a "Catholic state" were part of his doctrinal teaching with the further consequence that such a state is an exigence of traditional Catholic doctrine, especially since great Catholic scholars in the past have taught this and texts of Pius XI and Pius XII may be cited in corroboration.

But Murray gives a different answer to this question. He connects the concept of "confessional state" or "religion of the state" with the transitory conditions which influenced Leo's doctrinal utterances.

> For my part, I think that the concept of the confessional state in Leo XIII is more properly related to the polemic than to the doctrinal aspects of his teachings; this is why I called it . . . the "historical" part of his work, wishing to imply that historical circumstance had much to do with its fashioning.

In this manner Murray argues that Leo's approval of a Catholic state was rather accidental. Murray's attempt here is very significant. Essentially he seeks to interpret Catholic tradition. He "contextualizes," as it were, papal statements in order to discern what is Catholic church-state doctrine, in what manner it develops, and what relevance it has for radically new sets of circumstances.

We may summarize Murray's basic argument against the concept of "the religion of the state" as follows: (1) If the constitutional concept, "the religion of the state," is required for the doctrinal concept, "the freedom of the Church," then the former is an exigence of Catholic doctrine as a means necessary to the latter. (2) The basic question then is: "Is it [the constitutional concept of the religion of the state] a permanently necessary means apart from which the freedom of the Church cannot be properly secure?" (3) The answer to this question is negative; hence, the constitutional concept of religion of the

31

state may be able to be defended in a particular context but does not merit defense as "ideal" or "thesis" or doctrinal.

If one views the notion of the "state-church" as a reflection of a highly peculiar phenomenon cast up in a particular historical context, then the Catholic Church is not permanently welded to the notion. The Catholic Church must, argues Murray, "consent to other institutionalizations of Church-state relationships" than that of the "religion of the state" wherein the Catholic Church is either legally established or preferred; other forms of relations must be regarded as vital and valid "adaptations of principles to legitimate political and social developments." Concrete situations require consideration on their own grounds.

The Modern Constitutional Democracy

Carefully distinguishing the modern constitutional democracy—i.e., a constitutionally self-limiting democracy such as the American—from nineteenth-century absolutistic continental democracies, Murray asks: Does not the modern constitutional democracy represent a legitimate sociopolitical development to which the Church must adapt her principles of freedom, harmony, and cooperation? Murray states his reasons for an affirmative answer to the question:

> First, this form of state is presently man's best, and possibly last, hope of human freedom. Secondly, this form of state presently offers to the Church as a spiritual power as good a hope of freedom as she has ever had; it offers to the Church as a Christian people a means, through its free political institutions, of achieving harmony between law and social organization and the demands of their Christian conscience; finally, by reason of its aspirations towards an order of personal and associational freedom, political equality, civic friendship, social justice, and cultural advancement, it offers to the Church the kind of cooperation which she presently needs, and it merits in turn her cooperation in the realization of its own aspirations.

In the modern constitutional democracy, Murray contends, the freedom of the Church to reach persons in the temporal order no longer requires juridical assurance in the way it may have formerly in politically less-developed societies. Consequently, the issue of the juridical relationship between church and state is set aside, and the question of the Church's relation to civil society assumes prominence.

New political realities, such as the American secular or "lay" (not secularistic or laic) state, invite "a commensurate development in the theory of Church-state relations." Murray declares the fundamentally new fact in this modern political order to be, in the words of Pius XII, the appearance of the "autonomous person." The citizen of the American form of government is self-governing. He has certain responsibilities and duties in society. That this is so implies that he possesses certain rights and liberties as a person—i.e., the rights and liberties necessary to perform the duties expected. The Church, then, must now accommodate her principles to the self-governing citizen and his constitutionally guaranteed civil liberty.

> It is with this new "ruler," armed with his democratic instruments of rule, that the Church is now confronted. It is with his new *libertas civilis* that the old *libertas ecclesiastica* has to establish proper relations.

Popular share in power, political responsibility of rulers to the ruled, the effective right of citizens to express opinions about duties imposed on them—all these and more are included in the democratic concept of *libertas civilis* and sustained by constitutional means. "It is precisely at this point," in Murray's judgment, "that the problem of the relation of the two powers arises in its contemporary phase." This is true, contends Murray, because "the historically realized concept of *libertas civilis* has come to include 'religious liberty' in a sense as ample as the concept of civil liberty itself." Murray shifts the emphasis in contemporary Catholic thought away from the narrow problem of the "rights" of the Church in direct relation to the state and stresses instead the freedom of the Church to permeate human society in all of its dimensions, indirectly through Catholic be-

33

lievers. In order to support his contention, Murray develops a theory of the "indirect power" of the Church, hinged concretely on the dual nature of man as Christian and citizen, and affirms the freedom of the Church in society without compromising the genuine independence of the properly secular state.

The "Indirect Power" of the Church

The question is: How is the Church to express herself in the temporal order without becoming identified with a particular historical expression of authority and without being tempted to ignore the proper autonomy of the temporal order? What are the bases for the Church's action in the affairs of the political world? In what manner and to what extent is the Church's "spiritual authority" to be exercised and made effective in the sociopolitical order?

In order to arrive at a solution to this inquiry, Murray formulates a theory of the Church's indirect power in the temporal order. He asserts that it is more accurate to say that the Church "indirectly has a power" in the temporal order than it is to say the Church has an "indirect power," since the *magisterium* of the Church is an authoritative spiritual power directly affecting the spiritual order and this same spiritual power only indirectly has effects in temporal matters. That is, there are temporal after-effects, but the power of the Church does not terminate in them directly; they are repercussions in the temporal order of an action which itself, with its effects, remains purely spiritual.

In modern governments, Murray argues, as the church-state problem has emerged through history and modern political forms have evolved, the concept of the "indirect power" has been clarified, for "the Church no longer as in medieval time or in the classic confessional states, directly confronts 'the temporal power' in concentrated, centralized form" such as the person of a king. Rather the Church comes into actual relationship with the state only indirectly and incidentally "inasmuch as the two powers have a common subject or (what is the same thing) inasmuch as the one man is a member of [the] two societies. . . ." Hence, because the same man is both Christian and citizen, the two powers meet indirectly as they seek directly to serve him in different respects. The individual Christian who is also a citizen is the one who participates in shaping the political affairs of the world, and it is only through the citizen that the purely spiritual power of the Church indirectly has repercussions in the temporal order.

> The action of the Church on him [the Christian citizen] terminates at conscience, forming it to the sense of its Christian duties in all their range and implications for temporal life. The Christian then as citizen, in the full panoply of his democratic rights, prolongs, as it were, this action of the Church into the temporal order, in all the matters in which Christian doctrine and law has [sic] implications for the life and law and government of society.

What is essential to Murray's theory of the Church's "indirect power" in the temporal order may be summarized. First, the Church and the state are to be sharply distinguished, each supreme in its own order, each having its proper end, the hierarchy of ends of human life, and each having its proper, though limited, power. Second, it is requisite to maintain, on the one hand, the primacy of the spiritual end, hence of the spiritual order, hence of the ecclesiastical power. On the other hand, it is necessary to uphold the relative autonomy of the temporal end, hence of the temporal order, hence of the civil power. The Church's indirect power in the temporal order is a spiritual power inasmuch as ecclesiastical authority properly deals directly with the consciences of men. Finally, a harmonious relation should exist between the two societies and their powers.

In Murray's theory the indirectness of power derives from the fact that the Church acts only for a supernatural end; the spiritual power is supreme in all matters pertaining to the eternal end of men. The manner and extent of the exercise of the spiritual power are limited both logically and actually to purely

35

spiritual matters, to affecting the consciences of citizens. In Murray's view the Church has no authority or right, even in exceptional instances of grave danger to citizens, to intervene in the affairs of the autonomous temporal power. Murray's theory asserts the right of the Church to produce effects, or after-effects, in the temporal order; but for Murray the manner is always indirect (via the conscience of the Catholic citizen) and the extent is limited not only by circumstances but by the state's own secular nature and end as reflected in natural law. There is no instrumentality of the temporal power in the logic of Murray's view, since the civil power is never subject to the ecclesiastical power.

Two things then are central to Murray's theory of the indirect power with regard to its nature and the manner and extent of its functions. First, the spiritual power is limited to spiritual matters, in operation and effect, and produces only after-effects in temporal matters. Second, the spiritual power may "reach" the temporal power only by means of the consciences of Catholic citizens.

The "Care of Religion": The Person's Religious Freedom

In his many essays interpreting the concept of religious freedom as a juridical right—as in his role as a *peritus* at Vatican Council II and in his specific task as chief architect of the Declaration on Religious Liberty (*Dignitatis Humanae*)—Murray carefully chisels a view that extends his church-state theory. In relation to the problem of religious freedom, the church-state issue is: What is the nature and what is the extent of *cura religionis,* the "care of religion" by the secular authority, in contemporary societies? Stated briefly, Murray's answer is: "The state can and should do no more than guarantee freedom of religion." More adequately expressed, the entire civil society and all of its governing elements are to "care for religion" by caring for the person's civil right to religious freedom, a right that is grounded in the very nature of the person and that must be recognized, respected, and guaranteed in the juridical structures and processes of society.

Murray charges that traditional Catholic arguments for religious liberty are essentially irrelevant in relation to the *civil right* to religious freedom. Traditionally, for example, Catholics have argued *from* the formal theological notion of the freedom of the act of faith and the correlative formal ethical notion of the freedom of conscience. From these presuppositions an inference was drawn: that there should be free exercise of religion (or, for many Catholics, the true religion) in the political society. Murray declares that the supposed inference does not follow as Catholics have presumed. He maintains that the civil right to religious freedom is not deduced from the truth or untruth of one's conscientiously held belief, nor is it extrapolated from the abstract notion of one's freedom of conscience. Abstract notions of truth and freedom of conscience are not immediately relevant to the concrete civil right to religious freedom in society. The question of truth or untruth of one's inner convictions, for example, is a politically and juridically irrelevant question. It is politically and juridically irrelevant because a government is incompetent to judge the truth or untruth of one's convictions.

Murray argues that religious freedom must be considered at the outset to be a juridical matter, the *civil* right of persons and groups in society, because persons are inexorably social and are always members of concrete political societies. Advancing Catholic thought beyond a difficult problem, he maintains that it is proper and requisite that a political society guarantee the immunity of persons from coercion in religious matters to the extent that their actions do not seriously disrupt the *public order* (not the "common good"). Hence a person's religious freedom is to be juridically recognized, and sufficient reason must be given if the person's freedom is restrained. Restraint is possible only on grounds of the serious disordering of public life; that is, since the government is completely incompetent in religious matters, in no instance may it coerce in matters that

37

pertain to religion except on the juridical ground of public order. This argument is relatively new in Catholic thought, and it is an important contribution to the renewal of Catholic social thought on the contemporary scene.

With originality and brilliance, Murray shifts contemporary Catholic social thought away from meaningless or misleading anachronistic terms and formulas: "error has no rights," "dogmatic intolerance and civil tolerance," "thesis" and "hypothesis," a "Catholic state." He challenges the adequacy of notions, and the arguments built exclusively thereon, of the "rights" of the Church and the individual's freedom of conscience. Such notions, argues Murray, are profound insights, but they are too abstract and simple for clarity of analysis and argumentation in the modern world.

The new church-state problematic and the narrow issue of religious freedom as a juridical right require analysis and argumentation informed by concrete and complex historical conditions. In the present moment of history, the Church must adapt herself to whatever authentic currents emerge. As development of personal and political consciousness occurs—i.e., as the awareness of man's personal, social, political, and juridical dignity increases—former church-state relationships simply dissolve or are shattered, and conditions for a new problematic appear.

In order to be relevant to the "signs of the times" and yet remain loyal to former insights, a new church-state synthesis must be wrought. With consummate skill, Murray fashions a contemporary synthesis in terms of the freedom of modern man in constitutional democracies. For example, the "signs of the times"—man's present personal and political consciousness —are synthesized with the freedom of the Church and the fully secular autonomy of the sociotemporal order. A person's freedom as a Christian and as a citizen becomes the hinge for the contemporary church-state problematic.

It is man as Christian who knows that the freedom of the Church must not be engulfed by the political society; it is man as citizen who shapes the affairs of his society. The modern church-state problematic therefore centers on men who are both Christian and citizen, who conjoin in their very being, as it were, the freedom of the Church and the freedom of society. The renewal of the Church in the modern world and the proper human development of the sociopolitical society meet in such men. This conclusion, it seems, is requisite in the present moment of history. The profound significance of Murray's complex theory of the interrelation of church and state is that it reaches this conclusion: in his concrete and historical existence, man must be free—in faith, in conscience, in society. It is man's freedom that assures the freedom of the Church vis-à-vis the political society.

JOSEF HROMADKA

BY

Charles C. West

There are great minds whose genius stands alone on the land-
scape of life, peaks from which the world around may be sur-
veyed and understood. There are others who are so much a
part of the history they interpret that one discovers them
rightly only when one explores the mountain ranges of turbu-
lent events. Josef Hromadka is a theologian of the second kind.
He is a Czech, born under the domination of the Austro-Hungarian empire, a friend and adviser of Thomas Masaryk and
Eduard Benes, and one of the spiritual architects of the modern
Czechoslovak state. He has been part of the rise of that state,
its precarious life between Stalin and Hitler, its betrayal at
Munich by the Western powers, its revival, and its communist
domination. He is a Protestant, born of a Lutheran family, later
a leader of the Evangelical Church of the Czech Brethren,
which traces its ancestry to the Bohemian Reformation of Jan
Hus a century before Martin Luther nailed his ninety-five the-
ses to the Wittenberg church door. This special heritage has

placed him in the midst of centuries of church conflict as a reformer of his own church and a modern challenger of Roman Catholicism, as a reconciler of the churches and friend of Catholics amid storms of opposition from his own communion, and as witness for the whole of Christendom to the atheist leaders of modern society.

He is an intellectual rebel. Living in a conforming age, he savored to the full the challenge of philosophical skepticism and of biblical and historical criticism, and is to this day never satisfied when he is running with the hounds. But he found that the radical crisis of human existence when man confronts the living God, as well as the theology that starts from the biblical revelation of the action of this Lord in history, is a more profound challenge and a more invigorating promise than any the world can bring forth with its own resources. He has therefore become Eastern Europe's leading theologian of crisis and renewal. He is a socialist, not in the "scientific" sense set forth by the theories of Karl Marx, but in his profound feeling for the revolt of the masses against the crumbling structures of traditional and bourgeois society. From his earliest years he sensed in the Russian Revolution and its consequences throughout the world a force which, for all its cruelties and injustices, expressed the judgment of God on an unfaithful and unimaginative Christendom. He accepted, therefore, the communist coup of 1948 and has become since then his church's leader and spiritual guide, its chief interpreter of the word of God to an all too human socialist society.

Thus, the story of Hromadka is the story of his time and place in the history of modern times, of the external events of this history and their inner meaning, as his mind has illumined it.

Josef Hromadka was born June 8, 1889, in the village of Hodslavice, Moravia. His father was a respected farmer, a pious Lutheran and an active churchman. In secondary school young Josef was plunged into the ferment of his day which was calling into question the structure of nineteenth-century

Europe. At that time he probably heard Thomas G. Masaryk, the Prague philosopher who later became the father of the Czechoslovak nation. For a while he wavered between philosophy and theology as a university course but finally chose the latter. When he entered the University of Vienna, he was already caught in the conflict between his childhood faith and the skeptical attitude toward all religion that pervaded the intellectual circles of prewar Austria-Hungary.

In this, as in all later controversies, Hromadka was no man for half-measures. He drank deeply of the critical and historical method and became its ardent defender in Vienna, and later in Basel and Heidelberg. The historian Ernst Troeltsch was among his teachers who left on his mind a lifelong mark. He tried humanism and relativism, but, as a way of life, he could not make it his own. Instead, with the help of other professors— Bernhard Duhm in Heidelberg and D. S. Cairns in Aberdeen where he completed his study—he moved to a rediscovery of the witness of the Old Testament prophets to the sovereignty of God. In his own words, it was after he had returned to Prague as a pastor, around 1918, that "it became clear that the central problem of theology is the problem of God; that what matters is not religious experiences but their absolute truth; that God is no mere principle of life but the first starting point of any theological thinking; that it is not important what men experience, but what they are called to experience; that the problem of faith is no problem of the human mind and of internal spiritual process, but the question who is God, what does He want us to do, and what are His plans with the world." From this starting point Hromadka moved on to become in an ever more profound sense a theologian of crisis. In 1924 he discovered Karl Barth, with whose name this modern movement is usually associated. It was the beginning of a long friendship and professional association. But Hromadka was a colleague, not a pupil, of Barth. He came independently to his basic conviction that human thought, as well as life, begins with response to

God's primal action, and his accent in theology has always been significantly different.

After finishing at Aberdeen, Hromadka served two parishes in his country: one a small town in Moravia; the second in Prague where he was at the same time a doctoral candidate. The end of the War found him a chaplain in the Austro-Hungarian army on the eastern front, a disturbing experience both theologically and politically. Here he saw an empire collapse, and sensed for the first time what was to occupy him so intensely in later years: the power of the Bolshevik Revolution over the minds of men.

Back in Prague, however, the first act in another drama was already in progress. In October 1918 the Czechoslovak Republic was proclaimed. In December of the same year the Lutheran Church and the Reformed Church in Bohemia and Moravia united to form the Evangelical Church of the Czech Brethren in a conscious reassertion of the tradition of the fifteenth-century Bohemian reformer Jan Hus. In 1920 the Hus (since 1960 the Comenius) Protestant Theological Faculty of the Charles University in Prague was formed and Hromadka became instructor in systematic theology there, a post which he was to hold as professor after 1927 to the day of his retirement in June 1966. In 1920 also the Czechoslovak Church was formed as a national non-Roman but Catholic church, and during the next few years over a million Czech Christians moved from Roman Catholicism to these other two communions. A vigorous and controversial critic of this trend was Josef Hromadka.

This controversy has a history of many centuries. Already in 1400 Bohemia was alive with ideas for the reform of the Church, coming largely from the English scholar John Wyclif. They soon found their spokesman in the powerful preacher of the Bethlehem chapel in Prague, Magister John of Husinec, or Jan Hus. Hus was more conservative than Wyclif but far more effective. Preaching in Czech he appealed to the common people, the native Bohemian nobility, and the intelligentsia who

43

gathered in the university founded by Emperor Charles IV only a few years before. He was a vigorous defender of the sole authority of Scripture and tried to reform popular worship and common life in the light of it, as did John Calvin more than a century later. He struggled with Pope John XXIII over indulgences, maintaining long before Martin Luther that neither priest nor pope could forgive sins but only declare them forgiven where faith and repentance are sincere. He was an ardent reformer, even spiritualizer, of the priestly office. He did not deny the validity of sacraments administered by unworthy clergy, but he distinguished between a veritable priest, bishop, or pope who possessed the spirit of Christ, and one merely ordained or consecrated by legitimate means. He pleaded for a spiritual concept of the Church and a fellowship of those who had the spirit of Christ, those predestined for salvation, rather than for a legal institution under an earthly authority. In this fellowship, he believed, clergy and laity were distinguished only in the form of their ministries, not by special authority. He demanded that the cup as well as the bread be given in the eucharist to all members of the Church.

It is not surprising that Hus came into conflict with the papal court of John XXIII over these ideas that he and all other parties hoped to have resolved by the Council of Constance in 1415. At the Council, however, Hus was betrayed, condemned, and burned at the stake. Emperor Sigismund, who had guaranteed him safe passage, broke his word, and John XXIII imprisoned him. After Hus's flight the Council Fathers persistently refused to debate with him while he, in prison, refused the total submission they demanded. He died—a martyr in the eyes of his people—and a wound was cut in Christendom which it is still trying to heal today.

For two centuries, through a series of battles, compromises, and finally an agreement for mutual toleration, Bohemia and Moravia defended the reforms of Hus against both empire and papacy. The Church there was in correspondence with Luther. It absorbed many Lutheran and Calvinist influences during the

Reformation which modified its Czech nationalism and brought a certain reconciliation with German neighbors along with influences from which the Czech nation has never been free.

However, in 1620, catastrophe came for both Church and nation. In the battle of the White Mountain—an event that every Czech schoolchild knows today—the Bohemian and Moravian nobility were overwhelmed by the forces of Emperor Ferdinand II, an Austrian. Religious toleration was annulled, and the country was forcibly reconverted to Roman Catholicism. Surviving leaders were forced to flee the country. Thousands took refuge in Germany, Poland, and Hungary, where Czech literature was still produced and Czech hymns were sung by exiled congregations. The Moravian Brethren, offshoot of a radical movement inspired by Hus, moved its headquarters across the Saxon border to Herrnhut, and from there went out into the whole world as the first eighteenth-century modern missionaries. But many simply remained in the country, secretly Hussite though outwardly conforming, so that in 1781, when the liberal Emperor Joseph II of Austria granted religious toleration once more, Lutheran and Reformed congregations came into being at once and slowly grew.

The tolerance of this period, which continued with some changes up to 1918, was certainly far from what we would call religious liberty today. It was a right of private exercise, not of public proclamation. All kinds of extralegal obstacles were set in its way. The production of literature was limited. Only much later was any provision for the education of pastors given, and those in office were hampered and limited in their work. A Czech historian compares the situation with that prevailing in Spain today. Another analogy would be the degree of tolerance, combined with aggressive countermission, which is granted to all religion in the Soviet Union. Furthermore, Protestantism in Bohemia and Moravia was subject to special limitation, because it was still a carrier of Czech nationhood and of resistance to German cultural and Austrian political dominance.

The victor, finally, in all of this was not the Roman Catholic

Church or the Reformation, but the secular Enlightenment. Hromadka describes the situation in a sharp contrast: Protestants gained permission to worship openly

> in the time when human reason was opening out in freedom. Thrones were falling, dark powers of political and spiritual slavery were intimidated and even for a certain time, pushed aside. Joy in the dignity of man and moral maturity rose up to heaven. In such a glorious time were the fetters of the clandestine Bohemian Protestants struck off. That is the bright side of our Reformed tradition.

On the other hand, these Protestants were forced to suppress everything

> that would ring like a bell in the open world and would announce like a church steeple the greatness of Reformation faith. The church of the toleration period was pushed to the margin of public life, and its own Reformation tone which should have borne witness to the grace and the saving work of the Lord was muffled by the rationalism (I will not say the reason) of the Enlightenment.

Deist rationalism was a special temptation for the barely tolerated Christians of the Hussite Reformation between 1781 and 1918. It brought allies and opened doors even in nominally Catholic circles. It brought access to literature and prospects of success, both denied to those more theologically inclined. The opposite temptation of sectarianism and pentecostalism, so hard to control when the church cannot function in a responsibly public way, polarized the Protestant community. The result was that the new leaders of the Czech nation in the nineteenth century—many of them, including Masaryk and Benes, of Protestant background and nominal members of Protestant churches—were fed intellectually at the table of secular humanism. Czechoslovakia, when it was established in 1918, was led by men who drew their inspiration from Locke and Kant, from Goethe, and even from Karl Marx—who were often, in a vague humanist way, Christian though strongly opposed to the dominance of the Roman Catholic Church. But

the faith of Jan Hus, of Luther, or indeed of Augustine and
St. Paul, was for many of them a message never truly heard.
Small wonder. The General Synod which formed the Evangelical Church of the Czech Brethren in 1918 directed a message
to the Czech people, two-thirds of which devoted itself to
proving that the Catholic Church is a contradiction of the Czech
nation and a danger to its freedom: "And therefore we call
into our midst all our fellow countrymen who have fallen out
with the Roman Church but who do not want to be without a
religion and a church." Hromadka, a delegate to that synod,
remarked ruefully afterward,

> The old confessions crumbled in our hands and the Bible
> was for the larger part of those who sought this union, not a
> really living but only a formally acknowledged authority.

The problem of all Christians then—Protestant and Catholic
alike—in the new Czechoslovakia was to rediscover the Church
of Jesus Christ in the modern world by turning again to the
living Word, rather than to attract members of a diminishing
"religious-minded" community by nationalist appeals.

> As the Word sounds and works always anew, so the
> Church is ever newly formed by the prophetic word and the
> apostolic preaching. It is not possible to press the Word of
> God into set theological formulas or dogmatic articles. But it
> is also not possible to enclose it in set ecclesiastical orders
> and laws. The Church is the daily gathering anew around the
> Word and the present Jesus Christ according to the Scrip-
> tures. The Church is an ever fresh receiving of the wealth of
> the Holy Spirit.

Hromadka was not without his criticisms of the Roman Catholic Church. It "has grown to such an extent into the structure
of public political, social, and cultural life," he wrote in 1949,
"that its clergy and laymen find it difficult to see the frontiers
at a moment when the past structure of history is breaking
into pieces and with it also the forms of the Church-state relationship. The Roman Catholic Church was supported from all

sides by this . . . structure . . . in a way which was so natural and at times unobserved that we ourselves were almost unaware of the privileges from which it benefited. It was especially hard to distinguish to what extent it lived by its inner strength and out of its own resources and to what extent it drew on the wealth and culture of the society around it." As the church most deeply wedded to the old society, the Church of Rome has the most profound struggle to discover its mission and therefore itself in a world where the old securities have been swept away. But this challenge faces all Christians of every communion. There is no gospel in seeking a cultural revenge for the battle of the White Mountain.

> Man and history cannot undo anything. Only God is able to undo—through the forgiveness of sins and through the reconciliation of man to Him. But a believing mind cannot help seeing that many of the things that happen are also a judgment of God. What the people consider as settled and unchangeable, God is pulling up by the roots. "See I have this day set thee over the nations and over the kingdoms, to root out and pull down, to destroy and throw down, to build and to plant" (Jeremiah 1:10).

This is the vantage point from which Catholics and Protestants alike are called to understand and act in world events, thrown together as they are by the challenge of secularist liberalism in the 1920's and of communism in more recent times. For this task the resources of the whole Church are needed. Therefore, Hromadka in 1925 wrote *Catholicism and the Struggle for the Church,* in which he held up to his own people those values in Catholicism that must not be lost. The book is unavailable today, but something of its argument can be gleaned from a very recent article welcoming the new directions of the Second Vatican Council:

> The true universality of the Catholic Church as it manifests itself in the powerful Catholic thinkers and monastic movements, the real sense of tradition, anchored in the realization of Christ's presence amidst the communion of the

Church, the real spiritual struggle of the Catholic saints, men of prayer, humble shepherds, transcended the limits of modern Catholicism as manifested in the policy of the Curia, in the traditionally Catholic countries, and in many Catholic hierarchs and statesmen.

The full tradition of so great a church could not help but lead to renewal. "A constant inner struggle for a genuine communion with Jesus Christ and for a creative interpretation of dogma, liturgy, the mystery of the Church, and on the shaping of human society according to Catholic principles" was going on within it, also in modern times. But Protestants must not remain observers of this process with self-righteous satisfaction. "In our ranks too the desire for a renascence and fullness of Christian faith and existence must grow."

A genuine unity of all Christians is the object of our hope, our prayers, our spiritual struggle. The point is not whether the changes and paths of contemporary Catholicism correspond with our conceptions and norms, but whether we ourselves return to the Biblical message and a living apostolic tradition. It is a matter of understanding ourselves, and the contemporary revolutionary happenings or, at least, being ready to meet them, of being able to help humbly, but resolutely, modern man and society on their way toward real freedom and righteousness, toward true love and fraternity. Only thus can we hope that Christians will come closer together and unite.

Thoughts such as these are acceptable enough today. But in 1925, against the background of Bohemian history, they aroused a storm of controversy. For Hromadka was bringing to bear a criterion of churchmanship that all of Christendom had nearly forgotten and that came, therefore, as a new and radical message: the criterion not of a particular heritage, national or ecclesiastical, but of the perpetually challenging and reforming word of God.

Yet the controversy which arose around Hromadka's ecclesiology was as nothing, compared with the tempests his political orientation aroused. From his earliest years he was a Christian radical, impatient with bourgeois conservatism. He wrote in 1920,

> What a comfortable religion it is when one sees how the self-satisfied Bohemian Brethren rejoice that we have *in the past* had Taborite Communists and other Bohemian Brethren who fought against sin and the world! This kind of Christianity doesn't belong to us modern enlightened men. . . . It does not please us that the Christian brotherhood is born only out of broken, repentant hearts purified by the Cross, because then we would have to take the brotherhood *really* seriously, and that would have consequences that would make our hair stand on end. We would like to have a church, but as cheaply and easily as possible, so it won't hurt us and so that we needn't agonize over it.

In the same year he warned the Czech people for the first time—he was to repeat it thousands of times in later life—that the Bolshevik Revolution in Russia, whatever its cruelties, was a call to the Church to repent and to the nation to take seriously the demands of the poor for justice and social hope. It was the spirit of dedication and the historical power of the communist movement that fascinated him. "How did it happen?" he asked a church convention in 1923, "that there are men who wish to build a new society entirely on nonreligious and materialistic foundations? How much concentrated scientific thought and effort exist in Marxism, syndicalism, and revolutionary communism! How much despair, but also idealism, enthusiasm, and devoted service! . . . Socialism and communism cannot be brushed aside with a mere phrase such as 'materialism' or 'atheism.'"

Yet Hromadka was a loyal follower of Masaryk and later of Benes, a social democrat and defender of liberal society and the popular front. "My own sincere hope," he wrote in 1948 after the communist coup, "and desire, was that we should succeed in preserving Czechoslovakia as a kind of meeting place where the best and most creative elements of the East and West would come together and construct a common ground of cooperation. That was, I suspect, the guiding idea of President Benes' statesmanship." From the moment of Hitler's rise to power he became a militant antifascist, dedicated to arousing the conscience of his people to the evil and the danger of Nazism. He was shocked by and deeply critical of the Moscow purge-trials of 1936, the more so because of his collaboration with communists in antifascist work and his respect for them as representatives of the working class. He threw himself into the support of the loyalists in the Spanish Civil War and found in the Franco rebellion further evidence that "real democracy cannot depend . . . on the bourgeois elements. If the socialistic working class were to be defeated, the bell would soon toll for democracy as well." But he did all these things out of a profound sense that the political catastrophes and dangers of Europe revealed the action of God and could only be understood and responded to in this knowledge. "Only men who had been living in Europe in that period," he wrote later, "could have sensed the hellish magnitude of the crisis in its social, political, and spiritual implications. . . . All was at stake, humanly speaking." However, "the crisis had unveiled the cracks and crevices in the structure of modern life and thought. The future depended on whose name and what banner we would assume in rebuilding the shaken walls of our spiritual cathedral and political order. . . . If we, under certain historical circumstances, join with certain political groups in common action we do so on other grounds, the end and goal of our drive differing from that of our temporary allies and collaborators. . . . We may genuinely and honestly cooperate with the most radical movements, but we ought to do so in an attitude both of sovereign spiritual freedom and boundless compassion for suffering man. The reality of Christ is an unshakable rock, and provides, on the one hand, the only reliable angle from which to approach the events of history, and, on the other, freedom and security for the human soul." On this basis Hromadka was more open than any other major theologian of his country to collaboration

51

with socialists, communists, and all others in the antifascist cause. Before such an audience he put it thus:

> My friends, I am not going to speak to you in the name of your ideology or of any other political ideology. I am going to address you in the name of my Lord, who is my supreme authority and to whom I have committed myself, in the name of the crucified and risen Jesus Christ. But it is exactly because I believe in him that I am ready to help anybody struggling for freedom and liberty, for the welfare and righteousness of all who are poor, oppressed, downtrodden and despised.

Into this struggle came the Munich Pact of 1938, in which the French and British governments surrendered Czechoslovakia to Hitler's dismemberment and eventual occupation. It would be hard to overestimate the disillusionment with the non-communist Western world that this event created in Prague. The Czechoslovaks were a "Western" nation in culture, taste, political experience, and industrial development. With Munich, nevertheless, they were consigned to the East in the power division of Europe in order that the Western democracies might a little longer enjoy "peace in our time." The implications of this for the spiritual foundations of Western culture, its crumbling self-confidence, and its loss of vision for the future became Hromadka's major themes during the War and postwar years. The one consolation he received on the occasion of this —for him, historical catastrophe—was from the Swiss theologian Karl Barth, who wrote him as Hitler's armies were crossing the Czech borders:

> The really terrible thing is not the stream of lies and brutality that comes out of Hitler's Germany, but the possibility that in England, France, America, yes even here in Switzerland, we may forget that the freedom of Europe, and perhaps not only of Europe, stands or falls with the freedom of your people. . . . Every Czech soldier who fights and suffers, does so also on our behalf, and—I say it without reservation —he does so for the Church of Jesus Christ which in the clutches of Hitler can only be rooted out or become a parody of itself.

These words soon became public. Hromadka, marked by the Gestapo, had to flee his country to Switzerland, and had spent the war years teaching at Princeton Theological Seminary in the United States as well as working with the Czech government in exile. During those years he lived with the hope that the wartime cooperation of the Western allies with the Soviet Union would at last bring forth a new age of collaboration in which Christendom and bourgeois society would find a new vision while communism would be cured of its extremism. But the hope was overshadowed by a premonition which proved better founded—that the revolution which overthrows the old order must come upon it from without.

Returning then to Czechoslovakia in 1947, Hromadka cast his lot with an Eastern country, his own, already under strong communist influence, and with the church there. The final period of his active life, as guide and counselor of a church in communist society, has proved the most controversial of all. To understand it rightly, however, let us pause to examine the very structure of his thinking as a theologian and as an analyst of the world around him.

One dominant powerful note resounds in everything Hromadka has written during the past few decades—the note of total historical crisis, of revolution, and of the Lord of History, the Savior Christ, behind the events. Nowhere did he express this conviction more eloquently than in his effort to communicate it to the Christians of America while on their soil. Because it is his direct address to the writers and readers of this book from a volume now out of print, let him speak for himself at some length.

> How difficult it is to read and to grasp the essential issues of the Theology of Crisis! [of Karl Barth, Emil Brunner *et al*.] . . . And yet all becomes clearer and more relevant if we realize that a sinister earthquake is shaking the foundation of our civilization. Man has lost all sense of the Truth; the human soul has become confused as to what is the ultimate authority to which we owe our unqualified allegiance; the Church has forgotten her identity, and her ministers have

53

prostituted their calling through a primary occupation with the irrelevant, secondary, and tertiary issues of life. The modern mind has obscured the line between God and the world, between justice and injustice, between eternity and time; we have not realized the subterranean crumbling and breaking of the pillars on which our norms and standards rested. How can we bring home to the careless citizen, to the Church and her ministers, to philosophers and educators, to statesmen and technicians, the terrible fact that all is at stake?

The crisis of our civilization is deep, deeper than many of us are prepared to admit. The civilization as it existed prior to 1914, and, in a way, until 1930, is gone. The cathedral of common norms and ideas, standards and hopes, disintegrated from within. The present world war manifests in an unparallelled way the destruction of the (certainly imperfect yet real) unity on which the community of the civilized nations had rested. . . . We are living on the ruins of the old world, both morally and politically. Unless we understand this state of affairs, we cannot help groping and stumbling at noonday as in the night. All is literally at stake. No one single norm and element of our civilization can possibly be taken for granted.

The title of the book from which these words are taken, *Doom and Resurrection,* epitomizes his message. The doom of Western civilization is the end of an exhilarating, dynamic bourgeois idea, of a "free, autonomous, self-determining humanity," which had replaced both the Catholic vision of a politically integrated Christian civilization and the Reformation hope for a secular society redeemed and given direction by the free word of grace proclaimed in its midst. There is no saving idea today.

We cannot go back. We cannot save civilization by conservative caution or by reactionary devices. We cannot impose our abstract formulas and blueprints on the events of current history. Behind the history, the Risen Lord is doing His work. What does it mean that the close cooperation of Nazi Germany and Soviet Russia was prevented by vulgar and mean and stupid action on the part of the temporary lords in Germany? What does it mean that the vast spaces of Russia and the hundreds of millions of Soviet people found themselves on the side of the Allies? What does it mean that the spiritual and moral motifs of Russian history have been released by revolution and war and are shaping the days to come? . . . What does it mean that the liberal and democratic world has undergone a trial of blood and sweat?

What does it mean, in short, that there is no security, no place of refuge in the world from which we can observe the passing scene. Everything depends on how and in what faith man grasps and moulds the future.

Do not engage in abstract and artificial, cold and detached theories, or try to understand the footsteps of the Almighty God and of the Crucified in the light of the surface events of the days in which you live! . . . Do not moralize, do not be disillusioned. Rather fight for the victory of that in which you believe. The great mission of faith, philosophy, and theology is exactly to face and untangle the realities of history in the name of the Truth of the sovereign, holy, and merciful God.

This eloquence is not only Hromadka's response to the shock of Nazi invasion and the war. It is a recurring theme of his thought and the deepest experience of his whole life. It is a conclusion he draws from the analysis of historical events and a premise he brings to them from the prophets of the Old Testament who are constantly on his lips. However, he found this prophecy expressed most profoundly in modern times by two contrasting figures, the Russian novelist Fyodor Dostoevski and the statesman-philosopher Thomas Masaryk.

Dostoevski, more than any other nineteenth-century thinker, was in Hromadka's eyes a Christian prophet who foresaw both the doom that threatened Western man from within and the hope for all mankind that lay beyond. It was he who saw in the liberal humanism of his time the breakdown of all that is truly human. "This is the point at which modern man has arrived," as Hromadka summarized him.

55

First he declares himself to be the sovereign lord, and his reason to be the supreme authority; in the name of his reason he launches out into rebellion against the eternal sovereignty of God—and in the end by his reason he denies his reason itself and declares himself to be a powerless expression of the processes of nature or of the social milieu. This confusion of modern thought is gradually disintegrating everything that holds society together and opens the way to chaos and confusion.

This is not just a crisis of ideas. Human beings themselves, as Dostoevski demonstrates over and over again in the characters of his novels, become the victims of the uncontrolled passions of their bodies or souls. Again in Hromadka's paraphrase,

> Cut loose from the discipline of standards, and without awe before what is unconditionally sacred [human beings] are doomed to perish in incurable disease and self-destruction. Modern civilization is a macabre dance of men without bones, without sense of rhythm and melody, without order and discipline, without beauty and joy. A macabre dance at the edge of an abyss. . . . The wall protecting us from the horror of passions and impulses, from the powers of moral chaos, lust, debauchery, licentiousness and death, has been torn down by a deliberate, conscious and responsible act of the human mind.

Salvation then lies through suffering and death. It comes through taking on ourself the tragedy of man, like Sonia in *Crime and Punishment*. In the depths of human lostness, when there is no other help, we awaken to the companionship of Christ. "He is our companion in doom; he is the Lord of resurrection." He "challenges the power of death and sin by his real presence—without moralizing and patronizing, without sanctimonious poise, without orthodox self-complacency." He forgives with the weakness and yet with the power of love. "Only through him can we build a new cathedral both on the debris of impotent, dumb, and dull reaction and on the ruins of destructive revolution."

The emphasis on a new cathedral is significant. It binds Hromadka, despite his Reformation background, to the Eastern Orthodox vision of a sacred community giving structure to the whole earth. There is a nostalgia in his spirit for the very thing whose pretensions he most vigorously attacks wherever it appears—the unity of culture, religion, and political power that will inspire and integrate mankind in devotion to an ultimate loyalty and to human justice. More than once he appeals to America and to the Western world as a whole to prove him wrong in his baleful prophecy of its inner decay.

> Let me repeat it over and over again: all Europeans, eastern not less than western, would be terribly impoverished, intellectually, morally and politically, if the "West" should break down under its own weariness, exhaustion and lack of vision. The "East" of Europe, in its present stage of history and way of life, is lacking in many of the great values and achievements of western civilization. The destiny and mission of "Mother Europe" are tied up with the achievements and heritage of western Catholicism, the Reformation, the Renaissance, the Enlightenment and Democratic Humanism. If the West should waste its treasures through a lack of faith, through spiritual indifference and self-complacency, an atmosphere of a graveyard would, for a long time, deprive the whole European orbit (the East included) of its inward resilience and creativity.

But his standards for such a unity are higher than human beings can meet, and the relative patterns of obedience to be found in sinful men strike him as signs of doom rather than of evidences of grace. This contradiction between his yearning and his faith is expressed politically most sharply in his judgment on the father of his country, Thomas Masaryk.

To couple Masaryk with Dostoevski seems at first incongruous. Masaryk was a disciplined philosopher, a liberal, and an optimist though not a utopian. He was a man of action. "There was nothing academic, abstract or impersonal about Masaryk," wrote Hromadka. "He saw the old world crumbling and asked what to do about it." But Masaryk was at one with Dostoevski in his picture of the inner collapse of the old society, with its authorities, values, and loyalties rooted in the consciousness of the whole community. He also believed that nineteenth-century humanism brought no creative reconstruction.

> Postitivism, monistic Hegelianism and Marxian socialism deprived the human moral and spiritual freedom of all onto-logical, metaphysical and religious safeguards, and subjected the human personality to history, to the state, to the masses, to the absorbing, devouring Leviathan of the all-powerful society.

But Masaryk did not probe the depths of doom and resur-rection. He believed in "Jesus, not Caesar," as the organizing power of society and set himself to bring out all the humanizing insights of man's spiritual heritage as the basis for a renewed social and political order. He believed that the breakdown of society could be halted and that "the morally and spiritually vigorous democratic mind would do its upbuilding, constructive work in the postwar world."

This was also Hromadka's hope as a man of politics, though he was always aware of the limitation of Masaryk's faith. He saw in Masaryk a statesman who understood the depth and promise of the revolution that had succeeded in Russia, as well as its cruelties and excesses, and who was aware of the striving of the Russian people for "the fellowship of full and responsible love" that came to distorted expression there. He believed in him as the greatest apostle of the high calling of Western democracy—to build a creative, dynamically just soci-ety that would bring the communists into cooperation and dia-logue, and the working masses into full participation. He found Franklin D. Roosevelt and Henry Wallace (to whom he dedi-cated *Doom and Resurrection*) to be statesmen of the same faith and hope.

Finally, Masaryk's hope—and Hromadka's as well—was disappointed, and Hromadka came to look on his former ideal as one more illustration of the failure of the Western world this side of the total revolution of which communism in Czech-oslovakia was the expression. "The second world war revealed the greatness and worth of his personality and of his political and spiritual activity. He stood like a monument of a great epoch of humanistic ideals."

But soon after the war it became clear that he had in fact become a monument, and that his epoch had passed. I myself have had to wrestle with his heritage in order to realize that he belongs to the past, and that our future cannot be formed according to his patterns. Despite his fabulous knowledge of Russian history and Russian thinkers, he misunderstood and underestimated the historical meaning of the Soviet Revolution of 1917. . . . My own attitude toward this revolution was from the beginning more open and affirmative [than his]; but I hoped nevertheless that men like Masaryk—and in America Franklin D. Roosevelt—would be able to work creatively on the synthesis . . . between East and West. History has decided otherwise. Soon after the war it became clear that the preconditions were lacking on the western side for carrying out Masaryk's program, and that eastern communism, disillusioned by the west European politics of 1936–39, were not prepared to reckon with a bridgebuilder like Masaryk. Both west European socialism and Russian communism pushed Masaryk aside. . . .

Furthermore, it is clear today that Masaryk was a child of the nineteenth century, of the Enlightenment and of a positivist understanding of man. His philosophy, noble and sublime as it was, is out of date and unusable today in coming to grips with the upheaval of peoples and the needs of the contemporary world. He did not correctly judge the hard reality of a disintegrating humanity. Even in his understanding of Christian faith he was not able to see beyond the limits of rational and moral values, the religion of Jesus. . . . He has become a classic, but he is no longer a valid lodestar for our actions and our decisions of faith.

With these remarks Hromadka finally settles accounts with Western society, both theologically and politically, in the person of its most admired representative. He accepts the coup d'etat of February 1948 as both a judgment and an opportunity given by God. There is no turning back and there is no political qualification that can be made, he told the World Council of Churches at Amsterdam in 1948.

The fear and anxiety of a Maginot-line mentality which tries to preserve old treasures instead of creating new ones are not strong enough to meet the challenge of the present day. They reveal a spirit of self-defense. The people who are afraid and uncertain about what they believe or what they ought to establish are under a constant temptation to yield to a political or social reaction, or to an urge to stop the morally and socially justifiable processes of history. They will yield to the peril of being destroyed by the explosive elements accumulated by blindness and weakness, instead of shaping and forming the fluid lava of the present spiritual and social life. From my own experience I know of many instances—even in my own country—where the noncommunist groups have failed precisely because of their lack of common convictions, and of a united morally and politically dynamic program, whereas the communists know what they want, are well disciplined, and are hard working people.

This does not for a moment mean that the Christian is to surrender his prophetic freedom or identify with the communists. "The center of gravity of my own life and position is on another plane from that of the present masters of Czechoslovakia," he wrote to American friends soon after the coup. "The perspective of my political decision essentially differs from the perspective of communism." But "the social and economic transformation of our life along the lines of socialism cannot be contained and halted." To do so is to risk a greater social explosion than has already occurred. Furthermore, only the Communist Party has the discipline and devotion to carry out this socialization. "Communism is partly an heir of the agelong craving for social justice and equality, partly a child of the errors, blindness, and greediness of decadent bourgeois society." Its driving force is "an engrossing, fascinating idea of a society in which man will be free of all external greed, mammon, and material tyranny and in which a fellowship of real human beings in mutual sympathy, love, and goodwill would be established." This is, of course, a Christian's vision of what God is doing with the communists. By itself communism is inadequate to achieve its goals, just as Enlightenment humanism was before it. Dialectical materialism cannot grasp the heights and depths of human nature or historical destiny. When it exalts itself as the final answer, it becomes one more idolatry tempted to absolute power and destructive of human freedom, one that is unsure of the judgment of God on all men.

The Christian faith calls out to the revolutionaries: Avoid new injustice, for the wrath of the Holy Lord will come upon you and your children if you arbitrarily and arrogantly trample on eternally valid laws of right and mercy and truth. It reminds victorious revolutionaries: Do not boast of your victory. Do not consider yourselves anything more than the servants of men, and especially do not think that your revolution is the last stage in human history! The Lord God is Lord even over communism, and already today is preparing new forms of social life which will grow high above even the best that communism can offer.

But all this must be said and lived by Christians who have accepted the victory of the revolution and the fact of communist power without reservation or regret and who are prepared to play a constructive part in the socialist society which is being built. In the words of Jeremiah to the Hebrew exiles in Babylon, "Seek the welfare of the city where I have sent you into exile, and pray to the Lord on its behalf, for in its welfare you will find your welfare" (29:7).

Thus far we have spoken more of doom than of resurrection. This is true to Hromadka's starting point, but it is not fair to the quality of his faith. The center of this faith is his experience of the absolute sovereignty and living power of the risen Jesus Christ ruling and overruling human history. The fullest expression of it is the calling of the Christian to go with Christ into the deepest places of man's despair, to seek out the hope that is waiting to believe. In conclusion let us say a word about each of these. Hromadka wrote in 1950,

The Church of Christ is strong, because she clearly recognizes who her Lord is, and whom she should obey above everyone else. And she is free because she does not depend on human orders, she does not depend on worldly goods, but desires only to give testimony of the living God, serve and help the people no matter what may happen in this world.

The Church is a fellowship of pilgrims in this world. It "is not at home under any political regime nor under any social and economic order." By this very freedom, by this very acceptance of the events of history from the hands of God alone, Christians are able to be the bearers of new life and hope to people caught in its breakdowns—victims of its injustice and fearful of the future. In 1959, in a volume published in Germany, Hromadka put it this way after discussing the special burden of guilt and sin which lay upon the history of Czech-German relations:

> The Gospel frees us also from the burden and the fetters of history. The past loses, in the light of the Gospel, its binding power. Peoples live in history and are formed by their past. They are divided from each other by historical events and prejudices. But when the word of the Gospel sounds, those who have heard its voice come to the crucified and risen Christ as sinners. They are freed from that which has historically divided them and can truly begin to write a new chapter.

The Christian community gathers around the table of the Lord and his word is the place where the rule of Christ becomes clear and is confessed. It is the starting place for the redemption of the world.

But Christ is not only on high. "He, the Crucified, knows about the gates of Hell; he was a man of sorrows and acquainted with grief. He went through the shadow of death in the company of sinners." We too are called to go this way with him. This is the heart of Hromadka's ministry to communists and to the victims of communism, to the poor and to the powerful laden with their responsibility. "The Gospel of God's approach to man and of his presence in Jesus of Nazareth," he writes in a recent booklet, *Gospel for Atheists,* "among the sinners, sick, wandering, needy, hungry, and thirsty, and even

62

among the doubting and those who flee God, warn against every power front, against every attempt to mobilize the Church in an alliance with a 'Weltanschauung,' or a social-political, or cultural crusade. . . . In the light of the Gospel witness the atheist appears, not as an enemy, but at the most as an unhappy victim of our spiritual weakness, our dogmatic-churchly coldness, and the general corroding skepticism of modern humanity. . . . We must not forget that we find ourselves on the same level with the atheist, or better, that we descend with him into the depths of his doubts and of his spiritual weakness, and throw our lot in with him. . . . How can the sinner be brought to real repentance if one does not go directly to him, and in serving love take the burden of disbelief, doubt and helplessness upon oneself?"

This action of service and identification must not wait until the unbeliever is ready to receive us, until he "repents." Christians are called to serve even where they will be despised or reviled for doing so, to shoulder their responsibilities on the lowest levels of society, to which in the Stalinist era they were often consigned. They are called to show what it means to live responsibly but in freedom in the midst of the human problems and frustrations that bedevil a socialist society as much as any other. This is how they become the counselors and the helpers of communists and noncommunists alike. A new dialogue is already emerging from this situation as communists become less ideological, and Christians less fearful, about what it means to be human. Hromadka writes of this dialogue in his most recent work.

> Only in the depth of faith or conviction do the Christian believer and the communist understand how they are after all concerned with man in his pure humanity, with his liberation to true freedom and sacrificial service.

The heart and purpose of his ministry to a communist society is expressed in that confidence and that hope.

BERNARD HÄRING

BY

Stanley O. Weselowsky

Bernard Häring was born in Böttingen, Germany, in 1912. He received his doctorate in theology from the University of Tübingen. He was a member of the preparatory Theological Commission, *peritus* at the Second Vatican Council, and secretary of the commission that drafted Schema XIII, "On the Church in the Modern World." He is now secretary of the Papal Commission on Responsible Parenthood, which commission is continuing the Council's study of Catholic doctrine as it relates to modern problems of family life, population control, and individual conscience.

Considered one of the leading moral theologians in the Church today, he is best known for his three-volume work, *The Law of Christ,* which has appeared in eight languages, and for his *Christian Renewal in a Changing World*, translated into seven languages.

Bernard Häring has lectured widely in Europe and America and was recently a visiting professor at Brown University. His special interests include Lutheran theology, nourished by his contacts with major Lutheran figures, and Russian spirituality, which he traces to the years spent in Russia as a member of the Medical Corps and as a prisoner of war.

He currently lectures at the Academia Alphonsiana; he is professor of moral theology at the Lateran University and professor of pastoral sociology at the Pastoral Institute of the Lateran in Rome.

In his early major publication, *The Sacred and the Good, Religion and Morality in their Mutual Relationships* (*Das Heilige und das Gute,* 1950), Häring inquires, by means of a phenomenological and philosophical analysis, into the possible components and structures of "the sacred" and "the good." Following this preliminary step, he makes a concrete investigation of the way in which religion and morality, corresponding to the sacred and the good respectively, are treated in the philosophies of Nicolaï Hartmann, Emmanuel Kant, Friedrich Schleiermacher, Emil Brunner, Rudolf Otto, and Max Scheler. In this task the explicit interest of the author is to elucidate the fundamental attitudes of these philosophers in holding a variety of positions: religion as founded in morality (Kant); the independence of morality in relation to religion (Hartmann); the dialectic between religion and morality (Schleiermacher); the mutual penetration of Christian morality and Christian religion (Brunner); the mutual relation of the sacred and the good considered in their ideal forms (Otto); the sacred as the foundation of the good (Scheler).

The most intriguing sections of this work, however, are its concluding chapters. Häring writes: "A morality, therefore, which culminates and absorbs itself in the care for the salvation of its soul certainly remains, for us, a very reasonable enterprise, but this cannot be considered as a *religious* morality; even better, it cannot even justify itself as an absolute morality."

Within this context the question is posed: "What, now, could be the perspective that would make of morality a religious morality, and of religion precisely a religion that is morally efficacious, without therefore identifying religion and morality?"

The reply to this question is found in the direction that the phenomenology of the sacred and the good indicated to us: religion is essentially dialogue; it is a communion of persons, a communion of the love between the holy God and man who appears to him and consecrates himself to him. But morality equally manifests an essential tendency for the personal encounter between man who morally struggles and God who claims his obedience. Morality also seeks to be dialogue in the plain sense of the word, not a dialogue between the human person and a principal, but a response of man to the call of the Lord who commands and imposes his law.

According to Häring, the morality of the following of Christ fills in a supereminent manner, which is absolutely unforeseeable, what is required by the essence of the good as well as of the sacred. He does not, however, intend to make the following of Christ into a category which could be deduced from the results of phenomenology and which, in consequence, would be placed on the same level as other phenomena.

Though it is admitted that the quality of model and that of leader are categories of human communion, the following of Christ is seen to include all this, but it also signifies something infinitely more, something infinitely more profound. It cannot be deduced from anything, for it is disclosed in an absolutely unique manner by the love of God in revealing himself, in giving himself, and in instructing us. "But in denying the possibility of deriving the following of Christ from the results of phenomenology, we, however, can say: in the idea of the following of Christ there is present, in a supereminent manner, what the essence of the sacred and that of the good indicate and require."

Furthermore, this theme of the following of Christ reveals itself, precisely in the face of the morality of human self-perfection, as authentically religious through its dialogical character.

Out of this opposition Häring brings forth a number of implications. First, in the following of Christ, the proper value of man cannot be what is most superior within him; here the center of the self is not the center of all values. For here the subject that engages in moral effort moves beyond his self. His entire self rushes towards the value of the person, at once good and holy, of Christ. Second, there is not before the self an abstract image of the value of the self, an image which could be continually confused with the concrete self. On the contrary, there is before the self a loved Thou who incarnates the plenitude of all values, in whom and with whom can be discovered for the first time what the being of value is, the ideal essence of the proper self. Third, the proper image of value, the ideally proper person is born exactly because this is not viewed unilaterally in relation to the concrete self, but is received from the Lord, in sacred love for him. In the love of the Lord for the disciple, it is the essence of the disciple which is the theme: the Lord wishes the salvation, the perfection of the disciple.

This presentation of the marriage of morality and religion, so to speak, is discussed finally in relation to the way in which it transcends both formalism and legalism, how it transcends the categories of autonomy and heteronomy, and how it is best described as a loving obedience and obedient love.

Not unrelated to this early publication, therefore, is the massive three-volume work *The Law of Christ* (*Das Gesetz Christi,* 1954). The originality of *The Sacred and the Good* is slowly and carefully orchestrated throughout these volumes in the author's treatment of theological anthropology (man's following of Christ) as part of Christology (the primacy of Christ's invitation to man).

Because of the basic incompatibility of Christian morality and religion with all forms of individualism, the irreducible character of a simultaneous life in fellowship with God and fellow man becomes the subject of the second volume. This perspective is then carried out to the full in the third volume, with the presentation of the all-encompassing loving dominion of God over all forms of life and endeavor from the Christo-

67

logical center of the realization of the love of Christ in community.

Häring's intense preoccupation with the theme *persons-community-communion* is constantly displayed in this three-volume work; this is the case throughout all his writings, be they philosophical, theological, or ecumenical. On this same topic there should be added the following observation derived from a different point of view. His wide range of familiarity with the history of moral theology from the Church Fathers to the Middle Ages, through the Reformation period into the Enlightenment and the present era, all this, leads him quite naturally into inquiries in the fields of the sociology of knowledge, the sociology of religion, the ethos of cultural forms in the West, and the dynamics and scope of social life-forms.

Within the same year that *The Law of Christ* was published, there appeared another work entitled *The Sociology of the Family* (*Soziologie der Familie,* 1954). This work, which treats of the structure of the family in relation to religion, culture, society, economics, and technology, was later expanded and given a more detailed treatment in *Marriage in the Modern World* (*Ehe in dieser Zeit,* 1961). Commenting on these two works, Häring considers that

> from the start it was evident that the pastoral implications would have to be brought out more systematically, but finally it was clear that in view of the immense advance in the sociology of the family and the increasingly pressing need to integrate its findings into an overall survey of the moral and pastoral aspect of Christian marriage and the family, the scope of the first attempt was too limited. The result was a completely new work, combining sociology with the pastoral treatment of marriage and the family.

Already in an earlier book, *Power and Weakness of Religion* (*Macht und Ohnmacht der Religion, Religionssoziologie als Anruf,* 1956), he had made a penetrating investigation of the role that theology can play in religious sociology and of the place of the sociology of religion in the service of pastoral theology and the apostolate of the Church. Häring considers this study to be "an indispensable complement of the moral theology presented in *The Law of Christ*." The core of his thought evolves out of a set of theological reflections on the person in relation to community.

Häring's manner of clarifying this issue is to focus on Christology. In the Word becoming flesh there is an all-encompassing as well as a specific social side. Any attempt to ignore this would lead into a kind of Docetism, since, in concrete man, individuality and social relations belong indissolubly together. He considers that this

> is not less true of Christ, but rather more so: he is the head of all humanity; that also means he is in a unique way related to the whole of the human community and to every single person in the social milieu. His incarnation in the virgin Mary tells us at the same time that his universal position as head of all humanity does not exclude a concrete relation to a limited milieu, but rather presupposes it.

In the unfolding of this theme, Häring also treats of the constantly new projection of ecclesiastical structure and proclamation into changing human society. This embodiment is treated within the perspective of the sociology of knowledge in order to illustrate from it the vitality and variety of tradition. According to Häring, within this context moral theology is a special problem that is still insufficiently considered.

He claims that the same basic law of embodiment is true for the Church in all times. Because she is the fullness of Christ, she must continually imitate the self-emptying of Christ in a kind of "disincarnation," in the abandonment of her past time-conditioned forms in which she strives for a detachment from what she is used to, from the way things have been until now, in order to take on flesh and blood once again from the social and cultural elements of those peoples and times to which she wishes to proclaim and impart the power of the Incarnation of Christ.

This same theme of embodiment and detachment must also

69

be applied to the case of human language. Language is the instrument "of revelation and tradition precisely insofar as it is *life* and thus encounters the supernatural truth which is life in an infinitely higher measure. There is no absolutely static or even somewhat fast-frozen language; for language is the expression not only of the unity of the human spirit but just as much the variety of the formation of the human spirit. The entire culture of a people reflects itself in the language, but also at any given time in the particular stance of the social position of the one speaking."

In this way Häring indicates that numerous theological controversies and battles of faith must also be thoroughly examined from the perspective of the sociology of knowledge. The Christological and Trinitarian quarrels that broke out over the word and concept "person" are a classic example.

> The greatest efforts of the sociology of knowledge are perhaps still necessary in the area of moral theology, for it is precisely here that the existential character—the association with a definite situation—of many statements must not be overlooked if one does not wish unintentionally to put a false construction on earlier teachings coming from a completely different milieu. Moral theology—perhaps even more than dogmatics—of necessity always stands in a positive and negative confrontation with the spirit of the times.

Out of this position Häring concludes that the history of Catholic moral theology offers more than enough material for investigation by the sociology of knowledge. He claims that a systematic consideration of the viewpoint of the sociology of knowledge could lead to a more just evaluation of earlier moral theologians and at the same time to a position detached and free from any resentment towards the immediately preceding epoch. It could likewise lead to a more fruitful meeting with earlier epochs that stand intrinsically closer to our present-day Christian existence in a pluralistic society. It is admitted, however, that in these investigations we find ourselves only at the beginning.

This methodological study of how to engage in an evaluation and critique of the Church in the world in the past and present is complemented by another volume of that same year, *The Liberty of the Children of God* (*Der Christ und die Obrigkeit,* 1956). Here the theme of love and obedience in relation to Lordship and discipleship, a theme that was already sketched in *The Holy and the Good,* is now taken up in greater detail. Because Häring's theological exposition of obedience and love is Trinitarian and Christological, he correctly presents the gift of obedience as being as charismatic as the gift of love.

He begins by describing the life of the Trinity as

> a mutual giving in which all three persons are forever involved. This mystery is made known to us through the Incarnation and anointing of Christ as king of all creation in and through the action of the Holy Spirit. In him all authority has stability and dignity. Our Lord said to his disciples, "As the Father has sent me, so I send you" (John 20:21). This, the most sublime announcement in the history of the world, places ecclesiastical authority expressly in the ambient of the splendor of the highest of all mysteries, of the procession of the Son from the Father and of his being sent by the Father. The Father sent the Son out of his infinite love so that, through the kingdom of his love and grace, he might announce to men the glory of his love. Human authority should cooperate in this mission through the power of the Holy Spirit and in a "spirit of truth and love."

Within this context the following understanding of Christ in relation to the Church is most important for Häring. "Christ has merited the gift of the Church for himself through his obedience on the cross. He suffered *for* the Church—and what was perhaps even more difficult, he suffered *in* his Church, not only in Judas but also in Peter and in all who in the beginning fought but in the hour of trial took to flight."

And yet, the author mentions, it was also during Christ's life on earth that he joyfully announced to us that " 'all things had been given to him by the Father' (Matt. 11:27). Thus in him in whom all things have been created, all earthly authority has its value. He, the Incarnate God, gives in a mysterious way to the Church authorities a share in his own service of love and in its splendor."

For Häring, therefore, to speak of Christian liberty means to think above all of the liberty of Christ and, secondly, of that liberty by which Christ has made us free. It is the resurrection that is the great sign of the liberty that has triumphed in humility and in meekness without any use of violence or restriction. The measure that is placed before our eyes is the full participation in Christ's liberty, and the way to attain it is his way of humility, meekness, and love that does no violence to another man's liberty.

Häring's attitude to renewal and change is based as much on the sociology of knowledge and the sociology of religion in the service of pastoral theology as on the view that the Christian's life is one of obedience and love in relation to his being called (*vocatio, conversio, confessio*).

His investigations over a period of more than a decade anticipate, in many respects, the achievements of Vatican II. The volume *Christian Renewal in a Changing World* (*Christ in einer neuen Welt,* 1961), written a few years before the Council, seems, in retrospect, prophetic in various places. This work is an inquiry into the means and sources of strength for a genuine Christian renewal in our present involvement or lack of involvement in the modern world. For Häring, such a general survey of the Christian way of life must necessarily unfold the mutual interpenetrations of religion and morality, which procedure he had already developed in *The Sacred and the Good* and in *The Law of Christ*.

Once again, moral theology is placed within the context of faith in " 'the height and depth of the love of Christ, which surpasses all understanding' (Eph. 3:18)." The centrality of that to which the Christian is called, namely, " 'to be the light of *the world,*' " becomes the means by which he inquires into the many aspects of a fruitful Christian life. For it is only in the context of the glad tidings of the gospel that the Christian's obligations and duties reveal their genuine beauty and deep significance.

What we have here, quite literally, is a condensation of the first two volumes of *The Law of Christ,* which condensation is in one respect also superior to the original because of its greater emphasis on the law of the beatitudes and its de-emphasis on the Aristotelian presentation of virtue.

The comprehensive and original treatment of the sacramental character of Christian existence in *A Sacramental Spirituality* (*Gabe und Auftrag der Sacramente,* 1962) is yet another confirmation of the timeliness of Häring's inquiry in relation to Vatican II.

Commenting on the fact that for many Christians there is a wide gulf between liturgy and ethics, he also confesses that this rift is far from being healed everywhere. In spite of the many patient, and sometimes even impatient, movements for liturgical renewal, for Häring it is quite clear that we are still suffering from the consequences of that unfortunate catechetical and theological systematization which treated the sacraments *after* the commandments—or only as an *adjunct* to the commandments of the covenant of Sinai—and which regarded them principally as a new "set of duties" and at most as special "means of grace" given to help us keep those commandments, which are expounded without any reference to the "sacraments of the new law." Häring asks if it was not the "moralists" themselves of the last hundred years who unconsciously and involuntarily prepared the way for this sad phenomenon of the separation between liturgy and ethics.

This work, being acutely aware of past inadequacies, leans heavily on a Christological and ecclesiological understanding of the life of *all* Christians. More exactly, Häring's moral theology is here truly *theo*-logical in that it is founded on Christology (the Spirit of *Christ*) and pneumatology (the *Spirit* of Christ), which foundation *is* the *pietas* of the Father.

God, the Three-in-One, by an act of overflowing love beyond human understanding, has called men to be, as it

73

were, members of the family of the intimate society of love, the society of the Three-in-One, which is his own life. It is because of this *pietas* of God, by which he sees us not only as creatures, but as beloved children, that he is so deeply affected by our sins, so violently aroused to anger and so powerfully moved to pity. This is the *pietas* of God, or rather the *pietatis misericordia* of God, the almighty and merciful. . . .

The greatest sign of the *pietas* of our heavenly Father is the Incarnation, the suffering and the death of the Son of God himself *propter nos homines et propter nostram salutem*. In complete unity with the *pietas* of the Father, the Incarnate Son of the Father makes himself one with us. . . . The consecration of the sacred humanity of Christ to the high-priestly office in the Incarnation is one with the self-emptying of the eternal Word: "He emptied himself, taking the form of a servant" (Phil. 2:7). He consecrated himself to this service: "The Son of Man came not to be served but to serve, and to give his life as a ransom for many" (Matt. 20:28). His life is one of uninterrupted service; and the climax of his high-priestly work, his sacrifice on the cross, is the most perfect expression of obedience, of self-emptying and service.

Just as the *pietas* of the heavenly Father is visible to us in the heart of Christ, so it is the part of the Church, as guided by the Spirit of Christ, to bring into our experience the *pietas* of Christ, his identification with us as our brother, for our salvation.

Thus the proclamation by the Church of the message of salvation reaches its climax in the celebration of the sacraments. It is at this point that Häring lays great stress on the fact that the sacraments are not to be looked on as something apart from Christ; they are to be seen above all as powerful "words of the Word"—*verba Verbi*. Because they are the words of the Lord which effectively give something to us, they are no less than the act of salvation made present to us in a dialogue with him who alone possesses " 'the words of eternal life' (John 6:68)."

In order to state this even more precisely, Häring mentions

that because we live in the last age, the interval between the first and second coming of Christ, this means that it is the joyful age of grace and at the same time a period of longing for the full revelation of the glory of Christ and the Father. This can also be put in the following way: the interval between the event at Pentecost and the second coming of Christ is *the age of the sacraments.*

Therefore the sacraments are not to be thought of principally as a means of salvation, and far less as external aids to help us carry out a law which has already been given. They are themselves an effective and joyous proclamation of the decisive law for Christians, the "law of grace," and they bring all God's commandments into their proper place within this law.

The sacraments also have an eschatological character because, when the grace of the Lord speaks to us personally in the sacraments, this always means that his kingdom is claiming us. The sacraments are the mighty acts of God, the joyful news of the almighty Word of the Father in the love and power of the Holy Spirit.

It is of immense value to take a deliberate look at Christian life and the imitation of Christ from the point of view of the gift of God. "This prevents us from separating the good news of the Gospel from him who himself is the Word of the Father to us in person; we do not set up the sacraments as some sort of 'thing' apart from the Word of God; we do not separate the ethical commandment from the good news. Instead, we see in Christ himself, in his works of grace and in the good news of his Gospel, our salvation and the law of our life."

In this instance, Häring's understanding of *persons-community-communion* is seen to be deeply rooted in the sacramental character of Christian life. It is this character that truly indicates how human life points beyond itself in its being incorporated into the life of God. He emphasizes the fact that this fully personal and individual life to which the Bible and the sacraments call us is based on the heavenly Father's love, that is, communion, on the *pietas* of God in Christ. Man's fully personal prayer

and his consciousness of being responsible to God are truly
Christian when they are based on the part played as members
of that community called into being by God, on the praise of
God in common, and on the responsibility for one another.

This communal or ecclesiological aspect of Christian existence is itself under the tension of its present weaknesses and
the eschatological fulfillment that it longs for. On this issue
Häring is equally lucid.

> The Church knows that in the eyes of God and men she
> does not yet shine in the radiant glory of the heavenly Jeru-
> salem. Though she believes that Christ "loved her and gave
> himself up for her, that he might sanctify her, having cleansed
> her by the washing of water with the word, that the Church
> might be presented before him in splendor, without spot
> or wrinkle or any such thing, that she might be holy and
> without blemish" (Eph. 5:26f.), the Church makes no claim
> that all this has in fact been fulfilled already. Rather, it is
> a grace and calling which is binding on her, and humiliates
> her in her knowledge that she so inadequately lives up to it.

Because the Church is called into being through the *pietas*
of God expressed in Jesus Christ, she proclaims this mercy and
cries for mercy for all who have sinned. Accordingly, when the
Church seeks so urgently to make sinners conscious of the evil
of sin, for Häring this means that the Church is bound to proclaim not sins but the forgiveness of sins to her members and
to all men, so that all may turn around to the Father's home.

> The truth proclaimed so clearly in the liturgy, that the
> Church is *unum corpus poenitentiae*—one body in penance
> and atonement—bears an important message for us concern-
> ing the expectation and the duty that we should have in
> regard to the Ecumenical Council, which is certainly one of
> the decisive events in the life of the Church in the twentieth
> century.

One year later, in the middle of the Council, Häring brought
forth a theological interpretation of the ecumenical mission of
Vatican II: the Church's task of becoming a witness to unity,

which is stated in his work *The Johannine Council* (*Konzil im Zeichen der Einheit,* 1963). We find here what, by now, is to be expected—since it is one of his constant themes—a critical evaluation of the Church's love and obedience, viewed in relation to her response to the Master.

The very center of this theological analysis is Christ's prayer to his Father for his disciples. Continuing from this point, Häring presents the theme of unity in Christological and Trinitarian terms.

> Christ came forth from the Father into the world to render testimony of his substantial union with his Father in essence and in love (see John 16:27–28). The salvation of all mankind rests in faith in this mystery. This faith gathers up all men, making them truly one family in God.
>
> Christ is the Word of the Father unto us, his ultimate and absolute Word, in which he utters all his love. But he is also the Covenant, the response to the Father, the genuine and authentic response of love in the name of all mankind. His sacrifice of expiation for prodigal mankind who deserted the house of the Father is the work of love, a manifestation of the love of the Father. And at the same time it is the sign of the new love present in the heart of creation. In loving obedience and loving zeal for the glory of the Father, Christ manifests the intimate union of his own life with the Father and his incomprehensible solidarity with the human race.

Since the grand theme of the Council is the Church as she ponders her mission, her nature, and her forms of life in the light of her own basic mystery, for Häring this signifies that the Church seeks to renew herself in a manner whereby all can recognize that truly the Lord uttered the high-priestly prayer for her and that it is she who is the community of the faithful disciples bound by the double commandment of love. The Church, therefore, must inquire whether or not her whole structure and vesture, her liturgy, her preaching of the faith, her moral message, and her juridical forms are stamped by the mystery of unity and love, whether they are calculated in the present hour to serve the testimony of this mystery.

77

This same questioning is applied to the theme of relations among Christians. Häring stresses that vital theology, vital proclamation of the eternal Truth, exists only where faith is at work as well as hope and love. An anti-Protestant complex, or for that matter an anti-Eastern bias or any other disdainful bearing towards the men of our time, must have catastrophic results in the formulation of the truth. He maintains that this holds good not merely because such an attitude would render a disservice to unity but also because revealed truth itself would be disfigured.

He states that it is equally true that we cannot have an authentic theology in our time without dialogue with contemporary men. This holds for all to whom we announce the revealed truth: the faithful of today, the separated brethren, and even ourselves—simply all men. In stressing that the formulation of the message must be lovingly open to the contemporary manner of thinking, the Council enunciated the fundamental principle that the doctrinal magisterium is to be viewed in its pastoral function, indeed, as the expression of pastoral love. Thus the prevailing formalistic attitude towards doctrine, in Häring's view, must be corrected since the diffusion of sacred doctrine is essentially and entirely a service of love rendered by Christ through the Church to men of all times.

Applying one of his principles from *The Power and Weakness of Religion,* namely, that of projecting ecclesiastical structure and proclamation in changing human society to the Council itself, Häring claims that "the social message of the Church of the Second Vatican Council cannot be made acceptable to the twentieth-century mind if it is presented in the garb of the so-called European Christian culture." In any such presentation the cultural association would obscure the absolute and transcendent quality of Christianity in the minds of all those men of good will who question the validity of Western culture. In Häring's view the culture of the West with its origin and development in the Christian setting has become increasingly suspect to these men. Becoming more questionable day by day, this culture reflects discredit on Christianity through all too close association. For Häring it is clear that "in the vivid impression created by the unspeakable cruelty of two world wars, for which responsibility rests above all on peoples reputedly Christian, the myth of the superiority of Western culture over all others is definitely exploded."

He further argues that Christian social doctrine in the garb of an epoch in decline cannot attract even though it is proposed as distinct from Christian dogma. The person critical of Western culture would not look upon the Christian social message as offering an essentially dynamic structure for a new social order. Neither East nor West today finds in Western culture an approach to the transcendental and absolute in Christianity, an accessory motive of credibility.

As a foundation for his approach, Häring presents us with the parable about the call of Abraham. "As Abraham had to abandon his homeland and his own people in order to build the future promised him, so the Church today is called to divest herself of her Occidental past and to assume a position of service on a worldwide scale." Here, it should be noticed that even in his earlier investigations of Christology on the subject of embodiment and renunciation, he was led to the conclusion that one of the Church's permanent characteristics is to display this twofold reality of transcendence in commitment and commitment in transcendence: the Church's relation to God and to man grows in direct, not in inverse, proportion.

Häring mentions four "unquestionably positive" points, which he sees as the result of the first session of the Council, that could revitalize the Church's relation to the world: 1) there is to be no favoring whatsoever of any scholastic theory; 2) dogmatic utterances are to have an essentially pastoral character as is demanded by revealed truth; 3) a theology that conceives its own nature as bereft of pastoral interest is an impossibility; 4) the primacy of charity is an essential demand for dogmatic doctrinal proclamation.

In closer relation to his own field, Häring believes that the

Council introduced very clear and concrete bases and perspectives for the further development of Catholic moral theology. He notes, in following the example of the Constitution on the Sacred Liturgy, that the proclamation of morality will once again have to be more deeply inspired by the gospel, by the great perspectives of Sacred Scripture, more than in previous centuries. From the Council's deeper penetration into the doctrine of tradition Häring concludes that this has inflicted a mortal wound on the arid conceptualism which attempted to reduce tradition more or less to a handful of formulas. From the Council's sharp emphasis on revealed truth as the truth of salvation, on *caritas in veritate,* and on the primacy of love in dogmatic theology Häring concludes that this assures moral theology of that same decisive vision. Moreover, the baneful divorce of dogma from moral theology would thus be healed. And finally, because of the Council's express statement that the Church's juridical elements are to be totally animated by love, Häring concludes that this also applies to the way in which duties and laws of Christian life must be based on mystery, service, and charity.

Just as this work of Häring is concerned with the call of the Church *to become* a witness to unity, so also do we find the underlying motif to be the call *to renewal.* This does not mean that a listing of proposals about renewal is itself the accomplishment of the Christian's task; it is, rather, a confession that there remains much to be done.

Strengthened by past efforts and hopeful of the future, Häring sees that "the forces at work for some thirty years for the renewal and deepening of Catholic moral theology truly owe much to the biblical, liturgical, and patristic renewal. The work already begun will surely be able to reach a stage of greater fruitfulness if in all things we are motivated by an ardent desire for the fulfillment of the will of the Lord, 'that they all may be one.'"

The fact that Häring's work in moral theology stands in such solid relation to the concerns of Vatican II is fully indicated in the two volumes, *This Time of Salvation* (*Die Gegen-wärtige Heilsstunde*, 1964) and *Toward a Christian Moral Theology* (1966). The first is broader in scope and considers the problems and creative opportunities of moral theology in its confrontation with a variety of cultures and social mores. It also treats of moral theology in the context of different environmental conditions (subcultural forms) and in relation to the problems posed by monopolism, collectivism, individualism, and the spirit of technology. In the second volume the investigations begun in *The Johannine Council* are continued. Here the impact of Vatican II on moral theology is given a more comprehensive treatment. These two works are, however, very similar in that they are both reflections on the method of developing moral theology and on the manner in which this development would transcend the limitations of past manuals. Häring claims that we are involved in much more than merely new individual problems. Rather, "the question is being raised whether we can be just to these new problems with the tools of the post-Tridentine morality of the confessional, or whether the very abundance of the new questions does not demand a new synthesis, a new over-all view. Added to this is perhaps the most decisive factor —that the majority of the faithful today live in what is in every respect a pluralistic society."

He argues that a thorough reassessment in moral theology, something that he himself is energetically engaged in, is urgently needed.

Ever since moral theology began to constitute a proper theological discipline there has been continual vigorous discussion and open self-criticism within the field. But its self-analysis has perhaps never before extended to essence, sources, methods, and goal as much as it does today. The casuistic-canonical type of *institutiones theologiae moralis* (moral textbooks), which were oriented towards the "court of penance" and which on the whole were uncontested for three centuries, has begun to waver for the first time, and seriously. Today a series of compelling factors has brought the apparently benumbed forms of moral theology to the thawing point in almost all countries. Probably most important among these factors are the present-day Bible movement, the newly deepened relation to the liturgical-sacramental life, and the dynamic character of modern society.

This need for a critical understanding of the limitations of past moral theologies can be seen in the question of the relation of moral theology to other cultures and social customs. Häring's views might best be summarized in the following illustration.

It is a real danger for the Christian teaching on the moral life when we proclaim it to cultures of completely different background in the categories of Aristotle, of the Stoa, of one of the two scholastics of the same stamp, or even in the garments of the old Roman or typical modern and Western jurisprudence. A very intelligent and sincere Vietnamese priest once told us that to him the teaching of Confucius still seemed more stirring and preferable to a *manuale theologiae moralis* of which three-fourths is legal casuistry while the rest is presented in more or less juridical form. When we became somewhat skeptical of this criticism of the Latin textbooks on moral theology which had been introduced into East Asia, the young Vietnamese would not rest until we had read the four holy books of Confucianism thoroughly and had declared to him that moral theology can indeed build upon them more easily than on Stoic ethics or Western legal thought. When in the thought of Confucius, for example, we find at the summit of the "basic virtues given to us by heaven" goodness, or benevolence, it is really incomprehensible why we, particularly in Asia, should rest with the Greek schema after we have once been made aware that the Greeks did not have as high an interpretation of love. Whereas in the thought of Confucius love is the highest gift of heaven, and it alone is able to establish a correct order within the heart, to the Greeks it was only a passion or an effort towards one's own fulfillment.

Perhaps it is Häring's openness to criticism and his ability to benefit from criticism that has enabled his work to indicate so many new horizons. These untiring efforts, no matter what different issues they address themselves to, always reflect the following profound center: "Christocentric moral theology of today joins the *personal characteristics* with the *mystic-sacramental* and the *social salvation-ecclesiological.*"

What Father Elmer O'Brien has said of *The Law of Christ* can be applied fittingly to the whole and single task of this author: "No one is better founded in his criticisms or more knowledgeable and balanced in his proposals than Häring. . . . Achievements even greater than those of Häring are, one trusts, in prospect. When they come, it will be to him one's thanks will be mainly due. Until they come, to him one's thanks are due—unreservedly."

EDWARD
SCHILLEBEECKX

BY

Marinus J. Houdijk

"The New Turn in the Dogmatic Theology of Today" was the title of an article written by Edward Schillebeeckx in 1961 in the first issue of *Tijdschrift voor theologie*. As one of the originators and as the present editor-in-chief of this journal, he has demonstrated his concern for a new understanding of the reality and the truth of faith. Intrinsically it belongs to the task of theology to ensure that Christian and ecclesiastical belief can really become our belief insofar as we stand in the world of thought and life peculiar to this age. For Christian revelation is not a reality that may be considered objectively as an entity outside and beyond the human experience of existence. Christian revelation is given to man so that he may have a personal understanding and realization of his belief. From the very nature of revelation it follows that belief is conceived of and shaped by man's world of experience. Therefore revelation will always have to be understood within actual existential experience, which may justly be called a *locus theologicus*. And to the degree that our way of experiencing existence differs from that of former times, our view and our wording of the faith will differ from those of earlier days.

But at the same time Schillebeeckx is anxious to stress that this "new theology" is by no means a novelty if that is understood to mean a break with the old faith. On the contrary, present-day religious thought is in need of being confronted with the past in order to find its own new form. The past is an indispensable operative source for our religious thinking; in our confrontation with the past the new form of the faith is passed on to us. The reason for this is that despite all the differences in the forms in which religious life is expressed, we were concerned in the past and are in the present with the same faith which expresses itself variously to each generation.

> We simply cannot believe *in the same way* as people in the Middle Ages believed, not even as the Apostles did. And yet we have and practice the same belief indentically the same, but in the dynamic identity of a religious existence in history.
>
> What is new in the theology of today should neither bewilder us nor make us suspicious. We are not concerned with *another* theology, but with the old, ecclesiastical theology itself, which takes possession of the reality of the faith in a more powerful way.

Here one more guiding principle of his theological methodology becomes evident: the interpretation of the faith from our present-day existential experience remains constantly directed to the reality of faith and ruled by the data of faith. A new interpretation of the faith should be anxious not to narrow its content or to empty it of meaning, but, remaining true to the theological data, to unfold it in all its riches. Schillebeeckx's way of thinking is characterized by a great respect for the mystery that comes *towards* us in revelation. Theology must always be docile to the reality of revelation as it emerges from the Scriptures and from tradition.

At this point one can better understand why Schillebeeckx is esteemed by his readers. He does not confine himself to a mere repetition of the theology of the handbooks. Rather his work is a *ressourcement,* and thus a renewal of that theology. There are those who view this approach with alarm. While among the "progressives" the opinion is heard that Schillebeeckx does not always leave sufficient scope for the existential experience of today, that he conforms too much to traditional patterns of religious thinking or church practice. This may well be the basis of the criticism leveled by some people in the Netherlands against his recent book *Het ambtscelibaat in de branding* (Priestly Celibacy under Discussion) and his first answer to Bishop Robinson's *Honest to God, Personale Begegnung mit Gott.*

Theology helps to carry man further in the mystery of revelation. The "new theology" is no different: it is "a new ethos of the theologian" (and of the pastor) to look for such expressions of the faith as deepen faith and do not confuse it. "Sometimes I have the impression that we have exchanged the moving respect for the tender mystery of newly discovered aspects of truth that enable us to breathe more freely, for the cracking effect of sparkling bangers which frighten people."

Edward Schillebeeckx was born in 1914 in Antwerp, Belgium. After graduating from the Jesuit High School at Turnhout, he entered the Flemish province of the Dominican order in 1934. He studied philosophy and theology in the Dominican houses of study at Ghent and Louvain until his ordination in 1941, after which he immediately became a teacher of dogmatic theology. During these years of study he was tutored primarily by philosopher D. de Petter, O.P., who had a profound influence upon him, especially in the field of epistemology. De Petter did not agree with the Scholastic views current at that time; he felt that the Scholastic philosophy of his day had taken a rationalistic turn by adopting a conceptualistic theory of cognition and that it no longer conveyed the wealth of medieval Scholastic thought, in particular that of Thomas Aquinas. On the basis of St. Thomas' original thinking, De Petter drew up an epistemology in which the living experience of man's reality and that of the world are central; but he did this in such a way that he affirmed the value and the indispensability of conceptual cognition within experiential knowledge. By doing so De Petter broke through established conceptualistic Scholasticism without giving up the value of conceptual knowledge *within* living experience. In this theory of cognition he disassociated himself from M. Blondel and J. Marechal.

Schillebeeckx adopted De Petter's way of thinking and developed it in his own theology. Two elements which were to prove decisive in his thinking soon appeared. First of all there was an attempt to fathom the original view of St. Thomas through the *Aufklärungstheologie* of later Scholasticism and a revaluation of the biblical and patristic inspiration operative therein. Next there was a marked receptivity, at the same time critical, to contemporary philosophical thought.

The two elements were further strengthened when Schillebeeckx went to Paris in 1945 to continue his studies. At the Dominican Theological Faculty of Le Saulchoir he was tutored chiefly by M.-D. Chenu, O.P., and also attended lectures given by J. Wahl, Le Senne, and Lavelle at the Sorbonne. Having successfully defended his dissertation on the sacraments, he received his doctorate in theology from Le Saulchoir in 1951.

Schillebeeckx has always adhered to De Petter's theory of cognition as well as to his criticism of Marechal (and consequently of Karl Rahner). He agrees with the contention of the school of Marechal that conceptual knowledge has no value *per se,* but that this value must be found in a nonconceptual element. Thus the conceptualistic approach has been abandoned. On the other hand, he disagrees with the latter's answer to the question of where the value of our knowledge does lie. Marechal's view is that the value of our concepts is founded in the dynamic power of the human mind which takes in the conceptual content and, as in a projective act, reaches reality through that conceptual content. In Schillebeeckx's view, however, the value of our concepts lies in a "nonconceptual element of knowledge"; that is, there is an objective dynamism in our conceptual content itself which refers to reality. For conceptual knowledge is part of a preconceptual experiential knowledge which is fed by reality, and the concept itself refers to the reality which is present in experiential knowledge. Therefore, our knowledge is not a projection of the human mind but rests on the objective dynamic power of reality itself which we experience and which we express conceptually, though always inadequately.

A number of important notions are related to this view. Schillebeeckx considers the philosophical affirmation of the objective nature of human knowledge as an absolute precondition to the possibility of any real knowledge of God. Therefore, he has disassociated himself from some phenomenologically oriented Catholic thinkers who, in his opinion, have disparaged the importance of the objective nature of knowledge.

He stresses that the "proof of God's existence" lies in our experience of the reality we live in, and consequently he rejects every form of fideism which occurs even in the teachings of some Catholic thinkers.

> Reality itself manifests itself to man as referring to God. In a projective act the human mind only follows this objective dynamic power that lies in reality itself, closely as it were, and thus the mind is carried along—not by a projection of the mind, but by an objective, I might say "ontic" dynamism of reality itself—to the personal existence of God, without which the content of our experience would become intrinsically contradictory.

In the exchange of views between Schillebeeckx and nonreligious humanism, he has stated that Catholic theology shares the following humanistic starting-point: the only approach to any knowledge is our human experience. This also applies to our knowledge of God. In order to remain true to the nature of man's being, belief in revelation demands that a recognition of God is accepted within the universally human experience of all that is. Moreover, this is required from the viewpoint of revelation itself. For if man cannot in the first instance justify the existence of a personal God from his existential experience, it becomes impossible and meaningless to speak of a special revelation.

Schillebeeckx's anthropology can be briefly summed up in the phrase *spiritualisme incarné;* man is defined as an embodied spirit. In this way he arrives at a new appraisal of the unique character of the human being within theology. On the one hand, the spiritual dignity of the human person is emphasized; on the other hand, man's body is seen as a sign, a manifestation of the spiritual life of man. In this manifestation man finds himself, since he is never "a pure spirit" but always an embodied spirit, man in the world.

This view pervades every field of his theology. The consequences for moral theology, where it is concerned with "the law of nature," are described by him as follows:

> The absolute and therefore compulsory character of moral rules cannot be based on [biological] nature as such, but only on man's being a spirit, a spirit nevertheless that is intrinsically connected with the body. This is the immediate basis on which moral rules for every human act can be drawn, precisely because the radical uniqueness of man's being consists in the correlation between the spirit communicating itself to the body and the body merely participating in the spirit. So biological nature as such does not determine moral law in any sense. As a biological datum it is only *materia circa quam* of the ethical rules, which can be defined neither spiritualistically nor physicistically, but only anthropologically. The drawing up of ethical rules is based on "a law of incarnation," exactly because it is not the biological apparatus, but the *incarnation* that has a say in the drawing up of ethical rules. In this connection we can say that "law of nature" is a less felicitous formulation.

Schillebeeckx is of the opinion that in the writing of St. Thomas Aquinas a basic beginning can be found to overcome the "physicism" in moral theology which tends towards a personalistic view. In his book *Marriage: Secular Reality and Mystery of Salvation,* he shows that in both patristics and medieval writings the biological finality of the marital act was never the moral rule, which contravenes the teaching of later Scholasticism down to our own day, but that the particular dignity of a human being is always the determining factor of morality, although within the framework of the Church Fathers' thinking and that of the medieval theologians this particular dignity was expressed in images and formulations which are untenable today.

In this context Schillebeeckx takes into account the fact that among philosophers of the last two centuries the special and unique character of the human personality has increasingly been treated thematically. It is precisely this element which was, understandably, absent in the theology of former days. It is the task of present-day theology, therefore, to reinterpret the ecclesiastical heritage from a personalistic view of man, that is, from a view which is authentically Christian in its essence. Personalism opens the eyes to the dimensions of the mystery of salvation in a profound and unprecedented way. Thus in his book on marriage he discusses conjugal love and intersubjectivity in earnest, for this new datum of modern conjugal love is "an opportunity for grace."

Schillebeeckx's first major publication was an expanded version of his doctoral thesis at Le Saulchoir. It appeared in 1952 under the title of *De Sacramentele Heilseconomie* (The Sacramental Economy of Salvation). This book contains his investigations in the field of sacramental theology from the point of view of dogmatic history. The outline of his systematic theology can already be discerned here; he had intended to write a separate volume on systematic theology. Instead he synthesized all of his sacramental teaching in the book *Christ: The Sacrament of the Encounter with God.*

Christian revelation not only communicates a number of truths; it is the revelation of the reality of salvation, expressed verbally. We are concerned with a *mysterion,* the reality of salvation occurring in history and manifesting itself visually on earth. This mystery of salvation was fully realized in the sacramental manifestation of Christ. The reality of salvation was consummated in the mysteries of Jesus' bodily existence on earth. In Christ salvation became visible once and for all. He is the "primordial sacrament." By virtue of the salvation come about in Christ, the mystery of salvation is present in the Church, and the sacraments of the Church are signs by which the mystery of grace is presented to us. In the sacraments Christ offers salvation to man. This offer is essentially "infallible," that is, it is absolutely prior to any human response to it. It is only in this authentic sense of the term that the sacraments can be said to operate *ex opere operato;* since the sacraments are Christ's offer of salvation, they cannot be *dependent* upon human response.

However, Christian revelation is concerned with the dialogue of salvation between the living God and man. What theologians call "sanctifying grace" must be defined as the personal relationship of man to God, a personal communion with God, offered to man in transcendent mercy and put within man's reach. From the outset the sacraments occur in this context of *encounter.* In modern phenomenology man's symbolizing activity is seen as material realities which appear to be an expression and a rendering of a spiritual experience. Thus the sacraments are to be regarded as the incarnation-in-a-sign of the inner religious life of the faithful. But the essence of a sacrament is that it express the belief of the cult-community, the belief of the Church. Thus the sacraments are most clearly seen as a *professio fidei,* a confession of the living faith of the Church. A sacrament is called "valid" because the authentic faith of the Church-community is expressed in it. Since we are concerned with the exteriorization of inner belief, we must attribute a value to the word over and above the *faits et gestes* of the sacramental act.

In this way Schillebeeckx has disposed of a view of the sacraments which regards them as "things" (*res naturae*). Starting from this assumption Scholasticism described sacramental life and the life of grace in terms of physical categories, whereas personalism views the sacraments as set within the encounter between God and man. This also places a premium upon the personal religious effort of the person receiving the sacrament. Formerly theology considered this personal effort merely as a condition prior to the sacrament itself, whereas Schillebeeckx, seeing the sacrament as personal encounter with the living God, considers the individual's religious attitude as part of the essence of the fullness of the sacrament.

In 1955 Schillebeeckx published his book *Mary, Mother of the Redemption.* Here he describes Mary's motherhood as the original basis of all of Mariology. He emphasizes that her motherhood should not be understood in a merely biological sense; its personalistic character must have first place. Mary became Christ's mother through a personal act of free acceptance, expressed in her eminent *fiat.* On the other hand, Mary did not only agree to become mother of the man Jesus but also accepted motherhood of the *Savior* of the human race. In this act of free acceptance she accepted the redemption of all of us and was herself redeemed in a special way. With respect to Mary's cooperation in our objective and subjective redemption, there can be no question of Mary contributing anything to this redemption together with and in addition to Christ. Christ is the only Mediator. Mary's cooperation in redemption is a cooperation *simply through acceptance.* Mary is the one person who is universally accepting and universally redeemed and *in that* she is at the same time our "co-redeemer."

If we keep in mind that divine redemption of human beings is a human, *freely-accepted* redemption and therefore meritorious for us, in other words, if we keep in mind the personalistic nature of our redemption, it is immediately evident that Mary's having been redeemed objectively and subjectively is exactly the ground of her being the universal co-redeemer and of her universal merits with regard to her own and also to our objective and subjective redemption. And this precisely because of her spiritual-and-physical, or in faith freely accepted motherhood, that is because of the eminent way in which Mary was redeemed objectively and subjectively on account of the unique object of her free acceptance, which contains a corresponding unique depth of faith and readiness to make sacrifices.

Schillebeeckx pays great attention to the matter of man's personal acceptance of the reality of salvation, a personal acceptance to which the offer of salvation is intrinsically directed. In an article on the Vatican II Constitution on the Church, he has discussed at greater length this aspect of encounter with Christ, at the same time considering the historicity of human life in relation to salvation within the Church. The Church has been given salvation, but grace operatively present within the Church must always be internalized in the living faith of the Church-community.

> The Church is not only the sacramental presence of salvation, the sign of Christ's reign; it is also the *personally accepted* presence of it (accepted in grace).

Thus the victorious grace of Christ is operative within the Church, and consequently the Church will not fail; she is "indefectible." At the same time this grace requires an existential assent by the Church-community, an assent that is co-essential to the Church.

> But it is this existential assent—co-essential to the Church itself—that makes ecclesiastical indefectibility *history;* history not only of human behavior, but of *grace* itself.

Thus it is not enough to conceive of the marks of the Church in an abstractly essentialistic way outside their concrete realization within the Church. Rather they should be regarded as functioning within the religious practice of the Church. Only in this way can it be understood how the Church, in which salvation is unshakably present, can be in constant need of evangelical purification.

> The two elements—*indefectibilitas* and *purificatio*—evoke a strong tension; one element does not destroy the other but, on the contrary, evokes it on account of the situation in the flesh.

93

On the ground of the promised indefectibility the Church in its concrete form is always purifying and reforming itself. Expressed in different terms: the self-reform, continuously undertaken in faith, is the historic modality of ecclesiastical indefectibility. This shows already that the *indefectibilitas* is not triumphant, but in weakness, in which God's grace is victorious.

Even though the Church is an earthly, visible community and as such is open, for instance, to a sociological sounding, yet the Church community is essentially distinct from any other human community. For the basis of the Church is Christ in his glorified humanity; in him all mankind has already been brought to God, fundamentally—i.e., in faith, hope, and charity—before mankind is in fact gathered into one historical community of grace, the earthly Church. The community of persons in faith, hope, and charity, as it is present within the Church, derives its origin outside itself—from the glorified Christ. And that is exactly why the Church is a transcendent, "supernatural" reality.

The reality of salvation, i.e., the uniting factor or unity of the Church community, and consequently the regulating principle of authority, are prior to the Church, are pregiven to the Church in the person of Jesus Christ. The unity and the unifying principle do not lie, in the first place, *in* this community of the faithful, itself, nor do they proceed *from* this community, from below as it were, but in Christ and from him this saving reality that unifies all men is realized within the Church on earth. The value that joins the multiplicity of persons together into a *"communio"* within a *"societas"* and also the authority that safeguards man's realization of this unifying value are *pregiven* to the people of God in Jesus Christ. Therefore the members of this community do not really *constitute* the visible Church community of grace, but they are grafted by the Father in the mission of the Holy Spirit upon a pregiven central point, Jesus Christ, and thus, in the unity of them all with Christ, they are themselves also *made into* a community of persons in faith, hope, and charity. By virtue of baptism and belief in Christ we are *planted* as a visible community of grace in the dimension of history and public knowledge; and on that account our addressing the *Father* ("Our Father") must be

94

considered as inwardly community-making and Church-founding on the strength of the charisma of the Holy Spirit given to us by the Lord.

The unity of mankind, pregiven in the person of Christ, is realized in the earthly Church and founds a community of faith and charity immanent in the Church; this community is as much inward as outward and visible. The reality of grace in Christ is interiorized in the community of the faithful and is incarnated in the Church of living people. The Church is "the People of God"—not a special people, but all mankind, made in Christ into a community of love which makes its way to the coming kingdom of God and which, bearing active testimony within this world and working in and at this world, awaits the coming of Christ.

Although there is something of a continuous upbuilding in the conception of the body of Christ, the idea remains static to some extent; it does not possess the same suggestive quality as the conception of a people passing through the sorrow and joy of daily life. People means history, a history-making event, a genesis, a human event in which the horizontal and the vertical lines are viewed together. Then the Church, as the divine planting of an utterly new reality, is not disincarnated; it is given human features, the features of an earthly event, in which God writes a straight history with crooked lines. "People of God" suggests that the Church does not exist of things, of rites, doctrines, and laws, but of living human beings. The Church consists of human beings, *"vivis ex lapidibus,"* "built from living stones," but human beings who by the saving action of God, under God's never-failing forgiveness, grow together into a *"communio sanctorum,"* a holy communion of persons, of which Christ himself is the pregiven uniting factor, the fundamental life-value, the living rule and the principle of authority; in which, therefore, the living person of Christ in his human shape, that is, in the visible shape of a loving human gesture of unconditional servitude, is himself the rite, the doctrine, and the law, of which the sacraments of the Church and the administration of the Word are the living relics. Somewhere Church and World fall together, if only we are well aware that the man Jesus does not so much come to sanction our pregiven human authenticity, but that only in the absolute *novum* of the humanity of Jesus, what is authentic humanity is revealed to us from above and is realized on the strength of this revelation. In Christ humanity, a fellow-humanity, becomes by definition one people of God.

The relation between hierarchy and laity in the Church should always be seen within the framework of the one People of God if one does not wish to distort the proportions right from the beginning. In this essay we cannot enter into the precise definitions by which Schillebeeckx delineates the uniqueness and mutual relationship of both. We may only mention that he lays much stress on the fact that the distinction between hierarchy and laity cannot be regarded in such a way as to suggest that in the Church there are two groups, each with its own status of being a Christian. On the contrary, there is only one status within the Church in which hierarchy and laity share alike. *All* Christians, hierarchy and laity, live the same Christian life which they have entered by baptism and belief in Christ. The members of the hierarchy, too, are and remain primarily Christians just as do all members of the People of God. The People of God, that is the entire Church, is neither clerical nor laical. First of all, we are concerned with the same Christianity of all the members of the Church. But the concepts of hierarchy and laity indicate that *within* the fundamental unity of the People of God there are several *functions;* the concepts clerical and laical are Church-functional concepts; they only indicate a difference in office or *diakonia.* Thus hierarchy and laity prove to be always dependent upon each other because each of them is, in its own way, subservient to building up Christ's community. At the same time we must affirm here, on the level of administration, the essential distinction between hierarchy and laity.

Moreover, the attention paid by Schillebeeckx to the Church as the People of God, as a community of human beings who in their totality are under the continuous activity of God's spirit, is especially apparent from his revaluation of the *sensus fidelium,* the sense of faith of the entire Church community. In their episcopal letter about the Council (Christmas Eve 1960), mainly drawn up by Schillebeeckx, the Dutch bishops explain how, apart from the "public revelation," the faithful are addressed by God in their inner selves in the "light of faith" (*lumen fidei*) through which they can also hear God's offer of salvation personally within their hearts. While this inward drive and illumination by the Holy Spirit are active in each of the faithful, they are also present in the community of the entire Church. This impulse works hidden in the various factors of the human consciousness and of human existence, but in the long run it may lead to a *collective* religious view of the entire Church community. And of this Thomas Aquinas says the faith of the universal Church cannot err. But at the same time it is precisely here that the special task of the ecclesiastical hierarchy becomes clear; in order to decide whether we are really concerned with a consensus of faith of the whole Church, the hierarchy acts as the accompanying, correcting, and ultimately judging body in virtue of its special office with which infallibility is connected.

Thus it is obviously wrong to isolate the office of the ecclesiastical hierarchy from the faith of the entire Church community; on the contrary, its very *Sitz im Leben* is found in the living faith of the Church as a whole.

> From all this it appears that the infallibility inherent in the papal ministration cannot be detached from the totality of faith in which it was placed by Christ. By reason of the early breaking-off of the first Vatican Council, the separate dogmatic definition of papal infallibility creates the impression that it stands entirely apart. In fact, this personal infallibility also exists in unity with the ministerial infallibility of the world-episcopacy, which itself is co-supported by the infallible faith of the entire religious community.

The orderly publication of Schillebeeckx's many scattered articles began in 1964 under the general title *Theologische Peilingen* (Theological Soundings). Three of the eight projected volumes have already appeared. The volumes are organized thematically; the first volume contains articles concerning revelation and theology.

Christian revelation is a history of salvation, a "salvific economy." This understanding of revelation became so de-emphasized during the later period of Scholasticism that it gave way to teaching about the Deity which was overly abstract and philosophical. In the introduction of his *Sacramental Economy of Salvation* Schillebeeckx demonstrated that the *heilsgeschichtliche* and Christocentric view was present in the structure of St. Thomas' *Summa Theologiae*. In Schillebeeckx's view we only know the God of revelation insofar as the God of our redemption makes himself known in the history of salvation; it is the first task of theology to unfold this self-revelation of God in history. But a merely *heilsgeschichtliche Theologie* is inadequate. In the history of salvation the faithful are confronted with the Trinity as it *is* and not only as it manifests itself.

> I can hardly accept that the Scriptures speak of the Holy Spirit in an *exclusively* functional way, for *exclusive* functionalism ultimately means denying the independence of the Son and the Spirit, and then the Trinity is looked upon as exclusively *heilsgeschichtlich*: modalistic or at least agnostic. If *in* the Trinity, understood in the context of the "economy of Salvation" (as the Greek Orthodox theologians call it), the inner, *ontological* reality of the Trinity did not glimmer through, or if it were not implicitly given *in the Bible itself* as well, the dogma of the self-subsistent Trinity would be deprived of any basis, and the Son and the Holy Spirit would only be manifestations of God who himself would not be Trinity.

Thus the Bible itself demonstrates the necessity of an ontology *within "heilsgeschichtliche Theologie."* Here speculative theology is indispensable. As in philosophical reflection a real metaphysical doctrine is both possible and necessary, so theology must not restrict itself to a *pure* "phenomenology" of the history of salvation. This would result in agnosticism both with respect to the personal God and to the God of salvation.

Nor can existential phenomenology replace metaphysics. Without doubt the salvation event finds its authentic expression in terms of encounter, of intersubjectivity. The communion of grace is a real mutual relationship between God and man. At the same time it should be realized that *in* this communion of grace between God and man, God always remains absolute; that is, vis-à-vis his handiwork, he "creates from nothing." God *creates* man's intersubjective response. This is the authentic meaning of what is called "created grace" in Scholasticism. This element— God as creator enabling man to respond to the offer of salvation—escapes purely phenomenological description. At this point it becomes necessary to "extend" existential phenomenology "in a metaphysical approach."

Schillebeeckx places great stress on the value of our objective religious knowledge; that is why concern about any form of *relativism* (with respect to human knowledge) is foreign to him. At the same time, however, he takes into account the limitations, the changeableness and the growth of man's acquisition of truth. By virtue of the historicity of human life there are varying perspectives, varying ways of viewing the reality of revelation.

Through our faith that is realized in an earthly human form, we can, only from a finite, limited, and historical point of view, see the absolute reality of salvation, which, naturally, we can never control, not even in the beatific vision of God. It is not the value of salvation that changes, neither do our religious concepts *change,* but the perspective in which we look at the reality of salvation through the conceptual cognition (which by nature includes images) changes in the course of time and from person to person, and thus the acquisition of truth or the personal belief and our religious concepts grow as well.

Similarly, in the field of moral theology there is a changing historical perspective *within* the permanent validity of absolute ethics. Within that perspective the absolute rules are translated into concrete ethical imperatives that may undergo evolution in the course of time.

In 1965, at a time when questions concerning transubstantiation aroused great interest in the Netherlands, Schillebeeckx wrote a first, mainly historical article on the Eucharistic "real presence." (This article and its sequel will appear in book form.) It is mainly concerned with an interpretation of the doctrine of the Council of Trent. The Fathers of that council started from what the Bible has to say about the real presence in the Eucharist (as distinguished from the real presence in the preaching of the Word). Holy Scripture indicates that Christ is so truly present in the bread and wine of the Eucharist that he was able to say: Here, this is my body . . . this is my blood. This is the biblical datum of faith from which the Fathers argued. Here began the activity which properly belonged to the council, namely, safeguarding this datum of faith at that particular moment of history in the given situation of the time. To accomplish this the council had to express that datum in the ideas and images of those days. In this case the council could only *understand* and *imagine* the special Eucharistic real presence as a change (*conversio*) of the substances of the bread and wine into the substances of Christ's body and blood. They reasoned as follows: since there is a specifically Eucharistic real presence (the datum of faith), there must be a change of substance into the other. So, according to their way of thinking, it was inherently *necessary* to believe in this change if their faith in the given datum were to remain constant. (We will prescind from consideration of the fact that the Council of Trent declared that this change is rightly called "transubstantiation.")

The real problem in connection with transubstantiation lies in the acceptance of a *conversio*. Some theologians have tried to show that Trent disassociated itself from Aristotelian natural philosophy. Schillebeeckx, on the other hand, is of the opinion that the Fathers of that council made use of a scholastically Aristotelian way of thinking, that being the regnant frame of reference in those days. They simply could not think otherwise. To project our distance from the scholastically Aristotelian way of thinking back to that age is a "hermeneutic blunder." The question which should be asked is: In spite of its statement in an Aristotelian frame of reference, is there an ontological dimension of the Eucharistic presence—which was illuminated by Trent—still valid for us because of its foundation in the datum of faith?

Next, Schillebeeckx shows that patristics, as understood in the East and the West, fundamentally has always accepted a real *conversio,* although each has understood this term in a significantly different manner. The *conversio* which patristics spoke of is the same as that of which Trent spoke; the only difference is that Trent's framework was an Aristotelian mind-set unknown to the ancient Church. Both affirm that the *reality* of bread and wine in the Eucharist has changed radically after the consecration.

> Thus the final question, independent of the Aristotelian system, is whether the Catholic view of the Eucharistic presence can be thought of without a *real,* and in that sense, *ontological* change of bread and wine. Is this implication a necessary way of thinking in consequence of the medieval philosophical attitude of mind, or—as appears from the affirmation, oriented in the same direction by what is after all the entire patristic and pre-Tridentine theology—is it not primarily an inner ontological implication of the dogma of the Eucharistic presence and *therefore* a universally valid necessity to think so, in other words, a dogmatic demand made by the faith? The affirmation of the Eucharistic real presence is so intimately identified with the affirmation of a real change of bread and wine, that this is exactly what has been affirmed concretely and dogmatically: the Tridentine dogma proper as an affirmation of reality.

Here the question arises of how we should conceive this ontological dimension of the Eucharist in our own days. Though this is to be the subject of the second article, Schillebeeckx has already indicated two elements that must play a part in a modern conception of the Eucharistic presence. He thinks that it is innately Catholic to affirm that in the Eucharist there is an ontological element of creation which can be described by the term "created grace," implied in every self-communication of God or in every granting of grace and possessing an unexpectedly profound and ontological density precisely in the Eucharistic self-surrender, because this divine gift seizes the secular reality of the bread. But, on the other hand, this *conversio* must never be considered isolated in itself and outside the concrete sacramental act (as Scholasticism is inclined to view it). Our concern must always be with a *conversio within,* a sacramental symbolizing activity of Christ, which is naturally directed to the response of the personal belief of the faithful. The ontological aspect of the Eucharistic presence is that of a sacramental action which must be interpreted primarily from a personalistic view.

The second part of *Theologische Peilingen* bears the title *God en Mens* (God and Man). This book contains Schillebeeckx's discussion of the phenomenon of secularization and his conception of "Christian secularity," especially in confrontation with Bishop John A. T. Robinson and with nonreligious humanism. (His 1958 inaugural address to the University of Nijmegen also treated of these questions.) This year the third part appeared under the title *Wereld en Kerk* (World and Church). The first series of articles in this third volume covers the period 1945–1955; they are, as the author says in his prefatory note, "an answer to the tension between religion and world, as I had experienced in rising existentialism and in the intoxicating discussions of Catholics and Marxists in Paris as it was during the first years after the war, still restless." For the most part the second series includes recent articles dealing with the relationship of the Church to the world and to mankind. The book also contains articles on such current problems as tolerance, charity and social service, the Catholic hospital, and the responsibility of the Catholic intellectual for the future of the world and the Church.

There is an increasing tendency in Schillebeeckx's theology to take "secular realities" seriously within the interpretation of the faith. Thus he wrote an article called "Christ's Psychic Life," in which he does justice to the real humanity and the unity of the psychology of Jesus, the Son of God, while avoiding any semblance of "monophysitism." In an article on "The Meaning of the Humanity of Jesus the Christ" he described human inter-subjectivity as the form in which Jesus carried on his function as Savior. At the same time Schillebeeckx is of the opinion that the *messianic* significance of Christ's universal love of mankind cannot be founded in interhuman intersubjectivity as such. That Christ acts "in our place" and "in the name of us all" and is thus the bearer of *our* salvation cannot possibly be explained from the phenomenological categories of human fellowship or intersubjectivity but only from a divine *constitution* in which the Father causes the man Jesus to be representative of all mankind which must be brought together in him.

The representative value of Jesus being our fellow man is only based on a saving act of God, realized *in* the humanity of the Son of God. Only *within* this transcendent datum can Christ's interhuman relations acquire the significance of salvation that the Scriptures and the entire tradition of faith attribute to it; this representative saving function is transanthropological and only intelligible from the divine, mysterious constitution of the man Jesus to Messiah, Son of Man and Servant of God.

At the end of his first volume about marriage as "secular reality and mystery of salvation" Schillebeeckx says,

It has become apparent at any rate that a dogmatic reflection on marriage will have to take two fundamental data into account: the uncurtailed affirmation of marriage as intramundane, fully human and therefore evolutive reality, and the unconditional affirmation that this very reality has been drawn into salvation, not in any added aspect, but, on the contrary, in its totally human dimensions; and this not only because Christian existence must also be lived in and related to the intramundane—which is the affirmation of Christian secularity —but especially because this secular reality, having become object of salvation, has itself become *sacramental* in the full sense of the word.

Schillebeeckx considers *in extenso* the consequences of the phenomenon of secularization for faith and theology. One of the valuable aspects of secularization lies in man's greater secular freedom in the world today. Another is that the experience of God's "absence" in the world—which means that God is neither imagined nor experienced as an entity *among* the intramundane realities—offers the possibility of expressing the faith more purely, to the effect that God's transcendence is put in a truer light. But conversely, secular man is constantly being confronted with the mystery of his existence, which presents itself in the fundamental experience of the contingency of human life. The danger of secularization is that people *enclose* the horizon of their existence within the secular. But that only occurs when secularization is given a fundamentally wrong interpretation. For secularization takes its appropriate place and finds its authentic meaning only in our faithful relationship to the living God.

> Considered objectively, the merely profane or atheistic laicization is only a *hairesis,* which means that the earthly reality is severed from the whole to which it belongs; namely, *in* the faithful existential relation to the living God; only outside this connection does human reality become "profane." Thus belief in God is no longer an alibi for the lack of man's devoting himself to the earthly dwelling-place and to a more humane society.

In his recent articles Schillebeeckx has described "World and Church" as "the two complementary forms in which the one Christianity is lived." God's activity cannot be limited to the Church alone, but God is also active in the world: God is already active wherever true humanity is practiced in the world. It must even be said that God's activity is not concerned with the Church as such but with unity, peace, and justice among men. The Church is merely an instrument of God's unifying action of salvation in this world, and therefore it is bound to a serving ministry. But what God is already bringing about in the world must be laid open in its religious significance within the Church as in a sacrament, in which it is expressed in an explicit way. Moreover, the Church is already the visible presence of salvation in our midst (although always in the mode of a continuous *metanoia*) and seen in this light the Church has value in itself, but in the sense of its being directed to its mission in the world. Thus it is the mission of the Church to exemplify in its life what is already implicitly operative in the entire human community, but which is still being sought in a concrete and explicit form.

The religious meaning of "being human in the world" is elucidated by Schillebeeckx as follows:

> From God's revealed name . . . [Exodus 3:14] we realize in faith that the religious attitude of life is not only to God, but—in an equally original way—to our fellow man and our world as well, and that under the coefficient of an ever-new expectation for the future of man and world. Religion is not a relationship to "God," but to the *totality* of reality, for religion is precisely a relationship to the living God, *ground of being* of all reality and *Promise* to man in the world. Therefore religion is—to an equally original degree—an affirmation given to our fellow man in the world. Vice versa the unconditional "yes," affirmative to the very end, spoken to mankind is therefore also—at least implicitly but actually—a religious act. From this belief in God as Promise to man a new hope also arises for the world. Coming to himself in going out to the world man cannot reach his *Eigentlichkeit* unless this world is also drawn into man's absolute future, which is the pure grace of God. In that way the history of the world itself is embraced by the activity of God's promise and thus the Christian view of man implies a worldly eschatology, too.

From this last quotation, written after the publication of J. Moltmann's *Theologie der Hoffnung,* it appears that in Schillebeeckx's writings a trend has been confirmed, namely, that the Christian neither can nor may practice his belief in God through Christ but in the immediate context of his life within the human community and in the world. The God of the Christian revelation is not an "object" *beside* the human world in which we live and in which we have an inalienable mission as man and fellow man. Christian belief includes encounter with the living God, precisely as the one who wishes to be God *of* the human community and *of* the world. On this very issue classical "theism" failed to get near the God of the Bible. Yet Schillebeeckx asserts that in theism an indestructible element has been given that is essential to a right understanding of the Christian revelation, in spite of the fact that classical theism is embodied in a way of thinking and in a way of representing things that can be maintained no longer. That is the element of the existence of a personal God whom we know in his own independence of being and who, as independent subject, stands facing man and world. God cannot *merely* be ground of our being; for *in* his founding our existence God is transcendent and independent. He shows himself as a being in and of himself absolutely personal, on account of which he is to be loved in himself and for his own sake. In the so-called natural cognition of God, man is already confronted with the transcendent, personal being of God as the ground of human existence; and this carries with it a desire of the "natural" man, powerless though it is, for a direct personal contact with God. Now, the offer of salvation in Christ is the personal gesture of the living God who offers us community with himself and renders it possible. It is essential to the Christian revelation that God's grace offers man a direct intersubjectivity with God. Although the faithful also meet God as he is present *in* human relations and *in* the world, yet this encounter with God urges them on to what is most essentially Christian: direct communication with God. Therefore, a *radical* "horizontalism" strains the essence of the Christian belief.

Schillebeeckx's writings aim at laying bare the implications of intersubjectivity between man and God. We are concerned with the *living* God, the God of the Bible who enters into a history of salvation with mankind, not with the God of an abstract philosophical theory. We are concerned with the God who reveals to us not only a number of truths but *himself* and who gives himself as salvation to us. We are concerned with the God who delivers man and the world from being shut up within the merely human and merely secular and who admits man and the world into the mystery of his self-surrender to us.

106

The "personal life-community of man with God" means for the believer free acceptance of and inner surrender to the offer of salvation by God. However, man is not only inwardness but a person in the world with fellow men. Our fellow man in his world—and so in human history—is, viewed from the primordial sacrament of the encounter with God, the *man* Jesus, the sacramental manifestation of God's offer of salvation to us. Therefore, the personal relationship of the Christian and his Church with God must be expressed in real and authentic *love of mankind*. Therefore, this love for one's fellow man is the touchstone of the veracity of intimacy with God. Finally the personal relationship of man with God is always under the sign of hope urging us actively to transform the world for a better future, for God is the One Who Comes, the Promise to man and to the world.

In this brief exposition justice has not been done to the breadth of Schillebeeckx's thought. His profound knowledge of present-day philosophical thought and an erudition which covers the history of theology come together in a synthesis which aims at making faith for modern man become a vibrant, personal "acquisition."

JOHN A. T. ROBINSON

BY

Lowell D. Streiker

It is not uncommon to see the word "God" on the front page
of a popular magazine, usually in a context such as the recent
Time magazine cover which read "Is God Dead?" The American news media have shown a phenomenal interest in religion.
Religion is again a lively topic. Religious personalities are appearing with regularity on television and in the mass circulation
newspapers and magazines.

Much of this interest focuses on so-called Christian atheism
or death-of-God theology. None of this attention would be
possible if it had not been for the appearance in 1963 of a book
by a distinguished New Testament scholar who is Bishop of
Woolwich, an outlying district of London. Though John A. T.
Robinson's little book was not intended for a popular audience,
but rather for theologically adept readers who would be familiar
with the authors and concepts discussed and with his previous
writings, the book was a run-away best seller on both sides of
the Atlantic and is now available in nine languages.

"It is a safe assumption," Robinson observes, "that a best seller tells one more about the state of the market than the quality of the product." Why has this particular book been so immensely popular? And what has prompted the public furor in which Bishop Robinson has been branded " 'the atheist bishop' " (as well as plenty of other things!).

David L. Edwards, managing director of SCM Press, Ltd., the original publisher of *Honest to God,* perceptively deals with the state of Robinson's market in his essay "A New Stirring in English Christianity." He insists "today change is obviously desirable in English Christianity." Statistics suggest that *"active* support for the churches comes from under ten per cent of the population. This is said to be about the same proportion as in Soviet Russia." He notes that approximately half of the Church of England parish churches are medieval or earlier and that "the prayer books used in them have not been revised officially since 1662." He sees no real hope for English Christianity "short of a renewal of the life and the teachings of its local churches."

Three recent trends have encouraged optimism: the biblical, liturgical, and ecumenical movements. But these have been concerned with life as it is lived *within* historic Christian communities, and not with the relevance of Christianity to those *outside* the Church, concerned with the fellowship of believers rather than with the contemporary clash of belief and unbelief. These "substantial movements" all share one defect: *"they do not necessarily concern the truth of Christianity."*

"A deeper renewal is needed," one which "has now begun to appear." This new movement that Edwards terms *Christian radicalism* "results from a desire to honour and to hear the modern secular world." The new Coventry Cathedral, consecrated in 1962, "stands as a symbol of Christian radicalism" both through its stunning contemporary architecture and the efforts and experiments of its team of priests and laymen.

"Christian radicalism" has found literary expression in such British periodicals as *Prism* and *Theology,* as well as in three semi-popular books by theologians associated with Cambridge

University: *Soundings* and *Objections to Christian Belief,* both edited by Dr. Alec Vidler, and, of course, *Honest to God.* Edwards illustrates the radical temper with a quotation from a broadcast by Robinson in February 1963, a month before the appearance of his book.

Radicalism represents the built-in challenge to any establishment, any institutionalism, any orthodoxy: and it is an attitude that is relevant to far more than politics. Indeed, the essence of the radical protest could be summed up in the statement of Jesus that "the Sabbath is made for man, and not man for the Sabbath." Persons are more important than any principles. He illustrated this by his shocking approbation of David's action in placing concern for human need, even his own, above all institutions however sacred. "Have you not read what David did, when he was hungry, and those who were with him: how he entered the house of God and ate bread of the Presence, which it was not lawful for him to eat nor for those who were with him, but only for the priests?"

Yet radicalism is not anarchy. It is not just being "bolshy" or individualistic. It knows well enough that persons can matter, and freedom can flourish, only in a context of order. But, dissatisfied as it is simply with "freedom from," it will always be asking: order *for* what? When the structures of order take over and persons become subservient to them, when the movement of the Spirit hardens into the institutional Church, then the radical voice will begin to be heard.

What the radical stands for can perhaps be more clearly seen by comparing him with the reformist on the one hand and the revolutionary on the other. The reformist—corresponding in political categories to the Tory reformer—continues to accept the basic proposition, that man is made for the Sabbath. But, he says, the Sabbath regulations have become too rigid; we must modify them and bring them up to date. So he steals the Whig's clothes while he is bathing and lifts planks here and there from the Liberal platform. He overhauls the institution and titivates the orthodoxy; and in this way everything is enabled to go on smoothly, and the revolution is averted. The revolutionary, on the other hand—in political terms the Robespierres and Lenins of this world—will have nothing of the Sabbath at all. The institution is rotten, the orthodoxy stinks and enslaves. The entire structure must be changed if man is to be free.

The radical will often be found siding with the revolutionary in regarding the reformist as the real enemy. For the reformist would lull people into supposing no revolution is necessary, whereas the radical knows that for man to be made for the Sabbath is ultimately death. But equally he sees that if man is to live—rather than be subjected to a different, and perhaps deadlier, Sabbath—another revolution is required. The radical's response is to go to the roots—hence his name. It is to ask what the Sabbath is for, what human values it exists to frame, and then to try to see, at whatever cost to the institution or the orthodoxy, that it does so. Unlike the reformist, the radical is concerned constantly to subject the Sabbath to man. Yet, unlike the revolutionary, he *believes* in the Sabbath—for man.

This introduces another important characteristic of the radical viewpoint. Being a radical means being an "insider," an insider to the Sabbath—as Jesus was. The revolutionary can be an "outsider" to the structure he would see collapse: indeed, he must set himself outside it. But the radical goes to the roots of *his own* tradition. He must love it: he must weep over Jerusalem, even if he has to pronounce its doom. He must believe that the Sabbath really is made for man.

This means the radical must be a man of roots. The revolutionary may be *déraciné,* but not the radical. And that is partly why in our rootless world there are so few genuine radicals....

But it would not be fair to equate the Christian outlook with the radical, to suggest that all Christians should be radicals any more than all radicals should be Christians. For radicalism is simply an attitude of mind and its relevance is to some extent a matter of degree. The radical cannot claim to have the whole truth. To remember that should help to keep him humble, for the besetting sin of the radical is self-righteousness, as complacency is of the reformist and ruthlessness of the revolutionary. Nevertheless, I believe that the radical temper is a uniquely precious element in our cultural inheritance. I have no doubt that the other two are needed—and I find myself embracing each at times. But, if I had to choose, I would rather rest my reputation (for what it is worth) on being a radical.

Christian radicalism attacks the notion of religion as a kind

111

of "intellectual antiquarianism supported by autosuggestion." It attempts to separate what one must believe as a Christian from the accretions of conceptual formulation which belonged to former eras but which are not basic to Christian faith at all.

JOHN A. T. ROBINSON

John Arthur Thomas Robinson, the son and grandson of Canons of Canterbury, was born at Canterbury in 1919. He was educated at Jesus and Trinity Colleges, Cambridge. In 1945, after a brief pre-ordination theological course, he entered the ministry of the Church of England. In 1946 he received his Ph.D. for a dissertation entitled "Thou Who Art: The Notion of Personality and Its Relation to Christian Theology with Particular Reference to (a) the Contemporary 'I-Thou' philosophy; (b) the Doctrines of the Trinity and the Person of Christ."

For three years Robinson was curate of the Church of St. Matthew, Moorfields, Bristol. Mervin Stockwood, now Bishop of Southwark (under whom Robinson is suffragan Bishop of Woolwich) was the vicar. It was during his years in this industrial parish that Robinson's concern for social questions developed.

In 1948, Robinson became chaplain and lecturer at Wells Theological College in Somerset. At this Anglican seminary he lectured on doctrine and ethics (drawing heavily upon the writings of Martin Buber, Emil Brunner, H. H. Farmer, and John Macmurray) and subsequently on the Pauline epistles.

He became Fellow and Dean of Chapel at Clare College, Cambridge, in 1951. While at Cambridge Robinson completed work on *The Body,* his important study of Pauline theology, and wrote several articles and reviews. In 1953, Robinson was named to a lectureship at Cambridge. Two years later, he was Visiting Professor at Harvard University, delivering the William Belden Nobel Lectures which were later incorporated into the monograph *Jesus and His Coming.* He visited the United States for a second time in 1958 as Reinecker Lecturer at Virginia

Theological Seminary. In addition to these responsibilities, Robinson served as a member of the New Testament Panel for the *New English Bible*.

Robinson became Bishop of Woolwich in southeast London in 1959, leaving his academic pursuits only after five months of careful deliberation. Since the appearance of *Honest to God,* Robinson has contributed to *The Honest to God Debate* and written *The New Reformation?* and *Christian Morals Today*. He again visited the United States in 1964, delivering the Purdy Lectures at Hartford Theological Foundation and the Thorpe Lectures at Cornell University.

His lifework and thought may be summarized by a remark of his which refers to *Honest to God:* "Indeed my book was born of the fact that I knew myself to be a man committed without reservation to Christ *and* a man committed, without possibility of return, to modern twentieth-century secular society. It was written out of the belief that both these convictions must be taken with equal seriousness and that they *cannot* be incompatible."

HONEST TO GOD

In the preface to *Honest to God* Robinson says, "It belongs to the office of a bishop in the Church to be a guardian and defender of its doctrine." Robinson finds himself a bishop "at a moment when the discharge of this burden can seldom have demanded greater depth of divinity and quality of discernment. For we stand on the brink of a period in which it is going to become increasingly difficult to know what the true defense of Christian faith requires."

The first problem with which Robinson deals is our concept of God. Though most believers are too sophisticated to think of God as a being literally or physically "up there," "an old man in the sky," "we have accepted, as part of our mental furniture, a God who is spiritually or metaphysically 'out there.' "

"This picture of a God 'out there,' " Robinson notes, "com-

113

ing to earth like some visitor from outer space underlies every popular presentation of the God drama of salvation whether from pulpit or from the presses." According to this view, theists are those who believe in the existence of such a being "out there"; atheists, those who deny that such a being exists.

But suppose such a super-Being "out there" is really only a sophisticated version of the Old Man in the sky? Suppose belief in God does not, indeed cannot, mean being persuaded of the "existence" of some entity, even a supreme entity, which might or might not be there, like life on Mars? Suppose the atheists are right—but that this is no more the end or denial of Christianity than the discrediting of the God "up there," which must in its time have seemed the contradiction of all that the Bible said? Suppose that all such atheism does is destroy an idol, and that we can and must get on without a God "out there" at all? Have we seriously faced the possibility that to abandon such an idol may in the future be the only way of making Christianity meaningful, except to the few remaining equivalents of flat-earthers (just as to have clung earlier to the God "up there" would have made it impossible in the modern world for any but primitive peoples to believe the Gospel)? Perhaps after all the Freudians are right,—that such a God—the God of traditional popular theology—*is* a projection, and perhaps we are being called to live without that projection in any form.

In his attempt to articulate a constructive answer to this quandary, Robinson synthesizes the insights of several previous writers.

Indeed, it is the number of straws apparently blowing in the same direction that strikes me as significant. I have done little more than pick a few of them up and I am conscious that in this book, more than in any other I have written, I am struggling to think other people's thoughts after them.

Chief among these influences have been Paul Tillich, Dietrich Bonhoeffer, and Rudolf Bultmann.

Tillich opened Robinson's eyes to the "transformation that seemed to come over so much of the traditional religious symbolism when it was transposed from the heights to the depths."

114

Tillich's doctrine of God as "the Ground of our very being" is the central key used by Robinson to unlock the puzzle of our concept of God. He quotes Tillich's sermon, "The Depth of Existence."

The name of this infinite and inexhaustible depth and ground of all being is *God*. That depth is what the word *God* means. And if that word has not much meaning for you, translate it, and speak of the depths of your life, of the source of your being, of your ultimate concern, of what you take seriously without any reservation. Perhaps, in order to do so, you must forget everything traditional that you have learned about God, perhaps even that word itself. For if you know that God means depth, you know much about him. You cannot then call yourself an atheist or unbeliever. For you cannot think or say: Life has no depth! Life is shallow. Being itself is surface only. If you could say this in complete seriousness, you would be an atheist; but otherwise you are not. He who knows about depth knows about God.

The other major influences were Bonhoeffer's call to twentieth-century Christians for "a form of Christianity that does not depend on the premise of religion . . ." and Bultmann's program of "demythologizing" the message of the New Testament.

Robinson's Tillichian rethinking of the concept of God develops the basic insight of Martin Buber.

When he . . . who abhors the name [of God], and believes himself to be godless, gives his whole being to addressing the *Thou* of his life, as a *Thou* that cannot be limited by another, he addresses God.

Robinson comments, "In the conditioned he has seen and responded to the unconditional. He has touched the hem of the eternal." For "reality at its very deepest level is personal, . . . personality is of *ultimate* significance in the constitution of the universe, . . . in personal relationships we touch the final meaning of existence as nowhere else." It is in this manner that Robinson understands the expression "*a* personal God," which for traditional theism has meant "a supreme Person, a self-existent subject of infinite goodness and power, who enters into a relationship with us comparable with that of one human personality with another. . . . a Person 'out there' [without whom] the skies would be empty, the heavens as brass, and the world without hope or compassion."

Rather than being the acceptance of such a Person, belief in God is "the trust, the well-nigh incredible trust, that to give ourselves to the uttermost in love is not to be confounded but to be 'accepted,' that Love is the ground of our being, to which ultimately we 'come home.' " But what are the implications of such a view?

If this is true, then theological statements are not a description of "the highest Being" but an analysis of the depths of personal relationships—or, rather, an analysis of the depths of *all* experience "interpreted by love." Theology, as Tillich insists, is about "that which concerns us ultimately." A statement is "theological" not because it relates to a particular Being called "God," but because it asks *ultimate* questions about the meaning of existence: it asks what, at the level of *theos,* at the level of its deepest mystery, is the reality and significance of our life. A view of the world which affirms this reality and significance in personal categories is *ipso facto* making an affirmation about the *ultimacy* of personal relationships: it is saying that *God,* the final truth and reality "deep down things," *is* love. And the specifically Christian view of the world is asserting that the final definition of this reality, from which "nothing can separate us," since it is the very ground of our being, is "the love of God in Christ Jesus our Lord."

Robinson denies that as a result of such a denial of "supranaturalism," we are simply left with "naturalism." The experience of God, he insists,

is distinctively and characteristically an awareness of the transcendent, the numinous, the unconditional. Yet that is a feature of *all* our experience—*in depth.* Statements about God are acknowledgements of the transcendent, unconditional element in all our relationships, and supremely in our relationships with other persons. Theological statements are indeed affirmations about human existence—but they are

116

affirmations about the ultimate ground and depth of that existence.

In other words, one cannot reverse the biblical statement "God is love."

To assert that "*God* is love" is to believe that in love one comes into touch with the most fundamental reality in the universe, that Being itself ultimately has this character. It is to say, with Buber, that "Every particular *Thou* is a glimpse through to the eternal *Thou*," that it is "between man and man" that we meet God, not, with Feuerbach, that "man with man—the unity of *I* and *Thou*—is God."

The name "God" is indispensable, for

being has depths which naturalism, whether evolutionary, mechanistic, dialectical or humanistic, cannot or will not recognize.
There are depths of revelation, intimations of eternity, judgements of the holy and the sacred, awarenesses of the unconditional, the numinous and the ecstatic, which cannot be explained in purely naturalistic categories without being reduced to something else.

The question of God is not the question "whether *a* Being exists beyond the bright blue sky, or anywhere else." "The question of God is the question *whether this depth of being is a reality or an illusion*. . . . Belief in God is a matter of 'what you take seriously without any reservation,' of what for you is *ultimate* reality."

The man who acknowledges the transcendence of God is the man who *in* the conditioned relationships of life recognizes the unconditional and responds to it in unconditional personal relationships.

. . . .

This, I believe, is Tillich's great contribution to theology—the reinterpretation of transcendence in a way which preserves its reality while detaching it from the projection of supranaturalism. "The Divine, as he sees it, does not inhabit a transcendent world *above nature;* it is found in the 'ecstatic'

117

character of *this* world, as its transcendent Depth and Ground."

This viewpoint is fully in harmony with the biblical recognition, "God is not outside us, yet he is profoundly transcendent. . . . God since he is Love, is encountered in his fulness only *'between* man and man.' "

> And this is the burden of the whole Prophetic tradition— that it is only in response and obedience to the neighbour that the claims of God can be met and known. This message is focused in a passage to which I constantly find myself returning in the book of Jeremiah, where the prophet is addressing Jehoiakim, the son of Josiah:

> > Did not your father eat and drink and do justice and righteousness? Then it was well with him. He judged the cause of the poor and needy; then it was well. *Is not this to know me? says the Lord.*

> God, the unconditional, is to be found only in, with *and under* the conditioned relationships of this life: for he *is* their depth and ultimate significance.

> In the parable of the sheep and the goats (Mt 25:31–46), Jesus made precisely the same point.

> > Now this links up with what Bonhoeffer was saying about a "non-religious" understanding of God. For this ultimate and most searching question has nothing to do with "religion." It rests our eternal salvation upon nothing peculiarly religious. Encounter with the Son of Man is spelt out in terms of an entirely "secular" concern for food, water, supplies, housing, hospitals and prisons, just as Jeremiah had earlier defined the knowledge of God in terms of doing justice for the poor and needy. Indeed, in Macmurray's words, "the great contribution of the Hebrew to religion was that he did away with it." A right relationship to God depended on nothing religious: in fact religion could be the greatest barrier to it.

Since Robinson is dealing with a concept of God which he believes is relevant to the Christian community, it is necessary for him to define the doctrine which is central to that community, Christology.

The doctrine of the Incarnation and Divinity of Christ is on any count central to the entire Christian message and crucial therefore for any reinterpretation of it. It is also the point where resistance to reinterpretation is likely to be at its maximum and where orthodoxy has its heaviest investment in traditional categories.

It is just as important to move to a position "beyond naturalism and supranaturalism" in our thinking about Christ as in our understanding of God.

Traditional Christology has worked with a frankly supranaturalist scheme. Popular religion has expressed this mythologically, professional theology metaphysically. For this way of thinking, the Incarnation means that God the Son came down to earth, and was born, lived and died within this world as a man. From "out there" there graciously entered into the human scene one who was not "of it" and yet who lived genuinely and completely within it. As the God-man, he united in his person the supernatural and the natural: and the problem of Christology so stated is how Jesus can be fully God and fully man, and yet genuinely one person.

Such thinking is haunted by the notion that God and man, two distinct ontological orders, became one in the "God-Man." Many presentations of this doctrine are almost irrational, and, as such, are glorified by thinkers such as Tertullian and Kierkegaard.

as long as God and man are thought of as two "beings," each with distinct natures, one from "the other side" and one from "this side," then it is impossible to create out of them more than a God-man, a divine visitant from "out there" who chooses in every respect to live like the natives. The supranaturalist view of the Incarnation can never really rid itself of the idea of the prince who appears in the guise of a beggar. However genuinely destitute the beggar may be, he *is* a prince; and that in the end is what matters.

Robinson insists that the supranaturalist estimate of Christ is jarringly disharmonious with the biblical picture. He notes, "Jesus never claims to be God, personally: yet he always claims to bring God, completely."

119

This paradox is the point from which our reinterpretation of Christology must start. As the summary of his ministry in the fourth Gospel, Jesus cries out and says "He who believes in me, believes not in me but in him who sent me. And he who sees me sees him who sent me." Jesus, that is to say, reveals God by being utterly transparent to him, precisely as he is nothing "in himself."

Some form of "kenotic" Christology is in order.

The "kenotic" theory of Christology, based on this conception of self-emptying, is, I am persuaded, the only one that offers much hope of relating at all satisfactorily the divine and the human in Christ. Yet the fatal weakness of this theory as it is stated in supranaturalist terms is that it represents Christ as stripping himself precisely of those attributes of transcendence which make him the revelation of God. The underlying assumption is that it is his omnipotence, his omniscience, and all that makes him "superhuman," that must be shed in order for him to become truly man. On the contrary, it is as he empties himself not of his Godhead but of himself, of any desire to focus attention on himself, of any craving to be "on an equality with God," that he reveals God. For it is in making himself nothing, in his utter self-surrender to others in love, that he discloses and lays bare the Ground of man's being as Love.

Robinson turns to Bonhoeffer's concept of Jesus as "the man for others" in developing his Christology.

Jesus is "the man for others," the one in whom Love has completely taken over, the one who is utterly open to, and united with, the Ground of his being. And this "life for others, through participation in the Being of God," *is* transcendence. For at this point, of love "to the uttermost," we encounter *God,* the ultimate "depth" of our being, the unconditional in the conditioned. This is what the New Testament means by saying that "God was in Christ" and that "what God was the Word was." Because Christ was utterly and completely "the man for others," because he *was* love, he was "one with the Father," because "God is love." But for this very reason he was most entirely man, the son of man, the servant of the Lord. . . . He is perfect man and perfect God—not as a mixture of oil and water, of natural and supernatural—but as the

120

embodiment through obedience of "the beyond in our midst," of the transcendence of love.

In his transparence to the Ground of our being, the Christ reveals "the new being" of each of us which overcomes our estrangement from others and ourselves. We are accepted; we experience grace. As Tillich says,

> It happens; or it does not happen. . . . It strikes us when our disgust for our own being, our indifference, our weakness, our hostility, and our lack of direction and composure have become intolerable to us. It strikes us when, year after year, the longed-for perfection of life does not appear, when the old compulsions reign within us as they have for decades, when despair destroys all joy and courage. Sometimes at that moment a wave of light breaks into our darkness, and it is as though a voice were saying: "You are accepted. *You are accepted,* accepted by that which is greater than you, and the name of which you do not know. Do not ask for the name now; perhaps you will find it later. Do not try to do anything now; perhaps later you will do much. Do not seek for anything; do not perform anything; do not intend anything. *Simply accept the fact that you are accepted!"* If that happens to us, we experience grace. After such an experience we may not be better than before, and we may not believe more than before. But everything is transformed. In that moment, grace conquers sin, and reconciliation bridges the gulf of estrangement. And nothing is demanded of this experience, no religious or moral or intellectual presupposition, nothing but *acceptance.*
>
> In the light of this grace we perceive the power of grace in our relation to others and to ourselves. We experience the grace of being able to look frankly into the eyes of another, the miraculous grace of reunion of life with life.
> [*The Shaking of the Foundations* 163 f.]

As a result the Christian community exists "simply to be the embodiment of this new being as love." And that means, Robinson adds by citing Bonhoeffer, "participation in the powerlessness of God in the world."

Christians range themselves with God in his suffering; that is what distinguishes them from the heathen. As Jesus asked in Gethsemane, "Could ye not watch with me one hour?" That is the exact opposite of what the religious man expects from God. Man is challenged to participate in the sufferings of God at the hands of a godless world.

He must therefore plunge himself into the life of a godless world, without attempting to gloss over its ungodliness with a veneer of religion or trying to transfigure it. He must live a "worldly" life and so participate in the suffering of God. He *may* live a worldly life as one emancipated from all false religions and obligations. To be a Christian does not mean to be religious in a particular way, to cultivate some particular form of asceticism (as a sinner, a penitent or a saint), but to be a man. It is not some religious act which makes a Christian what he is, but participation in the suffering of God in the life of the world.

[*Letters and Papers from Prison* 166.]

But what does it mean "to be a man," to "live a worldly life as one emancipated from all false religions and obligations"? What is the "worldly holiness" of which Robinson and Bonhoeffer speak? "Worldly holiness" rests on the recognition, in Tillich's words, that "religion is not a special function of man's spiritual life, but the dimension of depth in all of its functions." Robinson denies that sacred and profane, holy and secular, are polar opposites.

For Christianity, . . . the holy is the "depth" of the common, just as the "secular" is not a (godless) section of life but the world (God's world, for which Christ died) cut off and alienated from its true depth. The purpose of worship is not to retire from the secular into the department of the religious, let alone to escape from "this world" into "the other world," but to open oneself to the meeting of the Christ in the common, to that which has the power to penetrate its superficiality and redeem it from its alienation. The function of worship is to make us more sensitive to these depths; to focus, sharpen and deepen our response to the world and to other people beyond the point of proximate concern (of liking, self-interest, limited commitment, etc.) to that of ultimate concern; to purify and correct our loves in the light of Christ's love; and in him to find the grace and power to be the reconciled and reconciling community. Anything that achieves this or assists towards it is Christian worship. Anything that fails to do this is not Christian worship, be it ever so "religious."

Christian prayer, which has so often been regarded as withdrawal from the world to God, must be defined "in terms of penetration through the world to God."

For the moment of revelation is precisely so often, in my experience, the moment of meeting and unconditional *engagement*. How easily one finds oneself giving pious advice to a person faced with a decision to "go away and pray about it." But, if I am honest, what enlightenment I have had on decisions has almost always come not when I have gone away and stood back from them, but precisely as I have *wrestled through* all the most practical pros and cons, usually with other people. And this activity, undertaken by a Christian trusting and expecting that God is there, would seem to *be* prayer.

For Robinson, the ethics of unconditional personal commitment are as different from traditional morality as the theology of *Honest to God* is from the supranaturalist concept of God. There is nothing specifically Christian about conventional morality. "To tie Christianity to it is simply to ask for the one to be discredited with the other."

The "Christian ethic . . . is for all men: it is based upon the nature of man." Its moral precepts "are not intended to be understood legalistically, as prescribing what all Christians must do, whatever the circumstances. . . . they are illustration of what love may at any moment require of anyone." Thus, for the Christian, "there can . . . be no 'packaged' moral judgments—for persons are more important than 'standards.' "

Life in Christ Jesus, in the new being, in the Spirit, means having no absolutes but his love, being totally uncommitted in every other respect but totally committed in this. And this utter openness in love to the "other" for his own sake is

123

equally the only absolute for the non-Christian, as the parable of the Sheep and the Goats shows.

. . . .

Love alone, because, as it were, it has a built-in moral compass, enabling it to "home" intuitively upon the deepest need of the other, can allow itself to be directed completely by the situation. It alone can afford to be utterly open to the situation, or rather to the person in the situation, uniquely and for his own sake, without losing its direction or unconditionality. It is able to embrace an ethic of radical responsiveness, meeting every situation on its own merits, with no prescriptive laws.

In belief and practice, there is required of the Christian Church "a radically new mould, or *meta-morphosis.*" Christians must be prepared "for *everything* to go into the melting—even our most cherished religious categories and moral absolutes." Above all, the Church must realize that "the last thing the Church exists to be is an organization of the religious. Its charter is to be the servant of the world." To fulfill its task, the Church may have to undergo a "second Reformation." Robinson remarks in *The New Reformation?:* "And the second Reformation, if it comes, will be distinguished from the first by the fact that it is a time of reticence, of stripping down, of travelling light. The Church will go through its baggage and discover how much it can better do without, alike in doctrine and in organization."

Bishop Robinson has been placed by virtue of unparalleled public attention in the front ranks of the "new reformers." He occupies this role neither unwillingly nor undeservedly. The dimensions of John A. T. Robinson's contribution are described with discernment by Father Richard P. McBrien.

How is the Church to fulfil her mission in the modern world, a world industrialized, urbanized and—most importantly—secularized? Indeed, what is the mission of the Church? Is it simply to preach the Gospel, without particular concern for the mode of expression or the actual effects (as Barth and, to an extent, Cullmann have suggested)? Does her mission merely consist in outward expansion so as to grow and increase numerically in time and in space (as, perhaps, many Christians on both sides of the Reformation-divide believe)? Or does the Church exist as Servant to God and Son of Man on earth, as a Church in *diaspora,* as the *secular community?* John A. T. Robinson, under the impact of pastoral responsibility and especially since his consecration in 1959, has clearly aligned himself with those who propose the last thesis. In so doing he has placed himself in an ever-widening stream of Protestant theological thought which claims Dietrich Bonhoeffer as its source. In recent years there has been a convergence of this stream with another of a Catholic nature, that of Congar and Rahner in particular. . . . these currents—in our judgement—are flowing in the right direction.

[*The Church in the Thought of Bishop John Robinson* (London: SCM Press, Ltd., 1966) 129.]

BERNARD LONERGAN

BY

Frederick E. Crowe

Bernard Lonergan's career in theology has been a relatively hidden and largely tranquil one whose influence is not yet widely discernible outside the circle of his immediate followers and students but promises to grow steadily as his ideas, always on the most fundamental and difficult level, begin to spread and to take root in men's minds.

Born in Canada in 1904, he left Loyola College in Montreal to join the Society of Jesus in 1922, with a consequent formation that followed a pattern more or less normal for Jesuits: classical studies (Guelph in Ontario); philosophy (Heythrop College in England, with specialization in languages and mathematics for a degree at the University of London); theology (Gregorian University in Rome); and second novitiate or "tertianship" (Amiens in France). Graduate studies won him a doctorate in theology (at the Gregorian again), and he began his professorial career in 1940 at L'Immaculée-Conception, the Jesuit theologate in Montreal; then Regis College, the sister theologate in Toronto, midway through the year 1946–1947; and then the Gregorian in Rome in 1953. Major surgery in the summer of 1965 forced him to give up classroom duties, and since his recovery he has been back at Regis College working on his accumulated papers and preparing a study on method in theology that his disciples have for a decade impatiently awaited.

Twenty-five years in the theology lecture halls: it has not been a long career of public academic service; it was not marked by particularly voluminous writings, nor much involved in sensational controversies or great communal enterprises of scholarship. Yet his disciples sense a latent power in his thought, the gathering momentum of a truly significant impact upon some future period. I say "latent" power, for it emerges mainly in work that is marginal to most of the classroom courses he has taught during this quarter of a century; it lies less in the material content of the courses assigned him than in formal factors for which the material theology is a kind of vehicle. His undergraduate courses during his thirteen years in Canada covered most of the theological map and have left us a number of arresting compositions; his twelve years at the Gregorian allowed concentration on the Trinity and Christology, with a resulting four-volume work crowded with theological insights into those fields. But it is definitely on the formal and methodological and transcendental and subjective level that we discern the development of a tremendously fertile thought. The indications are scattered through the pages of his material theology, where they often seem disconcertingly digressive; they are found in the graduate courses he has given at the Gregorian and in the various lecture series with which he occupied the summers of the last decade in the United States and Canada; most of all, they are given a philosophical foundation in his *Insight,* published in 1957. What will issue from his present concentration and new interests is another question whose answer we can only await from the future.

This evaluation, vague and uncertain though it may be, is germane to any presentation of Father Lonergan's ideas simply because they have lain on the level of the transcendental and because his very style and manner of thinking, his principles of method, and their exemplification in his own work are so relevant to his impact as a theologian. This, I hope, will appear more clearly as I expose his style and methodology.

I

This section explores Lonergan's views on the human thinking process in close connection with his own thinking performance. As it happens, such an approach is suggested not only by the intrinsic logic of his work but also by the temper of the times. That is to say, in a world of readers who no longer limit consideration to the objective content of a book but talk about the author's authenticity and involvement, reserve the right to challenge his vocation in life, demand that he speak to them publicly and not merely to his fellow theologians, and so forth —in such a world it is important to offer some explanation of Lonergan's particular "vocation" and "style" of thinking; and this can be done in relation to his own ideas of the thinking process and its inner requirements.

A fundamental position here can certainly be determined in reference to his *verbum* articles (*Theological Studies,* 1946–1949), where he shows himself adamantly intellectualist in opposition to the conceptualist. Those terms, which may be variously used by other thinkers, have an extremely precise meaning for him. The conceptualist is concerned with concepts, judgments, and syllogisms and combines them in various ways, with concepts joining to give judgments and judgments linking into syllogistic reasoning processes, but he neglects the fertile source of all concepts, judgments, and reasoning in the power of understanding. That understanding is the specific concern of the intellectualist: it is direct understanding through insight into data that enables one to conceive intelligently rather than repeat definitions as would a parrot; it is reflective understanding that by reference to the here and now is a source of judgments that are rational self-commitments and not a mere rubber-stamped yes or no to an already formed position; it is developing understanding that gathers fields of data and combines experiences to give the truly creative syllogism, *faciens scire*.

There are two vital features of intellectualism. One is the link with data, or experience, or the image, or the presented or the represented: "The act of understanding leaps forth when the sensible data are in a suitable constellation."[1] "Both acts of understanding [direct and reflective] have their instrumental or material causes, but the direct act has this cause in a schematic image or phantasm, while the reflective act reviews not only imagination but also sense experience, and direct acts of understanding, and definitions, to find in all taken together the sufficient ground or evidence for a judgment."[2] "Reasoning in its essence is simply the development of insight; it is motion towards understanding. In the concrete such development is a dialectical interplay of sense, memory, imagination, insight, definition, critical reflection, judgment; we bring to bear on the issue all the resources at our command."[3] That is to say, intellectualism is a validation in Thomist terms of the *preconceptual* and the *unformulated,* which have become so important in modern studies of primitive peoples and deserve an equal importance in our analysis or cognitional processes in the artist, the scientist, the philosopher, the theologian, or the man-in-the-street. Of course, its very character as preconceptual and unformulated makes understanding difficult to talk about: "Because the act of understanding . . . is prior to, and cause of, conceptualization, because expression is only through conceptualization, any attempt to fix the act of understanding, except by way of introspective description, involves its own partial failure; for any such attempt is an expression, and expression is no longer understanding and already concept."[4]

[1] "The Concept of *Verbum* in the Writings of St. Thomas Aquinas," *Theological Studies* 7 (1946) 362.
[2] *Ibid.* 8 (1947) 35.
[3] *Ibid.*, p. 46.
[4] *Ibid.* 7 (1946) 372.

The second vital feature of intellectualism is the *emanatio intelligibilis,* or rationally conscious procession of the inner word (concept or judgment) from understanding: "The intelligibility of the procession of an inner word is not passive nor potential; it is active and actual. . . . Again, its intelligibility defies formulation in any specific law. . . . Thus the procession of an inner word is the pure case of intelligible law. . . . Thirdly, it is native and natural for the procession of inner word to be intelligible, actively intelligible, and the genus of all intelligible process. . . . To introduce a term that will summarize this, we may say that the inner word is rational, not indeed with the derived rationality of discourse, of reasoning from premises to conclusions, but with the basic and essential rationality of rational consciousness . . . with the rationality that now we have to observe in all concepts. For human understanding, though it has its object in the phantasm and knows it in the phantasm, yet is not content with an object in this state. It pivots on itself to produce for itself another object which is the inner word as *ratio, intentio, definitio, quod quid est.* And this pivoting and production is no mere matter of some metaphysical sausage-machine, at one end slicing species off phantasm, and at the other popping out concepts; it is an operation of rational consciousness."[5]

When the *verbum* series began to appear in 1946, there was little welcome for the act of insight (direct understanding) and the intelligible process by which concepts were formulated. Eleven years later several reviewers of the book *Insight* were making cautious admissions of the psychological fact, but I think that there is still little recognition of the virtualities of this fundamental position. Perhaps that is to be expected, but at the same time it is to be deeply regretted, for insight and intelligible emanation not only link what the artist does with what the scientist does (the one oriented to the image by insight, the other oriented to the conceptualization of insight), but also has

[5] *Ibid.,* pp. 380–381.

extremely important implications in various questions of theology, e.g., in understanding how the human Christ might have
the vision of God (understanding) and not yet have formulated inner words on various particular sets of data (conceptualization). As for the act of reflective understanding and the
judgment of existence that naturally flows from it, Lonergan's
position was so little understood when he wrote the *verbum*
articles that he was actually accused of idealism, and the appearance of *Insight* has left many Scholastic readers still uncompre-
hending. This is not only to be regretted but is also a grave mis-
fortune for Scholastic thinking; whether it be a matter of the
existence of God, or of a critique of Duméry, or of theological
understanding of the one person and two natures in Christ,
reliance on a mythical look at being leaves one helpless before
the real problems.

We turn to another viewpoint. Lonergan's decision for a live
intellectualism as against a dead conceptualism may have been
the fundamental option of his academic career; it was certainly
the salient on which he pushed his attack against a now fast dis-
appearing type of Scholasticism. But if one reads his *Insight*
or his *De Deo Trino,* to take instances from different fields,
one is struck by the stringent adherence they show to the laws
of conceptualization; the defining, reasoning, and verifying are,
to repeat a phrase I have used before, inhumanly rigorous.
Those who run logic-machines might be forced to define more
accurately and use words more precisely, but, in the context of
philosophy and theology written in a flowing and legible style,
one could hardly ask for more careful formulation and proof;
his work is even conceptual sometimes to the point of tedium.
So the question arises: Has Lonergan abandoned his own great
discovery and returned to a barren conceptualism?

As the reader knows, my question is in the highest degree
rhetorical. First of all, nothing Lonergan does is "barren." As
for "conceptualism," what one should really ask here is the
place of the conceptual in an intellectualist's program, and then
the answer is that the conceptual plays a very important role

131

provided it does not turn into conceptual*ism*. To be intellectualist does not mean the rejection of the conceptual; the very
force of his intellectualist trend, the term of the *emanatio intelligibilis,* is the conceptual. There was nothing wrong with the
conceptualist's program of defining terms, stating his position in
well-formed propositions, and proving it in processes subject
to articulation in syllogistic form; indeed, if he wished to be
scientific and not just talkative, such a program was *de rigueur*.
What was wrong was the self-enclosure of the whole procedure,
the ghetto into which he had retired with his terms, propositions, and syllogisms, the wall he had built up between his terms
and their fertile source in image and intelligence. And the *verbum* articles as well as *Insight* were concerned to remedy that
defect.

But one must attend also to the inherent deficiency, from the
cognitional viewpoint, of the unformulated insight, whether it
be found in the artistic, the interpersonal, or anywhere else in
the world of the preconceptual. Those who remain here do not
think out what is virtual in their understanding; they do not take
possession of their understanding. The viewpoint here is that
of the full range of the cognitional: of experience, understanding, science, reasoned dialogue, rational reflection, and judgment. It is not a claim that the author of *Hamlet* should have
written a treatise on decision and authenticity instead of the play
he did write; it is simply a recognition that, if a person wishes
to be heard in the circles of reasoned, academic discourse, he
has to know what he is talking about and offer rational grounds
for his position; that is, he has to go beyond the insight to its
formulation.

The foregoing is a rather common-sense statement of a position that is implicit in Lonergan's fundamental analysis of the
human cognitional process, but the point is worth emphasizing.
The cognitional process has its own built-in normative, an exigence for understanding, for conceptualizing and universalizing,
for reflecting, for judging and stating objectively, for understanding more deeply across wider ranges of experience, for

132

conceiving, reflecting, and judging again on the basis of the new understanding; finally, at every stage there is the exigence for intelligent, rational, and responsible decision that makes a man what he is and determines his authenticity.

To grasp this "exigence" of the human spirit is basic for an understanding of Lonergan's work. He would be the last to criticize the inquiring mind, the intelligent artist, the precise logician, the careful framer of the well-formed statement, the objective scientist, the enthusiast for verification—these types all represent integral steps in the total process of knowing intelligently and rationally, and he himself has profited continually from work done under the impetus of their respective dynamisms. But he would be the first to criticize any of them who might nourish pretensions to be *the* representative of intelligent, rational work, for none of them represents the *total* exigence that is the special characteristic and proper feature of human knowing. Each increment of knowledge added to our store depends on a structure whose totality has to be respected: "Human knowing . . . puts itself together, one part summoning forth the next, till the whole is reached."[6] Furthermore, each increment is *only* an increment added under the drive of a dynamism that reaches out to the all: "Man wants to understand completely. As the desire to understand is the opposite of total obscurantism, so the unrestricted desire to understand is the opposite of any and every partial obscurantism no matter how slight. . . . Nor is the existence of this unrestricted desire doubtful. Neither centuries of inquiry nor enormous libraries of answers have revealed any tendency for the stream of further questions to diminish."[7]

Thus the ideal is a position in which both understanding and

---

[6] *Spirit as Inquiry. Studies in Honor of Bernard Lonergan* (Chicago, 1964), from p. 231 of Father Lonergan's concluding word, "Cognitional Structure." The volume was first published as a special issue of *Continuum*, vol. 2 (see p. 531).

[7] *Insight. A Study of Human Understanding* (London and New York, 1st ed., 1957) 638.

formulation retain their places, and insistence on the latter is no abandonment of an emphasis on the former. When Karl Barth, after forty years of insisting that God is the wholly other, came out in 1956 with a lecture on the "humanity" of God, he expressly asserted that the earlier message had still to be uttered and could not be eluded, but had to be said now more appropriately in conjunction with the new message to be thought out. Something similar, I think, might be said by Lonergan. Twenty years ago the need was great for an intellectualism characterized most noticeably by its opposition to conceptualism. But intellectualism was never *defined* by opposition to concepts; rather it calls for concepts by the very orientation of the understanding it stresses; and now—in the vagueness and talkativeness of the artistic, the interpersonal, the preconceptual, the round-table discussion, the exchange of facile opinions in the "viewiness" excoriated by Newman—the need is for insistence on rigorous thinking.

Thus I should sum up in two short phrases the prominent features of the "style" of Lonergan's thinking: intellectualism as against conceptualism, rigorous formulation and verification as against vagueness and viewiness. These features mark his work in both the transcendental area which occupied his early years and the historical area which has been more his concern in recent years.

II

It is his work in the area of the transcendental that we take up in our second section. The topic here is linked with that of our first section, for it deals with method, which is concerned immediately not with the object but with the subject and his operations. For two centuries, largely under the influence of Kant, there has been developing the critical demand, that is, the demand for saying only what we know and, consequently, for determining what we can know and what we cannot. This has forced us into the region of interiority, of human operations, of the structure and possibilities of our cognitional equipment, to what Lonergan in *Insight* (where it was the central issue) called self-appropriation. Self-appropriation is the basis for method, the critical possession of our own powers enabling us to return to the object with assurance of efficacious achievement.

Method, though its general precepts deriving from the basic structure of human knowing are relatively simple, becomes rather complex in the application to different fields and to particular procedures. In its general notion it is simple: "What ultimately is the nature and ground of method but a reflective grasp and specialized application . . . of the dynamic structure immanent and recurrently operative in human cognitional activity?"[8] The structure rises on the triple level of experience, understanding, and reflection, and so empirical method in general means "to formulate . . . hypotheses, work out their implications, and test the implications against observed results."[9] But within that very general structure there is room for great differentiation; for example, there is the division in empirical method between the "classical" and the "statistical," which complement one another in procedures, formulations, modes of abstraction, verification, and data explained.[10] Again, there is the distinction between upper and lower "blades" in the "scissors-action" of heuristic method: "As was noted in examining the methods of natural science, there is a scissors-like action that selects the mathematical expression of physical laws by operating simultaneously from above with differential equations and from below with measurements and empirical correlations."[11] Furthermore, there is the contrast between classical and statistical together on one side, and genetic method on another: "As classical method rests on the assumption that similars are to be understood similarly, so genetic method rests on the assumption that an understanding of significantly dissimilar individuals is to be reached

[8] *Ibid.* xxi–xxii.
[9] *Ibid.* 105.
[10] *Ibid.* 114–115.
[11] *Ibid.* 522.

by subsuming their respective histories under common genetic principles. . . . As classical method is concerned with laws, so genetic method is concerned with emergent trends."[12]

Special interest attaches to Lonergan's views on method in the higher science of philosophy. Here, as always, we must distinguish general problems and principles of method from those peculiar to the science in question. What belongs to basic structure and cognitional process will be found in every field of human knowing; much therefore that is learned from the methods of empirical science can be exploited in the field of philosophy. In particular, Lonergan stands for a philosophy that is methodical, critical, verifiable, and comprehensive; it derives these attributes from its basis in cognitional theory: "The philosophy and metaphysics that result from insight into insight will be verifiable. For just as scientific insights both emerge and are verified in . . . ordinary experience, so insight into insight both emerges and is verified in the insights of mathematicians, scientists, and men of common sense. . . . Just as every statement in theoretical science can be shown to imply statements regarding sensible fact, so every statement in philosophy and metaphysics can be shown to imply statements regarding cognitional fact."[13] Such a philosophy "will be methodical because it transposes the statements of philosophers and metaphysicians to their origins in cognitional activity and it settles whether that activity is or is not aberrant by appealing, not to philosophers, not to metaphysicians, but to the insights, methods, and procedures of mathematicians, scientists, and men of common sense."[14]

Important here is the isomorphism of cognitional structure and its proper object. Lonergan holds "that human knowing is structured in a related set of three acts and that the contents of those acts must be similarly structured: human knowing, in

---

[12] *Ibid.* 479.
[13] *Ibid.* xi.
[14] *Ibid.* xii.

its proper field, is a unification of experiencing, understanding, and judging; and so what is known in this field will be a parallel unification of a content of experience, a content of understanding, and a content of judging. Further, knowing is objective; the pattern of cognitional contents is not just notional but reflects the ontological pattern of what is known. And so, corresponding to experience, understanding, and judgment in the human subject, we have potency, form, and act in the proportionate object of his knowing."[15] To quote Lonergan himself: "There exists a necessary isomorphism between our knowing and its proportionate known. But that parallel is missed by Spinoza's deductivist *ordo idearum est ordo rerum*. The correct locus of the parallel is to be found in the dynamic structure of our knowing. Inquiry and understanding presuppose and complement experience; reflection and judgment presuppose and complement understanding. But what holds for the activities, also holds for their contents. What is known inasmuch as one is understanding, presupposes and complements what is known by experiencing; and what is known inasmuch as one is affirming, presupposes and complements what is known by understanding. Finally, the contents of cognitional acts either refer to the known or are identical with the known, and so the dynamic structure of knowing is also the structure of proportionate being."[16] One should note the point of all this: it is not that Lonergan has discovered the potency-form-act structure of the object of human knowing, which has long been Scholastic doctrine; it is that he has systematically correlated this structure with that of cognitional activity. And that correlation is basic for method.

So far we have been concerned with the proper exercise of human cognitional powers, but there is also improper exercise

[15] Here I quote an article of my own, "St. Thomas and the Isomorphism of Human Knowing and its Proper Object," *Sciences ecclésiastiques* 13 (1961) 167.
[16] *Insight* 486.

and, as well, failure to exercise the cognitional structure. There arises a problem that acquires peculiar urgency in philosophy and makes dialectical method especially relevant here. "Besides insights there are oversights. . . . Hence, if insight into insight is not to be an oversight of oversights, it must include an insight into the principal devices of the flight from understanding. . . . In its philosophic form . . . [this flight] appears to result simply from an incomplete development in the intelligent and reasonable use of one's own intelligence and reasonableness."[17] And so a philosophy based, as Lonergan's is, on cognitional theory "will be critical because it discriminates between the products of the detached and disinterested desire to understand and, on the other hand, the products of the flight from understanding."[18] "Dialectic provides . . . the general form of a critical attitude. Each department has to work out its own specialized criteria."[19] In philosophy the dialectic is between the basic "position" on the real (the real is the concrete universe of being), self-knowledge (it is acquired in intelligent and reasonable self-affirmation), and objectivity (the consequence of intelligent inquiry and critical reflection)—between these basic "positions" and the "counterpositions" on those same issues. "One is forced to the conclusion that philosophic method must concern itself with the structure and the aberrations of human cognitional process."[20] As Lonergan said in his summary of a projected talk to the American Catholic Philosophical Association: "A new higher viewpoint in the natural sciences ordinarily involves no revision of the subject's image and concept of himself, and so scientific advance easily wins universal and permanent acceptance. But a higher viewpoint in philosophy not only logically entails such a revision but also cannot be grasped with a 'real apprehension' unless the revision actually becomes effective

[17] *Ibid.* xi.
[18] *Ibid.* xii.
[19] *Ibid.* 244.
[20] *Ibid.* 421.

in the subject's mental attitudes."[21] In other words, there is involved a conversion, and all the implications of horizon, authenticity, and the categories existentialism has made famous.

Scientific method flows into philosophical; philosophical problematic and method flow into theological; theology in turn supports and guides philosophy. "While it is true that natural reason can arrive at a correct philosophy, it also is apparent that very commonly it fails to do so."[22] "Just as reason is illuminated by faith so also method may be illuminated by faith; indeed, since method is simply reason's explicit consciousness of the norms of its own procedures, the illumination of reason by faith implies an illumination of method by faith. . . . Finally, since the principles of empirical anthropology, psychology, sociology, pedagogy, medicine, economics, politics, and so forth, are not primitive propositions peculiar to each of those disciplines but methodical rules that are more or less common to all, it is primarily through the illumination of method by faith that theology has to exercise her queenly rule."[23]

We may notice, as a preliminary point, that there is a community of procedures in theology and other sciences inasmuch as they are all involved in the twofold order of analysis and synthesis: analysis (*via inventionis*) beginning with what is first-for-us and ending with what is first-in-itself, and synthesis (*via doctrinae*) reversing the direction. "If one compares a history of chemistry with a textbook on chemistry, one finds that the course of discovery runs from sensible data to ever more recondite theoretical elements while the arrangement for teaching and learning begins from the theoretical elements and gradually shows how they may be constructed into explanations of all known phenomena."[24] I do not remember Lonergan's having

[21] *The New Scholasticism* 32 (1958) 97. This talk was never given; Lonergan substituted another in its place.

[22] "Theology and Understanding," *Gregorianum* 35 (1954) 639.

[23] *Ibid*. 645–646.

[24] *Ibid*. 635–636.

illustrated the procedure in philosophy, but we may borrow an illustration from Aristotle and St. Thomas, where they show the historical sequence somewhat as follows: A man comes to see me. Why? To get some money. Why does he want money? To pay a debt. Why does he wish to pay the debt? Because justice tells him to do so. Why should he be just? And so forth. One thus arrives, in a series of swift analytic steps (which may have taken many centuries in actual human history), at the last reason of all, the ultimate good.[25] However, a systematic treatise in ethics commonly starts from the simply good, proceeds to the human good and its divisions, and so to justice, paying one's debts, and so on—exactly the reverse order. Now this twofold order Lonergan finds also in theology, where in fact it has particular importance: there is a historical development from what is first-for-us to what is first-in-itself, and there is a systematic exposition which begins with the fundamental explanatory idea and adds specifying constructions till we reach again what is first-for-us, but reach it now with the depth of understanding the prior work has given us.[26] There is special point to the twofold order in theology, where it is imperative to link the system with the source through a study of historical development, but it is common to all sciences because it is based on procedures native to the human mind. I do not know whether chemistry and philosophy are often taught according to this division, but it would be interesting to see the experiment tried.

But the great differences of theological method have to be

[25] *Post. Anal.* I, 24, 85b 30–35; see St. Thomas, *In I Post. Anal.,* lect. 38, and *Contra gentes* I, 74, #3.

[26] See "Theology and Understanding," *Gregorianum* 35 (1954) 637–638; also Lonergan's treatise, *De Deo Trino,* of which one volume follows the order of historical development from the sending of Son and Spirit to the understanding of the triune God through the psychological analogy, while the other starts with the psychological analogy and proceeds to a new and deeper understanding of the presence of Son and Spirit in the world.

noted too. In presenting the assumption of Mary as an instance of the development of dogma, Lonergan took occasion to outline some of the differences between such a development and that of empirical science: "The development of Christian doctrine is not subject to the revolutions that are part and parcel of the development of science; the reason for this is ultimately that the development of understanding in science regards sensible data while the development of understanding in Christian doctrine regards, not sensible presentations which intellect has to raise to the order of truths, but a divine revelation which already is in the order of truth."[27] This is quite basic for Lonergan: theological understanding, in the lapidary Latin he wrote sixteen years later, "non a datis sed a veris incipit."[28] The fundamental category, then, is the word of God in its aspect of truth.

There results a crucial difference between the historical or analytical part of theology and the corresponding part of an empirical science or the historical in general. For in theology we have to distinguish the positive from the dogmatic in historical study. This differentiation has arisen only recently and is still not well understood, with consequent hostility on either side towards its opposite member. Positive theology studies the documents of faith and hence is biblical, conciliar, patristic, medieval, etc.; it is called theological, not because it proposes a doctrine on God but because it narrates the doctrine of others on God: what Paul said, what John, what Ireneus, what Aquinas (theology in *oratio obliqua,* Lonergan has called it) said; it is called positive because of the close relation of its proper method to the data ("proper" here is understood in distinction to what it has in common with other methods). It does not try to formulate universal laws as psychology, sociology, and others do, but

[27] "The Assumption and Theology" in *Vers le dogme de l'Assomption* (Journées d'études mariales, Montréal, 1948) 418. I give only one of a series of differences which Lonergan outlines.
[28] *De Deo Trino* (Rome, 1964) II, 20.

studies intelligibility in the singular, trying to bring to light the meaning in its every aspect of the author studied.

But dogmatic theology is not content with the intelligibility of a particular author, be he Paul or be he Thomas Aquinas; it seeks the catholic rule of faith. What positive theology achieves in piecemeal fashion, dogmatic theology tries to integrate. Where positive theology is divided into many specialized areas, dogmatic theology transcends divisions to relate them all to the common faith. Where positive theology studies the obscure and the rare and the doubtful, dogmatic theology turns to the clear, the common, the certain. Where positive theology uses the categories of the document studied, dogmatic theology makes explicit what was only implicit and so perforce uses other categories than those that found expression in the document. And so forth.[29]

Besides the historical part of theology, there is the systematic, where one is concerned to understand what one believes. I have already referred to the article Lonergan published in 1954 in *Gregorianum,* under the title "Theology and Understanding." You could hardly find two words that express more succinctly his lifelong interest: theology, the science of God and of all things in relation to God; and understanding, the basic need of the human spirit. Now theological understanding aims at the totality, hence at relating the bits of information it acquires, hence at system. The aim of such systematic theology is not the generation of indisputable certitudes; any certitude we have in this field derives from the sources of revelation in the historical part of theology. Its aim is understanding of the mysteries, in that imperfect way, of course, which alone is possible. "Still, though it generates neither new certitude nor perfect understanding, the *ordo doctrinae* [systematic theology] is most fruitful. With some approximation to a single view it gives rise to an apprehension of the exact content and the exact implications of the many mysteries in their many aspects. That single view both simplifies and enriches one's own spiritual life, and it

[29] *Ibid.* I, 5–14.

bestows upon one's teaching the enviable combination of sureness of doctrine with versatility of expression. Finally, the single view remains, for it is fixed upon one's intellectual memory."[30]

What settles the relations of these various parts of theology to one another? It is *method,* which Lonergan links here with the Thomist wisdom. In any treatise there are many integral parts: dogmatic theology in the strict sense; the documents, which are instrumental; the meaning of the documents, which is positive theology; systematic theology, which gives the total view of the object. And it is wisdom or method that presides over all, distinguishing parts, assigning each its role, directing all parts to the mutual help of one another.[31]

To talk about the method of theology and the structure of human operations in the theologian and believer seems very remote from the praying theology so much advocated today, but the relevance of such fundamental study appears in its application to one of theology's most pressing problems: that of the crosscultural. The problem arises whenever those of one culture try to understand the documents of another, but it becomes especially acute in theology, which is based on divine revelation. For divine revelation was made to a particular people at a particular time in a particular way, and is entangled in their cultural situation; nevertheless, the church of God is meant for all peoples of all times and places; it is a universal church, then, founded in a particular culture. A good illustration of the problem occurs already in New Testament times, where they fought out the concrete issue whether or not the Greeks were to be bound by the Mosaic law. But that is only an instance; the problem has a far wider scope, being limited only by the limits of the human capacity for change.

We have to return here to the distinction between the *prius quoad nos* and the *prius quoad se,* which, in discussing the twofold order of science, I translated first-for-us and first-in-itself.

---

[30] "Theology and Understanding," *Gregorianum* 35 (1954) 640.
[31]*De Deo Trino* I, 5.

A further distinction is needed now in the first-for-us: in the realm of nature it remains the same, but in the realm of spirit it changes. That is, colors, sounds, hot and cold, and whatever is known by sense are roughly the same always and everywhere with the sameness of the human body, and so the first-for-us in this area is a univocal category. But in the realm of spirit, in languages, customs, domestic and political structures, in mechanical and liberal arts, in religion and science—in all these areas there is unrest and fertility, perpetual change, and extreme diversity; further, in this area the first-for-us is what we first experienced as children and, since the experience of children in Toronto is not that of children in Tokyo, nor the experience of children in 1966 that of children in 1066, the first-for-us in the spiritual world is an equivocal category. Each epoch, each nation, each class of society has its own spontaneous first-for-us.[32] Thus there arises the problem of a crosscultural principle by which one can move systematically from the first-for-us of one culture to the first-for-us of another; specifically, the question is how to move from the biblical word of God to the word of God in our contemporary society.

The relevance of theology here is that its movement terminates at the first-in-itself, so it can relate to any first-for-us and thus speak to all cultures. The specialist can indeed immerse himself in Hebrew culture and learn to pass skillfully between that culture and his own, but he does not provide a general solution to the crosscultural problem, and even his own transition from culture to culture tends to leave aside anything touching principles, judgments, counsels of men, as if all this were doomed to relativism; the result is that different deficiencies in the thinking of the scholars produce different accounts of the culture they describe.[33] (A concrete illustration: the failure of many specialists to discover any recognition of the principles of noncontradiction in Hebrew thinking.) The church, however, not only

[32] *Ibid.* II, 42–43.
[33] *Ibid.*, pp. 43–44.

144

goes from one first-for-us to another, that is, from "relative" to "relative," but also ascends to the first-in-itself and makes the ascent definitive in conciliar declarations such as those we have from Nicea and Chalcedon.

The church did this spontaneously through history in the normal exercise of her function, but the theorist has now the task of explaining what happened. Here Lonergan's painstaking analysis of human operations stands him in good stead. "If you wish to ascertain the origin and evolution of cultures, you should turn to the field of human operations and see how they are carried out, joined to one another, modified according to circumstances, see how they coalesce gradually into more and more complex sets, until they reach that dynamic structure to be discerned proximately in men . . . working for particular goods . . . while only implicitly is the structure informed by the good of order and actuated by value."[34] Lonergan offers an extremely simple illustration of the "implicit" in human operations: everyone who says "is" or "is not" is concerned with being and metaphysics, but he may be completely ignorant of explicit accounts of that subject matter; his metaphysics is simply implicit in his operations.[35] Now the movement to theology makes explicit what was implicit and at the same time rises to that first-in-itself which is catholic, permanent, universal.

III

In passing now from Lonergan's formal theology to its material content, I make two preliminary remarks. One is already overdue in this essay, which appears in a volume called *Theologians of Our Time,* yet speaks much more of what readers may call the profane ideas of philosophy than of the religious ideas proper to theology. Perhaps the relation of Lonergan's ideas on method to the problems of theology has done some-

[34] *Ibid.* I, 89.
[35] *Ibid.* 12–13.

thing to meet objections from this quarter, but I make the general remark here that what distinguishes a theologian is his set of concepts—Lonergan likes to borrow from the Germans and speak of *Begrifflichkeit*. Theologians are believers and, as such, all hold approximately the same set of truths; but what makes a theologian rate a distinct chapter in a volume such as this, is the distinctive set of ideas he uses as tools to explore the revealed truths he holds. Nor does this put him in some inferior position religiously as compared to biblical and patristic and liturgical scholars. Ideas of bread and wine, light and darkness, and all the rest are likewise just a set of tools, no less profane in themselves than "person," "nature," "historicity," "method," and the tools of a theologian. The difference is not between sacred and profane, but between descriptive and explanatory terms, a difference spelled out in Lonergan's *Insight*.

My second remark concerns the influence a transcendental approach may have in determining even the objective details of a material theology. For one thing, Lonergan's study of operations, method, correlation of subject and object, and so on, enables him to use as analogies for the divine mysteries not only those categories of objective creation which could be presupposed by Vatican I in its decree on theological understanding, but also the categories based on the very procedures and methods of the human mind itself. This had been done long ago by Aquinas in regard to the procession of the Second Person in the Trinity; but in the Middle Ages that was a rather exceptional practice, whereas now we are provided systematically with a new set of analogues, as useful in our time as matter and form, substance and accident, were in medieval thinking. Furthermore, the critical and transcendental approach provides a criterion for judging the categories and determining which are peculiar to an age or culture, and which correspond to permanent exigencies of the human spirit. For example, is the doctrine of two natures and one person in Christ merely an ephemeral expression suited to the speculative mood of the fifth-century Greek fathers, which would leave it true, if you will, but decidedly irrelevant in our time, or does it correspond, under the technical terminology, to questions which are native to any human mind and therefore as relevant today as they were fifteen centuries ago? Such questions can be answered systematically by the transcendental approach, where, without it, we are apt merely to fume and bluster.

One will expect Lonergan's objective doctrine to be different, therefore, in correspondence to his methodology. However, since I cannot give his material theology in any detail whatever, I think the most useful procedure here might be merely to sketch the areas in which he has done significant work and suggest a few samples of his less well-known ideas that could profitably be explored by the reader. His doctoral dissertation was on the notion of *gratis operans* in St. Thomas (published in *Theological Studies*, 1941–42); it was not intended to be precisely a study of the Bannez-Molina argument, though it took a definite stand here (the verdict: no contest, within the terms of the Thomist doctrine of grace)—it was rather, as the subtitle of the dissertation stated, "A Study of Speculative Development in the Writings of St. Thomas Aquinas." It resulted in a positive grasp for Lonergan of certain great and key ideas: habits, psychological continuity, moral impotence, operation, freedom, the transcendence of God, and others that have continued to fertilize his thought ever since.

Longeran's next main work in theology was on the processions of Word and Love in the Trinity. The groundwork was again historical, a study of the ideas of Aquinas; likewise, it was basically philosophical, in the field of psychology and gnoseology. But the theological result was the dereliction of the view making the formation of images in the imagination as good an analogy for the Word's procession as the formation of an inner word in human intellectual consciousness. The movement was from the generality of ontology and causality to the specific richness of psychology and rational consciousness. His work on the Trinity received more systematic treatment when he began to teach this treatise in Rome in a course that subsequently

147

gave us his two volumes, *De Deo Trino*.[36] One does not summarize a theology manual, but the more significant sections of
original theology may be indicated: the movement towards
Nicea and the significance of Nicea itself; the category of
"mystery" in Trinitarian theology; the scriptural basis for the
"psychological analogy" (in volume I) and the theological
exposition of the analogy (in volume II); the introductory chapter of the second volume on theology in general; the resolution
of the various "insoluble" difficulties that arise for speculative
thought in regard to the Trinity; the question of consciousness
in the divine subjects (note the plural—there are three subjects
in God for Lonergan); the very personal theology of the divine
missions and the relation of Word and Spirit in the world to
the grace-structure of the universe.

Also the result of his classroom lectures in Rome are two
works of Christology: *De constitutione Christi ontologica et
psychologica*[37] and *De Verbo incarnato*.[38] The first, a mere booklet of 150 pages, is packed nevertheless with good things on the
ontology and psychology applicable to Christ; it contains also
Lonergan's first sally into the controversy initiated by Maurice
de la Taille with his views on the union of uncreated and created;
but it is especially noteworthy for the chapters on the human
consciousness of Christ, one of Lonergan's major contributions
to current questions of material theology, I should say, though
they have met little comprehension yet in the theological world.
The second work incorporates the results of the first into the
context of a total treatise, adding very useful studies of the

[36] To clarify the editions of this work, note that the 1964 edition has a
Pars dogmatica (vol. I) and a *Pars systematica* (vol. II), that vol. I had
a previous edition under the title *De Deo Trino: Pars analytica* (1961),
and that vol. II had two previous editions under the title *Divinarum
personarum conceptio analogica* (1957 and 1959).

[37] Rome, 1956; further editions (unchanged): 1958, 1961, 1964.

[38] Rome, 1960; further editions: 1961 (unchanged), 1964 (revised).
Technically, this work is not published but is available at the bookstore
of the Gregorian University.

movement of ideas in New Testament writings, a thorough historical study and original theory on human knowledge and its development in Christ, and a section on the redemption that likewise combines historical range and theoretical depth.

Besides these major works we have a small collection of stray articles: on marriage, on the assumption of Mary, on the natural desire to see God, etc. Perhaps even more important than these are certain ideas less expressly thematized, ideas more or less embedded in works on another theme. For example, there is the nucleus of a theology of history in his study on marriage, and there is the outline of a treatise on the grace-structure of the universe tucked away in a couple of pages of his Trinitarian work; his ideas on the relation of natural and supernatural are scattered up and down the length of his writings during a quarter of a century; his remarks on Barth, Bultmann, Duméry, *et al.,* occur sporadically as precious but undeveloped insights into the influential movements of our time. One could do a service to the theological world by collecting these *obiter dicta* and thematizing them in their own right.

As I look over this essay in the effort at self-criticism, two questions preoccupy me: Have I yielded to the temptation, normal enough in a volume like this, of "making a case" for the subject of my contribution? And have I failed—better, in which respect have I most notably failed—to give an adequate account of Lonergan's ideas?

The answer to the first question is probably not wholly within my competence. Many of us know well enough what we personally owe to Lonergan's thought; we have no doubt that as a thinker he is historically significant; but perhaps we are too close to him, too busy assimilating his ideas, to locate him accurately in the stream of history. However, one thing I do wish to state: anything in this essay that may tend towards popularizing Lonergan is hereby repudiated; he is not to be made popular. Not at least till his ideas have undergone a whole program of implementation. Does that mean he lacks "contemporaneity"?

No, but obviously his work is contemporaneous only in the sense in which fundamental ideas are always contemporaneous, even though they are likewise always remote, with an extent of contemporary influence in inverse proportion to their difficulty; here we may apply to Lonergan what he said of St. Anselm: "Only what is difficult seems to his taste."[39] I do not think his disciples ought to try to modify his "vocation" in this respect; the demand that thinkers occupy themselves with the problems of our time is legitimate, but what does not seem legitimate to me is the demand that they do their thinking in terms accessible at once to everyone.

With regard to my second question I have, oddly enough, a rather definite answer, though I am unable to remedy the inadequacy of my presentation. That is, the great difficulty of giving an adequate account of Lonergan's thought is not merely that its momentum is still so strong; even in a still developing movement, one could recognize past gains, discern new consequences, and predict with some accuracy coming achievements. The difficulty is that the present development of Lonergan's thought does not seem quite so homogeneous with the past as his development from the *verbum* articles to *Insight,* or from *Insight* to his lectures on method. There is a somewhat more radical evolution involved in the distinction which is most operative in the present trend of his thinking, that between classical consciousness (concerned with the universal and necessary and unchanging) and historical consciousness (concerned with the particular and contingent, the changing and developing). Earlier development occurred within the scope of the transcendental, but the distinction I outlined is effecting a shift from the transcendental to the historical. Some elements of the present concern were present in his earlier work (e.g., his ideas on genetic method), and some details of the new interest have been indicated: his ideas on development of doctrine; his explanation of positive

---

[39] "St. Thomas' Thought on *Gratia Operans,*" *Theological Studies* 2 (1941) 296.

theology; the role he attributes to conversion in intellectual work; his view of the problem inherent in a historically conditioned revelation. But such indications are far from being an analysis, and I am acutely conscious of not having done justice to this phase of his thinking. Hopefully, his own publications will soon remedy the defect and do so in definitive fashion.

JOHN HICK

BY

Lowell D. Streiker

John Hick has described the purpose of his first book, *Faith and Knowledge,* as "a bridging operation between philosophy and theology." Indeed, Hick's entire thought may be so described. What makes his effort worthy of special attention are the standpoints from which Hick undertakes this "operation." He is, in his own words, "philosophically to the 'left' and theologically to the 'right.' " He is committed to both contemporary analytical philosophy and to theological neo-orthodoxy, positions which cannot be easily harmonized.

John Harwood Hick was born in 1928 at Scarborough, Yorkshire, England. Educated at the Universities of Hull, Edinburgh, and Oxford, as well as Westminster Theological College, he is recipient of the M.A., Ph.D., and D.Phil., degrees. As an ordained minister of the Presbyterian Church of England, Hick served with a rural congregation at Belford, Northumberland, from 1953 to 1956. From 1956 to 1959, he was Assistant Professor of Philosophy at Cornell University. From 1959 to 1964, he served as Stuart Professor of Christian Philosophy, Princeton Theological Seminary, and is currently Lecturer in the Philosophy of Religion at Cambridge University. He was S. A. Cooke Bye-Fellow, Gonville and Caius College, Cambridge, and a Guggenheim Fellow. Hick describes his marital status as "one wife, four children." A complete bibliography of his books and principal articles is included with the conclusion of this volume.

Though Hick describes himself as a philosopher of religion, his resolve to take Christian faith as the foundation or presupposition of inquiry casts doubt on the accuracy of this identification. Quite clearly he is a Christian philosopher, one who looks theistically at all things, including intellectual dilemmas; thus his most fruitful contribution consists of the imaginative manner in which he seeks to remove unnecessary obstacles to faith. The manner in which he deals with perennial issues, such as the problem of evil and the question of free will, indicates that it is possible for Christian faith to heal and transform the human intellect in the same way that the reception of divine grace heals and transforms the will.

Analytical philosophers frequently dismiss the language of religion as cognitively meaningless. They contend that religious statements reveal much about the emotions of those who utter them, but nothing about objective, observable states. Such statements, they claim, tell us what religious people *feel,* but do not inform us about reality.

The Protestant neo-orthodoxy of Karl Barth and others has stressed the discontinuity of revelation and reason. The "Word of God," the subject of theology is regarded as *sui generis* and sovereign. Neo-orthodox thinkers feel themselves under no obligation to conform their interpretations of the divine message with current modes of thought. They deny that there is any knowledge of God apart from revelation. Human finitude and sinfulness have so incapacitated human reason that all human formulations of the divine are questionable, if not idolatrous.

For Hick to bridge the chasm between these two positivisms, both of which place in doubt the ability of man to describe the divine, he must demonstrate that religious language is meaningful. As Hick explains the concept of "meaningfulness":

> To say that a proposition has meaning or, more strictly . . . , that it has factual or cognitive meaning, is to say that it is in principle verifiable, or at least "probabilifiable," by reference to human experience. This means, in effect, that its truth or falsity must make some possible experienceable difference. If its truth or falsity makes no difference that could possibly be observed, the proposition is cognitively meaningless; it dose not embody a factual assertion.

The need to demonstrate that religious language is verifiable in human experience, at least *in principle,* forms the very center of Hick's activity as a philosophical theologian or, as he prefers to describe himself, a philosopher of religion.

Hick respects the traditional understanding of philosophy of religion as the presentation of demonstrative proofs for the existence of God. In *Philosophy of Religion* he examines the traditional arguments and finds them inconclusive. "None of the arguments which we have examined," he says, "seems qualified to compel belief in God in the mind of one who lacks that belief."

Hick rejects the notion of faith as the acceptance on God's authority of divinely revealed and promulgated propositions. Rather, he adopts "the Reformed view of faith," according to which, "the locus of revelation is not language but history, not propositions but events." According to this view

> the content of revelation is not any body of truths about God, but God himself coming within the orbit of man's experience by acting in human history. From this point of view, theological propositions, as such, are not revealed, but represent human attempts to understand the significance of revelatory events. This non-propositional conception of revelation is connected with the recent renewed emphasis upon the *personal* character of God, and the thought that the divine-human personal relationship consists in something more than the promulgation and reception of theological truths.

Both the religious and the nonreligious man see the same events. But the religious man sees them *as* the workings of God. Thus

154

Christian faith is the recognition of the presence of God in the historic events recorded in the Old Testament and, pre-eminently, in the life of Jesus of Nazareth. God discloses *himself* (rather than propositions *about* himself), and the believer recognizes and responds to the divine activity.

Hick identifies himself as one who cannot help but believing in God because he is aware of the presence of God in his life. Yet he feels compelled to explain the similarities and differences of the knowledge gained through such encounters and the knowledge gained through ordinary perception of the world, and to deal with the intellectual problems which such knowledge entails. His starting point is not the question of the existence of God, but rather the question of whether religious experience, i.e., the sense of the presence of God, is cognitively significant. In other words, does religious experience yield knowledge as trustworthy as that obtained from our ordinary perception of the world?

In seeking an answer to this question, Hick enumerates the similarities and the differences of "taking religious experience as cognitively veridical."

"What are the similarities?" he asks.

> . . . in each case there are certain data, and our interpretation of these data in terms respectively of a spatio-temporal world, and a divine Creator of this world who is related to us in and through it. In normal sense perception we are not conscious of sense data as such, or of the habitual interpretative activity which issues in our perception of physical objects. Likewise the man of faith, whilst he is conscious of standing directly in God's presence, is not aware either of "raw" religious data or of his own interpretative response to them.

Thus our ordinary experience of the world and religious awareness include an interpretative element. Hick continues:

> We have no special name for the interpretative element in our cognition of the world; however, the equivalent element in our cognition of God is traditionally termed faith.

> The data of religious experience are, for the most part, the

same in both cases. With the exception of extraordinary instances such as the "special phenomena of mysticism," the data of natural experience and religious experience are identical. "We may say that the same data are being used in two different ways, ways which are not mutually exclusive or competitive but which operate upon two different cognitive 'levels.'" The interpretation of the religious man presupposes the natural interpretation of the world. Both theist and atheist live in the same world; "but as a further characteristic superimposed upon its material structure he (the theist) experiences it as mediating the presence and activity of God." For example, the prophets of the Old Testament saw "the hand of the Lord moving powerfully and purposefully within human history." In like manner, the early Christian community was aware of the reconciling activity of God in the life of the carpenter of Nazareth.

One may see these acts merely as natural occurrences, i.e., events which do not require a religious explanation. But, "in neither case can we prove demonstratively, or even show it to be probable, that the object of our 'cognition' exists independently of those states of mind in which we suppose ourselves to be cognizing it." The religious believer finds that he cannot help interpreting the data in the way in which he does; nor can he prove that his interpretation of the data at this further level is not misinterpretation. Therefore, Hick concludes that the theist has as much right to trust his religious experience or interpretation as does the nontheist.

Hick realizes that there are important differences between sense perception and religious perception. First, whereas sense perception is coercive, religious perception is not. "If we try to ignore the perceptible world, for instance by treating a brick wall as though it were not there, we quickly learn that we must take account of the actual features of our physical environment, or be eliminated from it." But for God to make awareness of himself coercive in this way would greatly diminish the freedom of man to respond to him in faith.

Second, sense perception is universal; religious perception is not. "The sense experiences of any two individuals can be correlated in terms of the hypothesis of a common world which they jointly inhabit." On the other hand, many men appear to lack religious perception. The reports of religious experiences from various cultures cannot easily be correlated as reports of the same religious reality.

Third, sense perception is highly coherent. ". . . the perceived world exhibits continuity and order both in space and time," forming "a systematic whole, changing in accordance with discernible laws upon which accurate predictions can be based." In contrast, "the religious awareness of different individuals varies greatly in degree of coherence." For some it is sporadic and diverse; for others continuous and uniform.

At its "top levels" religious experience is coercive. As we have already noted, there are those who *cannot help* believing in God. Hick refers to the apostle, prophet, or saint as one who, at least at certain times, is "so vividly aware of God that he can no more doubt the veracity of his religious awareness than of his sense experience." During the periods in which such an individual is living consciously in the presence of God, "when God is to him the divine Thou," the question of the existence of God "simply cannot arise." This implies

> The awareness of God, for those who have it, can be as coercive as our ordinary awareness of other human persons and of our material surroundings. The difference, so far as coerciveness is concerned, is not in the vividness of the two types of experience themselves (when the religious experience is considered in its strongest instances), but in the fact that whereas everyone is compelled to have sense experience, no one is compelled to have religious experience. God does not force himself upon our attention as does our physical environment. The individual's own free receptivity or responsiveness plays a part in his dawning consciousness of God, even though once he *has* become conscious of God that consciousness may possess a coercive and indubitable quality.

To summarize, although the awareness of God is coercive to the one who has it in highest degree, no one is coerced into having it.

Short of the highest degree in which the awareness of God is "coercive (but not coerced)," there are many degrees of religious consciousness, "dwindling down to zero."

Hick's examination of the nature of the cognitive claims of religious experience has not established that religious assertions are cognitively meaningful. On the basis of the similarities of natural and religious language listed above, he concludes that the theist ought not to be inhibited from trusting his religious experience. However, his consideration of the differences between religious perception and ordinary sense perception suggests that religion employs language and claims knowledge which differ from the language and knowledge of sense perception in the degree to which the objects of each epistemological approach differ.

> In thus stressing the immense difference between God and the world, such that our status as responsible persons is not undermined by a compelled awareness of the latter, but would be undermined by a compelled awareness of the Supreme Being, the argument may now be in danger of running into an opposite difficulty. For if God is so utterly different from the world and from our fellow humans, perhaps there is after all no proper question concerning his existence or non-existence. Perhaps then the proper function of statements about God is not to make factual assertions of any kind, but rather to express some inner state of the religious mind, perhaps an ethical intention or a way of feeling about the world. In this case talk of "knowing" God would be symbolic rather than literal, and the biblical belief in a really existing personal Being who loves us and who can receive and respond to our worship would require to be radically reinterpreted.

What disturbs Hick is the tendency of a large group of contemporary philosophers and theologians to regard religious language as the poetic expression of aspirations, moral commitments, ideals, and so forth, rather than as factual assertions about God. But, for religious assertions to be regarded as factually meaningful, they must, according to the canons of contemporary philosophy, refer to observable states of affairs.

They must make an actual or possible difference within human experience. This standard cannot be ignored by the pious short circuit to which many religious thinkers appeal, i.e., the practical efficacy of religious belief. The question is not whether *belief* in religious statements makes an observable difference in human experience. The power of religious *belief* to transform lives and harmonize the strivings of large numbers of individuals is beyond question. Even a naturalist can admit as much. The question is whether or not religious statements literally mean anything. Is there anything in reality that corresponds to what the theist believes?

It is the responsibility of the theistic thinker to specify the set of conditions which would either verify or falsify his beliefs. If he is unable to do so, the nontheist may rightly suspect that religious beliefs are completely devoid of cognitive significance or meaning.

Hick insists that "the way in which . . . language operates within historic Judaism and Christianity is much closer to ordinary factual asserting than to the expressing of aesthetic intuitions or the declaring of ethical policies." Religious language is factual, that is, its truth or falsity makes some possible, experienceable difference. Hick is trying to escape the dilemma posed for the theist by John Wisdom's famous parable of the gardener.

> Two people return to their long neglected garden and find among the weeds a few of the old plants surprisingly vigorous. One says to the other, "It must be that a gardener has been coming and doing something about these plants." Upon inquiry they find that no neighbor has ever seen anyone at work in their garden. The first man says to the other, "He must have worked while people slept." The other says, "No, someone would have heard him and, besides, anybody who cared about the plants would have kept down these weeds." The first man says, "Look at the way these are arranged. There is purpose and a feeling for beauty here. I believe that someone comes, someone invisible to mortal eyes. I believe that the more carefully we look the more we shall find confirmation of this." They examine the garden ever so carefully and sometimes they come on new things suggesting that a

gardener comes and sometimes they come on new things suggesting the contrary and even that a malicious person has been at work. Besides examining the garden carefully they also study what happens to gardens left without attention. Each learns all the other learns about this and about the garden. Consequently, when after all this, one says, "I still believe a gardener comes" while the other says, "I don't" their different words now reflect no difference as to what they have found in the garden, no difference as to what they would find in the garden if they looked further and no difference about how fast untended gardens fall into disorder. At this stage, in this context, the gardener hypothesis has ceased to be experimental, the difference between one who accepts and one who rejects it is not now a matter of the one expecting something the other does not expect. What is the difference between them? The one says, "A gardener comes unseen and unheard. He is manifested only in his works with which we are familiar"; the other says, "There is no gardener" and with this difference in what they say about the gardener goes a difference in how they feel towards the garden, in spite of the fact that neither expects anything of it which the other does not expect.[1]

As Hick notes, "Wisdom is here suggesting that the theist and the atheist do not disagree about the empirical (experienceable) facts or about any observations which they anticipate in the future; they are, instead, reacting in different ways to the same set of facts." They are not contradicting each other but are expressing different feelings. Since neither position is verifiable, even in principle, we cannot say that one is right and the other wrong. Hick is keenly aware of the thrust of Wisdom's parable: The theist must either declare the possible, experienceable conditions which verify or falsify his beliefs or admit that they are without cognitive meaning.

In his essay "Theology and Verification" and frequently in his other writings, Hick develops the idea of "eschatological verification" as a solution to the problem of verification. "Eschato-

---

[1] "Gods," first published in *Proceedings of the Aristotelian Society* (London, 1944–1945) and frequently reprinted.

logical verification" is "a constructive suggestion" based upon the fact that Christianity includes beliefs that "some or all human personalities survive bodily death." Hick maintains, "It is this survival-claim that constitutes the experiential crux between naturalism and religion," and, in consequence, that the eschatological predictions of religion assure the cognitive status of religious discourse.

In unfolding his "constructive suggestion," Hick presents the following preliminary points.

1. "The verification of a factual assertion is not the same as a logical demonstration of it. The central core of the idea of verification is the removal of grounds for rational doubt."

2. "Sometimes it is necessary to put oneself in a certain position or to perform some particular operation as a prerequisite of verification." For example, one can only verify the presence of a table in the next room by going into the next room.

3. Although "verifiable" normally means "publicly verifiable," that is, capable of being verified by anyone, it does not follow that "a given verifiable proposition has, in fact, been or will, in fact, ever be verified by everyone." For example, "The sun will rise tomorrow at 5:37 a.m." is a factual assertion which may be verified (or falsified) by anyone who cares to arise at such an early hour.

4. "It is possible for a proposition to be, in principle, verifiable but not, in principle, falsifiable." It is the nature of some propositions that they may "one day be verified if . . . true but can never be falsified if . . . false."

5. The hypothesis of continued conscious existence after bodily death provides an instance of just such a proposition.

With these preliminary points in mind, "the idea of eschatological verification can now be indicated—following the example of other writers on this subject—in yet another parable." The following "parable" is quoted in full from *Faith and Knowledge,* pages 150–152.

Two men are traveling together along a road. One of them believes that it leads to a Celestial City, the other that it leads

161

nowhere; but since it is the only road there is, they must both travel it. Neither has been this way before, and neither is able to say what they will find around each next corner. During their journey they meet both with moments of refreshment and delight and with moments of hardship and danger. All the time one of them thinks of his journey as a pilgrimage to the Celestial City and interprets the pleasant stretches as encouragements and the obstacles as trials of his purpose and lessons in endurance prepared by the King of that City and designed to make of him a worthy citizen of the place when at last he arrives there. The other believes none of this and sees their journey as an unavoidable and aimless ramble. Since he has no choice in the matter he enjoys the good stretches and endures the bad. But for him there is no Celestial City to be reached, no all-encompassing purpose ordaining their journey; only the road itself and the luck of the road in good weather and bad.

During the course of the journey the issue between them is not an experimental one. They do not entertain different expectations about the coming details of the road, but only about its ultimate destination. And yet when they do turn the last corner it will be apparent that one of them has been right all the time and the other wrong. Thus, although the issue between them has not been experimental, it has nevertheless from the start been a real issue. They have not merely "felt differently" about the road; for one was feeling appropriately and the other inappropriately in relation to the actual state of affairs. Their opposed interpretations of the road constituted genuinely rival assertion, though assertions whose assertion-status has the peculiar characteristic of being guaranteed retrospectively by a future crux.

Hick's parable (like all parables) has its limitations. "I do not in fact wish to suggest that at the moment of death, the turning of the last corner, all ambiguities vanish away and there is no longer any need to interpret our environment aright in order to know it aright." The parable is designed to make one point: "Judaic-Christian theism postulates an ultimate unambiguous existence *in patria*, as well as our present ambiguous existence *in via*. There is a state of having arrived as well as a state of journeying, an eternal heavenly life as well as an earthly

162

pilgrimage." Hick recognizes that he cannot appeal to alleged future experience as evidence for theism as a present interpretation of experience. However, ". . . it does suffice to render the choice between theism and atheism a real and not merely an empty or verbal choice." The theist expects that when history is completed it will be seen in some unambiguous manner to have led to the fulfillment of a specific purpose, "namely, that of creating 'children of God.'"

Hick's concept of "eschatological verification" has evoked strenuous criticism, a full presentation of which is beyond the scope of this book. However, a few objections may be listed. First, even if we accept *post mortem* experience as public experience that can verify the claims of theists (which is much more than most philosophers will grant), must we not admit that the vast majority of religious statements have no such eschatological reference? Have we gained much if we are forced to admit all religious assertions except those which speak of life after death are cognitively meaningless? It would appear that Hick has chosen as paradigmatic the area of religious discourse which is the least significant in the lives of religious men and which is the most highly figurative in expression of all religious assertions in his attempt to demonstrate that religious language is factual. Thus it is difficult to accept Hick's appraisal of his presentation of "eschatological verification" in *Faith and Knowledge*: "[My] object has not been to offer a proof, or even probabilification, of divine existence, but to vindicate the meaningfulness of the theistic assertion."

Also, his reliance on personal encounter with God as the basis for indubitable knowledge is questionable. He fails to deal with the important respects in which encounter with the divine "Thou" is unlike encounter with a finite, human "thou" (a fault common to Christian theologians who borrow Buber's terminology). Hick's failure is quite apparent in his criticism of contemporary thinkers for whom "God is an idea, a concept."

In his *Philosophy of Religion*, John Hick attacks theories which "treat religious language as noncognitive," especially the "naturalism" of Professor J. H. Randall, Jr., of Columbia University.

Randall regards religion as making its own special contribution to human culture. Religion works with its own distinctive materials: a body of symbols and myths. According to Randall:

> What is important to recognize is that religious symbols belong with social and artistic symbols, in the group of symbols that are both *nonrepresentative* and *noncognitive*. Such noncognitive symbols can be said to symbolize not some external thing that can be indicated apart from their operation, but rather what they themselves *do*, their peculiar functions.*

Religious symbols, says Randall, have a fourfold function: 1) they arouse emotions and move men to action; 2) they stimulate cooperation and thus bind a community together; 3) they convey qualities of experience which the ordinary, literal use of language cannot express; 4) they evoke, foster, and clarify man's experience of the "Divine" aspect of the world, which Randall describes as the "order of splendor."

Hick finds in Randall's position a "radical departure from the traditional assumptions of Western religion," for he does not even imply that God or the "Divine" exists independently of the human mind. God is for Randall a projection of the human mind, a product of the human imagination.

According to Hick, Randall's theory of religion and religious language is characteristic of our contemporary culture. "This way of thinking," says Hick, "is epitomized in the way in which the word 'Religion' (or 'faith' used virtually as a synonym) has largely come to replace the word 'God.' " Where a former generation debated concerning the existence, nature, attributes, and purposes of God, the modern generation discusses "Religion, its nature, function, forms, and pragmatic value." This shift of center is indicated further by the fact that "Religion" has replaced

* *The Role of Knowledge in Western Religion* (Boston, 1958) 114.

"God" as the head of the linguistic family of terms used in these discussions.

The change of terms has brought with it a change in the character of the questions asked. "Concerning God, the traditional question has naturally been whether he exists or is real. But this is not a question that arises with regard to Religion. It is obvious that Religion exists; the important queries concern the purposes which it serves in human life . . . the question of the truth of religious beliefs has fallen into the background, and the issue of their practical usefulness has come forward instead to occupy the center of attention."

As refutation, Hick cites the reproaches of two agnostics, John Stuart Mill and Bertrand Russell, to such religious pragmatism. Mill, in his essay *The Utility of Religion* says: "If religion, or any particular form of it, is true, its usefulness follows without other proof." Says Russell: "I can respect the men who argue that religion is true and therefore ought to be believed, but I can feel only profound reprobation for those who say that religion ought to be believed because it is useful, and that to ask whether it is true is a waste of time."

Hick then contrasts these religious utilitarians (i.e., Randall *et al.*) with the great biblical pillars of faith. "There is a profound difference," he observes, "between serving and worshipping God and being 'interested in Religion.' " The God of these contemporary thinkers is merely a concept, and a concept can be "analyzed, defined, and even revised." But for Hick, God is "the living Lord of heaven and earth before whom men bow down in awe to worship. . . ."

The primary accusation which Hick makes in these passages is that, for thinkers such as Randall, God is merely a concept. The question which Hick habitually directs to such thinkers is whether they believe that God exists independently of their conception of him. This is like asking Hick if he believes that God exists independent of his revelation in Jesus Christ. Of course, Hick does so believe. But if he were asked how he knew that such were the case, his answer would probably be by reference to the revelation of God in Jesus Christ. The product of imagination, as Hick terms philosophical concepts of God, is not so very different from the "interpretation" of Jesus Christ to which Hick commits himself.

The most annoying aspect of Hick's criticism is his condemnation of "concepts" of God. It is quite unfair of Hick to contrast a *concept* of God with his *Lord*. If he desires to meet us on equal footing, he must compare a given thinker's *concept* of God with his *concept*. If he believes that his concept more adequately mirrors the divine reality, he must be prepared to offer demonstration. And if he does, one wonders if his "proof" will not be of the order so despised by John Stuart Mill and Lord Russell. Though Hick may be little inclined to argue in this vein, he should recognize that it is not a great move from claiming (as he does in *Faith and Knowledge*) that "the deity of Christ was mediated first through his moral character," to asserting that the proof of religion follows from its usefulness. If, as Hick admits, belief in the divinity of Jesus would have been unthinkable if men had not been attracted by virtues of this man which were reproduced and experienced in their own lives, he is himself answering the question of whether a religious doctrine is true by appealing to its meaning (or "usefulness") in human experience. Indeed, it is difficult to conceive how any religious doctrine can be understood apart from such "utility."

The Christ in whom the Christian discovers the moral perfection, love, and forgiveness of God by virtue of which he accepts him as divine Lord and reinterprets his whole life may be personally overwhelming and beyond demonstration, but as a subject for discussion, "the Christ" is merely "a concept," and one which can be "analyzed, defined, and even revised," as the history of Christology clearly reveals.

In a recent letter, Hick summarizes his own position:

> Faith, in its most fundamental sense, is not believing theological propositions (Thomism) nor commitment to an hypothesis (Pascal, William James, F. R. Tennant, etc.), but the interpretative element within a religious experience. The

kind of religious experience I am thinking of here is the (putative) awareness of God. This occurs in the sense of being in the presence of God, and of his activity towards us in and through the events of history and of our own lives. In the latter case, the concept of "experiencing-as" (developed from Wittgenstein's "seeing-as") provides an epistemological clue, e.g., the prophets' experiencing events *as* God's acts within his covenant with his people; the New Testament disciples' consciousness of Jesus *as* the Christ; believers in all ages conscious that in all of life they are having to do with God and he with them. The interpretative element within religious experience is continuous in character with the interpretative element within all conscious experience. Interpretation, in this sense, does not mean theory-construction or rejection of hypotheses, but interpretation in the sense in which this enters into our consciousness of a three-dimensional world of objects in space, and into the recognition of these objects.

Why does religious cognition, our faith, have this peculiar character? The answer of theology is that this is in the interest of man's cognitive freedom vis-à-vis his maker.

In dealing with the problem of theodicy, the same notion of cognitive freedom, and the epistemic distance from God, is important in connection with the origin of sin. As a creature given freedom in relation to God, man is created at an epistemic distance from God—created not knowing God. This is his fallenness, and the root of moral evil.

This view of faith leads to a conception of the nature of the Christian ethic. To experience the world theistically (among other things) is to be in a dispositional state to live in a certain way within it; and the moral teaching of Jesus is a description, with examples drawn from contemporary life, of the way in which someone naturally lives to see the world in its relation to God.

But contemporary philosophy asks: is not faith, so conceived, simply a way of seeing the world which terminates in the world itself?

Theism constitutes a factual claim open in principle to experiential (not experimental) confirmation in the future (*post-mortem*) Kingdom of God. It should be noted that the idea of eschatological verification is not intended to prove the existence of God. Nor is it suggested that the religious man does not *now* have knowledge of God. The experience of

167

God's presence justifies a present knowledge claim, and we do not have to wait until after death to find out that there is a God. The point is simply to show that the Christian claim, taken in its totality and therefore including its eschatological aspects, does constitute factual assertion.

ABRAHAM
JOSHUA HESCHEL

BY

Fritz A. Rothschild

It is customary to blame secular science and antireligious philosophy for the eclipse of religion in modern society. It would be more honest to blame religion for its own defeats. Religion declined not because its was refuted, but because it became irrelevant, dull, oppressive, insipid. Religious thinking is an intellectual endeavor out of the depths of reason. It is a source of cognitive insight into the ultimate issues of human existence. Religion is more than a mood or a feeling. Judaism, for example, is a way of thinking, not only a way of living. Unless we understand its categories, its mode of apprehension and evaluation, its teachings remain unintelligible.

These words, addressed to a seminar on religion in a free society held in New York in May 1958, indicate something of the ambivalence which Abraham Joshua Heschel feels toward the theological enterprise. There is no doubt that Heschel is one of the great theologians of our time. His influence is not only felt among the Jewish community but extends in ever widening circles to Christians who find his explications of biblical religion and their applications to contemporary problems relevant to all who believe in the God of Abraham.

Theologians expound in coherent conceptual form the teachings and beliefs of their religion. Yet Heschel is not only an exponent of religion but also a critic and gadfly of the religious status quo. He is convinced that more is needed than a presentation of the explicit teachings and ideas of Judaism, for he holds that faith has its roots in a "pretheological situation, the presymbolic depth of existence" that cannot be adequately verbalized in philosophical discourse.

> The primary issue of theology is *pretheological;* it is the total situation of man and his attitudes toward life and the world. It is from this point of view that we must realize that there are four dimensions in religion . . . four necessary components of man's relationship to God: a) the teaching, the essentials of which are summarized in the form of a creed; it is the creed that contains norms and principles about matters sacred or eternal, the dimension of doctrine; b) faith, inwardness, the direction of one's heart, the intimacy of religion, the dimension of privacy; c) the law or the sacred act to be carried out in the sanctuary, in society or at home, the dimension of the deed; d) the context in which creed, faith, and ritual come to pass, such as the community or the covenant, history, tradition, the dimension of transcendence.

The mystery of man's confrontation with God cannot be expounded in propositions; it constitutes what may be called "depth theology."

> Depth theology seeks to meet the person in moments in which the whole person is involved, in moments which are affected by all a person thinks, feels, and acts. It draws upon that which happens to man in moments of confrontation with ultimate reality. It is in such moments that decisive insights are born. Some of these insights lend themselves to conceptualization, while others seem to overflow the vessels of our conceptual powers. To convey these insights, man must use a language which is compatible with his sense of the ineffable, the terms of which do not pretend to describe, but to indicate; to point out rather than to capture. These terms

are not always imaginative; they are often paradoxical, radical, or negative. The chief danger to philosophy of religion lies in the temptation to generalize what is essentially unique, to explicate what is intrinsically inexplicable, to adjust the uncommon to our common sense.

The incongruity of dogma and mystery is the reason why Heschel engages in the paradoxical task of striving for a clear and coherent philosophical account of Judaism on the one hand, and of trying to point to the ineffable matrix of religion by evocative language on the other hand. The creative tension between the urge to articulate religious ideas in conceptual clarity and the need to remain sensitive to the ineffable source of all religious experience is central to his thought. He is aware that "the vitality of religion depends upon keeping alive the polarity of dogma and faith, of ritual and response, of institution and the individual." Without intellectual rigor faith tends to become subjective and vague; without spontaneity doctrine becomes petrified and distorted.

Heschel's work can perhaps best be understood as an attempt to achieve a synthesis between the two different worlds in which he lived before he came to America. He is the joint product of the traditional self-contained universe of Eastern European Jewish piety and the secular scholarship of Western civilization.

Abraham Joshua Heschel, born in Warsaw in 1907, is the descendant of a long line of outstanding leaders of the Hasidic movement, founded by Israel ben Eliezer, the *Baal Shem Tov* in the eighteenth century. He grew up among people whose whole life was devoted to the daily unremitting observance and study of Judaism. By the age of ten he not only was familiar with the Hebrew Bible and its medieval commentaries, but had attained proficiency in the difficult dialectic of the Talmud and had been introduced to the mystical speculation of the Kabbalah. What left a permanent imprint on his soul in these formative years was not only the study of the classical sources of Judaism, but the quality of life lived among people who "were sure that everything hinted at something transcendent, that what was apparent

171

to the mind is but a thin surface of the undisclosed." The sanctification of life and the experience of God's presence through the observant of the mitzvot commandments which punctuate all daily activities, created a sensitivity to the religious dimension of existence that could not possibly have been acquired by mere book learning.

At the age of twenty, after having privately prepared himself for the requirements of modern academic life, he left his native Poland and enrolled as a student at the University of Berlin. Here he experienced the clash between the claims of ancestral piety and the demands of modern secularism with full force:

> I came with great hunger to the University of Berlin to study philosophy. I looked for a system of thought, for the depth of the spirit, for the meaning of existence. Erudite and profound scholars gave courses in logic, epistemology, esthetics, ethics, and metaphysics. Yet in spite of the intellectual power and honesty which I was privileged to witness, I became increasingly aware of the gulf that separated my views from those held at the university. To them, religion was a feeling. God was an idea, a postulate of reason. They granted Him the status of being a logical possibility. But to assume that He had existence would have been a crime against epistemology."

The result of this confrontation was Heschel's attempt to examine the classical documents of Judaism anew in order to discover their relevance for contemporary man. In this enterprise he made use of the conceptual tools of academic philosophy, especially the techniques of phenomenology, but he was careful to refrain from forcing upon biblical thought categories derived from Greek metaphysics and Neo-Kantian philosophy, which in his opinion distorted the meaning of the biblical message. In his dissertation (which earned him a doctorate in 1933) he developed a novel conceptual framework that became the nucleus of his later philosophy of Judaism.

In 1937 Martin Buber chose Heschel as his successor to head the central organization for Jewish adult education in Germany and the *Jüdische Lehrhaus* in Frankfurt-on-the-Main. His activity during the brief but intensive cultural Jewish renaissance which took place under the challenge of the Nazi regime came to a sudden end when he was expelled by the German authorities together with the rest of the Polish Jews resident in Germany in October 1938. After teaching in Warsaw for eight months he emigrated to England. In 1940 the Hebrew Union College in Cincinnati invited him to teach philosophy and Rabbinics. In 1945 he moved from Cincinnati to New York to join the faculty of the Jewish Theological Seminary of America, where he is professor of ethics and mysticism. In 1965 he was appointed Harry Emerson Fosdick Visiting Professor at Union Theological Seminary in New York, the first Jewish theologian to hold this post.

Heschel has long been active in the field of civil rights and has addressed White House conferences on the problems of the elderly and of youth. When Pope John XXIII asked Cardinal Bea to prepare a schema on the Church and the Jews, he established contact with Heschel to consult with him about the wishes and suggestions of Jewish theologians with reference to Roman Catholic past and future attitudes towards Jews and Judaism. On September 13, 1964, the opening day of the third session of Vatican II, Heschel was received in an important private audience by Pope Paul VI. When asked later why he had let himself be involved in the affairs of the Ecumenical Council he replied: "The issues at stake were profoundly theological. To refuse contact with Christian theologians is, to my mind, barbarous. There is a great expectation among Christians today that Judaism has something unique to offer."

Heschel sees the task of the religious philosopher neither as the construction of a "religion of reason" which draws, among other sources, upon the Jewish tradition, nor as the analysis of "religious experience." The first substitutes philosophy for religion; the second tends to replace it with the psychology of religion. Heschel's own writings attempt to penetrate and illumine the reality underlying religion, the living and dynamic relationship between God and man, through the objective, yet sympathetic, understanding of the documents of Israel's tradition and of the life and experience of the pious Jew.

There are three starting points of contemplation about God; three trails that lead to Him. The first is the way of sensing the presence of God in the world, in things; the second is the way of sensing His presence in the Bible; the third is the way of sensing His presence in sacred deeds. . . . These three ways correspond in our tradition to the main aspects of religious existence: worship, learning, and action. To recapture the insights found in those three ways is to go to the roots of Biblical experience of life and reality; it means to delve into the religious drama of Israel.

Although he brings to this task the tools of philosophy, he points out repeatedly that no amount of rational analysis alone can ever exhaust the richness and fullness of this reality. He therefore emphasizes the fact that reason itself discloses its own limits and that the ineffable quality of the divine cannot be reduced without remainder to any scheme of conceptual categories: "We apprehend more than we can comprehend."

Heschel's lifework can thus be seen as consisting of two parallel strands: his studies and interpretations of the classical sources of Judaism and his endeavor to offer to our generation an authentic theology, resulting from the application of the insights gained from these classical sources to the problems and perplexities that the contemporary Jew encounters. Thus he started out with his book on prophecy, *Die Prophetie* (the basis of his expanded work in English, *The Prophets*), in which he presented a phenomenology of prophetic consciousness in the Bible, and followed it with his interpretation of Maimonides' life and thought, *Maimoides: Eine Biographie*, where the confrontation of scholastic Aristotelianism with Rabbinic Judaism is examined. Articles in the field of Kabbalah and Hasidism continue this enterprise. Since 1962 two volumes of a major study in Hebrew on two great trends in Talmudic thought concerning the nature of the Torah and revelation have appeared under the title *Theology of Ancient Judaism*.

174

The results of these and similar researches are utilized in the formation of Heschel's original philosophy of Judaism which has found its chief expression in two books: *Man Is Not Alone: A Philosophy of Religion* (1951) and its successor volume, *God in Search of Man: A Philosophy of Judaism* (1956). Religion is there defined as an answer to man's ultimate questions. Since modern man is largely alienated from the reality that informs genuine religion, Heschel is not content to present the traditional answers but tries first and foremost to recover the significant existential questions to which Judaism offers answers. This leads to a depth theology which, by going below the surface phenomena of modern doubt and rootlessness, tries to confront the reader with the living God of the Bible. In expounding the various approaches that lead one to an awareness of God's reality, he repeatedly stresses that we cannot *prove* the existence of God:

> Thus, the certainty of the realness of God does not come about as a corollary of logical premises, as a leap from the realm of logic to the realm of ontology, from an assumption to a fact. . . . In sensing the spiritual dimension of all being, we became aware of the absolute reality of the divine. . . . In the depth of human thinking we all presuppose some ultimate reality which on the level of discursive thinking is crystallized into the concept of a power, a principle, or a structure. This, then, is the order in our thinking and existence: the ultimate or God comes first and our reasoning about Him second.

God to the religiously sensitive man is an "ontological presupposition" rather than the conclusion of a logical statement.

Heschel describes three ways in which man can come to an awareness of God. First, by sensing the grandeur and mystery of reality. Through wonder we go beyond the mere givenness of the facts and become aware of the grandeur and mystery of reality. Such wonder can take different forms: as *curiosity* it can become the starting point of science which looks beyond given facts to the laws they exemplify; as *radical amazement* it can become the starting point of religion by perceiving that things point beyond themselves to the ground and power that stand behind all facts and perceptions of facts.

To the Biblical man, the sublime is but a form in which the presence of God strikes forth.

This evocative approach yields a panentheistic outlook: through created things man reaches an awareness of God who is within but also beyond all finite existence.

In the second way, man reaches an awareness of God by delving into the recesses of his own being, thus realizing that he is not an independent and self-sufficient entity but part of something greater and more encompassing than his individual ego. The fallacy of assuming that the self is a discrete isolated subject which can find God as another isolated object of cognition is shattered once the awareness is gained that the conscious self is itself the expression of something never fully expressed and that life and time are not our property but a trust.

What in my voice has originated in me and what is the resonance of transsubjective reality? The self can be distinctly separated only at its branches; namely, from other individuals and other things but not at its roots. . . . I am endowed with a will, but the will is not mine; I am endowed with freedom, but it is a freedom imposed on the will. Life is something that visits my body, a transcendent loan; I have neither initiated nor conceived its worth and meaning. The essence of what I am is not mine. *I am what is not mine.* I am that I am not. In penetrating and exposing the self, I realize that the self did not originate in itself, that ultimately man is not a subject but an object.

This second approach tends to a quasi-mystical world view. But it stops short of the danger of mystical absorption and annihilation in the Godhead by its articulation of God as the subject of all reality and man as the object whose dignity and worth are founded in his very consciousness of being the goal of divine concern and expectation. In principle any moment of life and any experience can be regarded by the sensitive believer as such divine address and summons. But in fact this awareness is only felt rarely in a clear and unambiguous manner.

There are moments in which we feel the challenge of a

176

power that, not born of our will nor installed by it, robs us of independence by its judgement of the rectitude or depravity of our actions. . . . Our sense of what is right and wrong may at times be uncertain. What is indubitably certain is our sense of obligation to answer for our conduct. . . . We are open and communicative to someone who transcends us and is concerned with our life.

It is this third approach by which man becomes aware of the voice of God. The "holy dimension" of hearkening to the voice and acting responsively and responsibly characterizes the biblical view of man as the recipient of divine revelation. It is in facing the transcendent God and his demands that one becomes a moral agent. The dichotomy of faith and works was never a real issue in Judaism since the two are not inimical but inherently complementary. By doing the *mitzvot* commandments of the Torah the Jew enters the holy dimension of God's challenge and guidance and by obediently responding to the divine demand he experiences himself as the object of God's address and concern, thus gaining faith in the Author of the Law by responding to his voice.

The claim of Judaism that religion and law are inseparable is difficult for many of us to comprehend. The difficulty may be explained by modern man's conception of the essence of religion. To the modern mind, religion is a state of the soul, inwardness; feeling rather than obedience, faith rather than action, spiritual rather than concrete. To Judaism, religion is not a feeling for something that is, but *an answer* to Him who is asking us to live in a certain way. It is in its very origin a consciousness of total commitment; a realization that all of life is not only man's but also God's sphere of interest. . . . The meaningfulness of the *mitzvot* consists in their being vehicles by which we advance on the road to spiritual ends. Faith is not a silent treasure to be kept in the seclusion of the soul, but a mint in which to strike the coin of common deeds. Spiritual aspirations are doomed to failure when we try to cultivate deeds at the expense of thoughts or thoughts at the expense of deeds. Judaism is averse to generalities, averse to looking for meaning in life detached from doing, as if the meaning were a separate entity. Its tendency is to make ideas convertible into deeds, to interpret metaphysical insights as patterns for action, to endow the most sublime principles with bearing upon everyday conduct. In its tradition the abstract became concrete, the absolute historic. By enacting the holy on the stage of concrete living we perceive our kinship with the divine, the presence of the divine. What cannot be grasped in reflection, we comprehend in deeds. Religion is not the same as spiritualism; what man does in his concrete, physical existence is directly relevant to the divine. Spirituality is the goal, not the way of man. In this world music is played on physical instruments on which the holy is carried out.

Heschel's emphasis that faith is not so much assent to a proposition but rather an attitude of the whole person, an engagement and attachment to God's demands, is not only important for his understanding of the significance of the law, but it is also crucial for his interpretation of God as *personal concern* and for his critique of the main trends of philosophical theology that have tried to assimilate the living God of the Bible to impersonal categories of Greek ontology or modern process philosophy. While the medieval tendency was in the direction of describing God as Being Itself, the modern inclination has been to raise the concept of God from the level of crude anthropomorphism by describing the Deity as the power that makes for goodness, the underlying structure or *nisus* of the universe, the moral dimension of reality, etc. This, however, is not only detrimental to religious life, but is in conflict with the biblical and rabbinical outlook. Heschel tries to do justice to the experience of the living God who stands in a dynamic relationship to man and who is influenced and affected by human actions. Hence he stresses the *divine concern* of the personal God as the most essential category for an adequate Jewish theology.

If God is merely a thing among things, even though the most powerful one, he is not truly God. If he is a general principle or power, he is an abstraction lacking religious availability. Therefore Heschel develops his doctrine of *the divine pathos*. The God of *pathos* described in analogy to the human personality is never exhausted in any of his particular manifestations. God cares for and is interested in all his creatures. Indeed, creation as a religious concept points at the divine care and concern for that which is to receive the gift of existence by the divine *fiat*. The doctrine that God shares in the joys and sufferings of his children and that their actions make a difference to him is the prerequisite for a mutual and vibrant relationship between creator and creature. As the rabbinic phrase puts it, "man is the partner of the Holy One, blessed be He," and what we do here and now is of cosmic importance. By doing the *mitzvot*—ethical as well as ceremonial—and thus cooperating in the building of the Kingdom here on earth, man finds his true vocation and develops his true humanity. Life, far from being a preordained process, reducible to a scientific formula, becomes a drama in which the unexpected, the novel, and the unique can always happen again The universe is not closed; the horizon is always kept open to new incursions of divine challenges and freely given human responses.

The idea of *the divine pathos* must not be confused with the seemingly similar view of paganism. While pagan gods were also personal, they acted in unpredictable, capricious, and selfish ways. Judaism, however, teaches that there is no dichotomy between a personal living God and the universal canons of ethics. "God's pathos *is* ethos."

To say that God is personal may, of course, be courting the danger of anthropomorphism. But to speak of him as mechanical or abstract compounds the danger since it makes him subhuman rather than superhuman. To affirm that God is always the subject and never the mere object of religious experience and thought, guards only partially against this error. Although his essence is incomprehensible and he is known only by his acts and expressions, human language must take the risk of referring to him as a person: the closest analogue to the prophetic encounter with the Deity is the encounter that takes place between human persons:

The Bible speaks in the language of man. It deals with the

179

problems of man, and its terms are borrowed from the vocabulary of the people. It has not coined many words, but it has given new meaning to borrowed words. The prophets had to use anthropomorphic language in order to convey His non-anthropomorphic Being. The greatest challenge to the Biblical language was how to reconcile in words the awareness of God's transcendence with His overwhelming livingness and concern.

The assertion that God shares in the mystery of personality must not be misunderstood as an attempt to reduce him to human scale. On the contrary, it indicates that man's ability to act with compassion, sympathy, and altruistic concern is the sign that he was created in the *imago Dei,* and that man's true fulfillment is found in *imitatio Dei.* Man leads the good life not only by following general rules as codified in the Bible and in tradition, although these rules are an indispensable part for the business of living. He must, in addition, respond individually and spontaneously to the demands of God in each new and concrete situation. This is the reason why scholars and saints are never done with the task of determining the divine intention for changing times and circumstances throughout Jewish history. The tension of fixed pattern *keva* and inner spontaneity *kavanah* is a pervasive trait of Jewish life. Though never completely solved by an individual, its resolution is an ideal toward which every Jew should strive. Joy and discipline, regularity and spontaneity are both aspects of Jewish living. But although it seems easier to abrogate the principle of regularity in order to avoid mechanical and perfunctory observance, Heschel warns against this temptation.

> Our spiritual resources are not inexhaustible. What may seem to be spontaneous is in truth a response to an occasion. The soul would remain silent if it were not for the summons and reminder of the law. Routine holds us in readiness for the moments in which the soul enters into accord with the spirit. *Kavanah* inner intention comes into being with the deed. Actions teach.

Three factors have influenced Heschel's views on the relationship between Judaism and Christianity in our time: the extermination of six million Jews under Hitler in a civilization that was nominally Christian; the crucial importance of the Hebrew Bible (called the "Old Testament" by Christians) as the common patrimony of Jews and Christians; and the rapid spread of secularism and nihilism in a world that repudiates the biblical message. He is convinced that these three facts are mutually connected and that the future of our civilization depends on the true understanding of this connection and its implications among Christians and Jews.

In his inaugural lecture at Union Theological Seminary in November 1965 he said:

> I speak as a person who was able to leave Warsaw, the city in which I was born, just six weeks before the disaster began. My destination was New York, it would have been Auschwitz or Treblinka. I am a brand plucked from the fire in which my people was burned to death. I am a brand plucked from the fire of an altar of Satan on which millions of human lives were exterminated to evil's greater glory, and on which so much else was consumed: the divine image of so many human beings, many people's faith in the God of justice and compassion, and much of the secret of power of attachment to the Bible, bred and cherished in the hearts of men for nearly two thousand years. . . . I speak as a person who is convinced that the fate of the Jewish people and the fate of the Hebrew Bible are intertwined. The recognition of our status as Jews, the legitimacy of our survival, is only possible in a world in which the God of Abraham is revered.

He pointed out time and again that mutual respect and genuine dialogue between Jews and Christians can only come about if the Church abandons its so-called mission to the Jews.

> Any conversation between Christian and Jew in which the abandonment of the other partner's faith is a silent hope must be regarded as offensive to one's religious and human dignity. Let there be an end to disputation and polemic, an end to disparagement. We honestly and profoundly disagree in matters of creed and dogma. Indeed, there is a deep chasm

181

between Christians and Jews concerning, e.g., the divinity and Messiahship of Jesus. But across the chasm we can extend our hands to one another.

But above creeds and dogmas which separate Jew from Christian there is a common commitment and a common faith in God and the Hebrew Bible that is holy to both. It is ironic that while there is hesitation among various religious groups to cooperate and overcome narrow parochialism, the antireligious forces in the world are attacking the religious heritage of biblical faith in a truly ecumenical way.

> Cynicism is not parochial. Should religions insist upon the illusion of complete isolation? Should we refuse to be on speaking terms with one another and hope for each other's failure? Or should we pray for each other's health, and help one another in preserving one's respective legacy, in preserving a common legacy?

As the last sentence indicates, Heschel does not plead for Jewish-Christian cooperation merely as a strategy for survival against a common foe; he is convinced that through the common legacy of the Bible and the core of biblical faith there exists a deep attachment to the same God: "I rejoice where His name is praised, His presence sensed, His commandment done." Of course, this must not lead to a vague syncretism in which interfaith becomes a substitute for faith and conformity reduces the different religions to their lowest common denominator. Thus both communication and separation are necessary.

There must be humility and a sense of reverence on both sides:

> None of us pretends to be God's accountant, and His design for history and redemption remains a mystery before which we must stand in awe. It is arrogant to maintain that the Jews' refusal to accept Jesus as the Messiah is due to their stubbornness or blindness, as it would be presumptuous for the Jews not to acknowledge the glory and holiness in the lives of countless Christians. "The Lord is near to all who call upon Him, to all who call upon Him in truth" (Psalm 145:18).

HENRI DE LUBAC

BY

William C. Russell

Several years ago, in The *Splendor of the Church,* Henri de Lubac traced the portrait of the *vir ecclesiasticus,* the "man of the Church." His description, remarkable for its completeness, its balance, and its finesse, speaks eloquently of a man who has "fallen in love with the beauty of the House of God" because the Church "has stolen his heart." Such a man "will love her past, he will meditate on her beauty, holding her tradition in reverence and exploring deep into it." Such a man is Henri de Lubac himself.

Born at Cambrai, France, in 1896, he entered the Society of Jesus in 1913 and was sent to Canterbury in England to begin his novitiate training. Shortly thereafter he was called to serve in the French army during the War of 1914–1918. Badly wounded at the front, he returned to England to continue his studies in philosophy on the Isle of Jersey and in theology at Ore Place, Hastings. In 1929, on his return to France, he was appointed professor at the Catholic Theological Faculty of Lyons and the following year was named to the chair of the History of Religions. That same year his first article, "Apologetics and Theology," marked the beginning of a literary activity that has set him apart, in the words of Jacques Madaule, as "the theologian most open to the aspirations of our times and yet most attentive and most faithful to Catholic tradition."

Time and again he has clearly stated his unique goal, and with each new study one is able to judge how very successful he has been in "stringing pearls" and in drawing upon and "repeating" —in the Kierkegaardian sense of the word—"the treasures, so little utilized, in the patristic writings," seeking only to understand them and to listen to what they have to tell us, "since they are our Fathers in the Faith and since they received from the Church of their times the means to nourish the Church of our times as well." By faithfully echoing the Christian tradition, by allowing it to speak for itself, he has enabled countless others to share "the recurrent thrill which comes from recognizing that impressive and undivided voice in all its modulations and all its harmonies."

And yet there is something paradoxical in the fact that it has been precisely this deep love and respect for the tradition of the past that has enabled him to approach Christian thought in the context of renewal. If he is looked upon today as one of the most eminent and respected advisors of the *aggiornamento* of the Church, it is primarily because he has understood, perhaps more than any other theologian of his generation, that the openness and renewal so important to this "second springtime" of the Church must be rooted firmly in a devotion to her tradition "which is not a burden but a source of strength and which will be at the beginning of bold and fruitful innovations."

It is this love of the Church and her tradition that has enabled him to place side by side with his definitive study of Origen his works on the Fathers of the Church and his monumental history of medieval exegesis, works which reflect, along with his time, on the eternal problem of God as it is debated in our present-day society. His works of a theological order have in no way kept him from directing his attention to a Proudhon, a Nietzsche, a Feuerbach, a Marx, and an Auguste Comte, and yet his guidelines remain unchanged and his purpose unwavering for they, too, are seen in the light of tradition; they, too, known for their "innovations," are shown to be far more "traditional" than one might readily suspect.

It has been said that the entire history of Christian thought is present in his works, and a familiarity with his more than thirty book-length studies, his countless articles, conferences, and learned papers tends to confirm this judgment. In his pages, frequently interwoven with citations, in the thousands of references where practically every Christian author—not only those who have left a name but also the great mass of forgotten writers whose testimony attests to the continuity of the Christian tradition and the unique essence of the Christian mystery—has been called forth to testify, Henri de Lubac establishes himself as the authoritative spokesman of the entire body of Christian thought over the ages.

THEOLOGY

It is in his works which figure under the rubric "Theology" that Henri de Lubac best realizes his goal to once again explore the early Christian tradition so as to highlight the incredible richness and the "unity amid diversity" of what he refers to as "that creative sap that even today is not yet dried up." Four examples, illustrated by four different studies, are of particular importance and significance.

It was while rereading the works on the ninth-century theologians in preparation for his role as examiner of a student's doctoral dissertation on Florus of Lyons that he was struck by the *corpus mysticum* of a Radbert, a Ratramne, a Godescalc, and a Raban Maur. In *Corpus Mysticum : L'Eucharistie et l'Eglise au Moyen Age* (1944), he retraces the surprising vicissitudes of the two words of its title throughout history, thereby showing the depth and complexity of the links which, both in

Christian life and Christian doctrine, unify the two realities: the Eucharist and the Church, as well as the relationship that binds together in the Catholic synthesis the most "mystical" element to the most institutional.

In his desire to discover the origin, the exact meaning, and the final significance of *corpus mysticum* he has, as in so many of his other studies, allowed an army of long-forgotten witnesses to speak for themselves. Their testimony, which forms the very core of this technical and minutely documented study, goes a long way in explaining why the significance of an expression— one which today is taken for granted and which from the very beginnings of Christianity was used with reference to a large context of words and ideas—was virtually unknown for so many centuries.

His patient study firmly establishes that it was due to a "gradual and unnoticed reversal of the expression" that *corpus mysticum*, initially used with reference to the Eucharist, was later extended to the doctrines touching upon the relationships between the Eucharist and the Church.

The history of the theology of the supernatural, because of the breadth of its subject—the entire mystery of man and God is included within its scope—and the extreme complexity of the notions and doctrines connected with it, as well as the many and profound changes in its problematic over the centuries, is a difficult one to write. It is not surprising that the theologian, when treating the question, feels obliged to "walk much like the explorer who makes his way across a continent whose soil is always moving and whose boundaries never cease to shift."

In *Surnaturel* (1946), Père de Lubac's controversial study of the problem of the relationships between philosophy and theology, reason and faith, the development of the resources of human nature and the eventual acceptance of a supernatural *donnée,* the reader is confronted with a wealth of erudition which is the fruit of a very long, attentive, and profound reflection on a question frequently discussed by theologians over the centuries.

186

Every Christian knows that his final end, as proposed by God, consists in the beatific vision and that it is the possession of this vision which will unite him forever with his Creator and Savior. He knows, too, that this vision has been promised him and that it will be given to him out of God's pure liberality. But he might ask himself if this end was proposed to humanity from the very beginning—at the moment of Adam's creation—or only after his fall in view of the merits of the Redeemer. In this second hypothesis should we look upon Adam, before his sin, as oriented by God towards a natural beatitude, merited by a holy and just life, such as the forces of nature would be able to assure?

If this hypothesis of a "pure nature" oriented towards a natural end is to be excluded, it nonetheless necessitates a closer study of this intuitive vision of God which is man's unique and supernatural end. This vision, which fulfills the aspirations of our nature but which is beyond its forces, is proposed to us at the end of our life as the reward of our faith and the meritorious acts which we shall have accomplished. We are drawn to God by his grace and sanctified by the Spirit which he sends us and which lives within us. Brought face to face with this gratuitous and sublime calling and confronted with the graces that "lift us up to God," other problems arise such as the source of this divine destiny. What possible title does man have to so high a calling and to so many graces that transform his very life, penetrate within him, and unite him to God in the most intimate and most mysterious of ways?

Theologians have long sought to illuminate these mysteries with the light of faith, and Père de Lubac has set as his task to make a careful study of their works. His own conclusions, presented in the form of a series of historical studies, show how theologians, in their desire to refute the positions of Baius and Jansenius, all too willingly adopted Cajetan's hypothesis of a third and purely natural state in addition to the two states of human nature prior to and subsequent to Adam's fall, and "though it never existed, we can nonetheless conceive of it as being possible."

187

What was first a mere philosophical hypothesis soon became a historical reality. Adam, before his fall, lived in this state of "pure nature," and his life was oriented not towards the intuitive vision of God but towards a natural beatitude. It was, it must be admitted, a handy distinction, and by differentiating between the two final ends and the two states of man the adversaries of Baius found a convenient means of substantiating the gratuitousness of grace. Not only was an orientation towards a purely natural beatitude possible: they saw it as being Adam's unique destiny prior to his fall. Such a line of reasoning resulted in the nearly complete abandon of an opinion generally agreed upon by all theologians: the natural aspiration within man towards the intuitive vision of his Creator.

Still another problem raised in these discussions was whether or not the early, authoritative tradition of the Church admitted the possibility of an impeccable spiritual nature. St. Thomas formulated his negative reply in *De malo* and went on to explain his reasoning in his *Compendium theologiae*, but his opinion is not based on the theory of a double finality, as some have thought, because he recognizes man's unique beatitude to be a supernatural one, and that very supernatural character rules out the possibility and the necessity of man being drawn towards it by a movement of his human nature.

It is apparent from the conclusions reached in *Surnaturel* that a certain dualist conception of the two orders, natural and supernatural, which was developed in certain schools of theology over the past four centuries and which results in the creation of a "separated theology"—itself generative of a "separated philosophy"—is neither fully consistent with Christian tradition nor favorable "to the full flowering of the life of the spirit."

In recent years Père de Lubac, at the urging of many theologians, has undertaken a considerable development of the complex notions expressed in his *Surnaturel*. He has completely rewritten the first and most important section of this study in *Augustinisme et Théologie Moderne* (1965), and the theoretical conclusions implied in an article on the mystery of the supernatural have been developed in *Le Mystère du Surnaturel* (1965).

Some years later, in *Histoire et Esprit: L'Intelligence de l'Ecriture d'après Origène* (1950), he directed his attention to an explanation of the early Christian interpretation of Scripture. In his study of Origen, whom most scholars have looked upon as being first and foremost an allegorist all too ready to sacrifice the historical for the symbolic, he points out that the word allegory is "vague and open to many meanings" and that when historians speak of his "exaggerated symbolism" and his "extravagant use of allegory," it is important to know if they are referring to a mere lack of moderation in his use of symbols or whether, on the contrary, they are thereby implying that his exegesis is to be rejected entirely. His study is meant "to bring this question out of the shadows so as to establish what Origen actually thought and said."

In choosing Origen, "its most gifted representative," as the focal point of his historical investigation into the fundamental notion of the early Christian interpretation of Scripture and in allowing him to speak for himself, he has succeeded in showing that his spiritual exegesis does not consist in taking the historical realities of the Bible and transforming them into pure symbols, but in being rigorously faithful to all the details of the text and in giving his complete attention "to both the elan and the meditation of the Spirit which inspires them and welds them into one." It is not merely a question of exegesis, as he points out in his introduction, "but a view of the world which wells up before us. It is an interpretation of Christianity of which Origen, despite many personal traits which were often questionable, was nonetheless the witness." It is through this "spiritual understanding" of Scripture that Christianity itself appears as "taking from itself a reflected consciousness." And this is the phenomenon that was so characteristic of the first Christian age and that Père de Lubac grasps so well in *Histoire et Esprit*. It is his "contribution to current research into the fields of philosophy and the theology of history as well as to the synthesis sought between biblical exegesis properly so called and the fields of dogmatic theology and spirituality."

In his authoritative four-volume study *Exégèse Médiévale: Les quatre sens de l'Ecriture* (1959–1964), he continues the study so impressively and so skillfully introduced in his study of Origen. It is a massive work, for he has "read as many texts as possible" so as to grasp "the doctrine of medieval exegesis in its essence," and just as *Histoire et Esprit* was "but one simple chapter of the history of spiritual exegesis," so *Exégèse Médiévale* is "but one important chapter of the history of theology."

If he speaks of his "contribution to the history of theology," it is because he looks upon this exegesis not as "an auxiliary science of theology but theology itself, and even more than theology, for it sets in motion a dialectic, often subtle, of the before and the after; it defines the relationships of historical and spiritual reality, of society and the individual, of time and eternity; it contains, as we would say today, a theology of history in connection with a theology of Scripture. It organizes all of revelation around a concrete center, marked in space and time by the cross of Jesus Christ; it is in itself a complete dogmatics and a complete spirituality, completely unified.

The subtitle, *The Four Meanings of Scripture*, seems at first reading to be somewhat provocative, for if there is a sterile sector in the exegesis of the Middle Ages, it is surely the childish theory that pretends to establish the arbitrary and the fanciful as doctrine. One can perhaps forgive the piety of the commentators, but to base the interpretation of the Bible on

> *Littera gesta docet, quid credas allegoria,*
> *Moralis quid agas, quo tendas anagogia*

either by dividing the content of Scripture into four neat compartments or, by an even more artificial procedure, pretend to find in each biblical text four different and distinct meanings at four pre-established levels is equivalent to "repudiating the Bible in the name of Scholasticism."

Yet though it would be vain to wish to restore what is recognized today as a cultural phenomenon, it must not be forgotten that up until the twelfth century the doctrine of the "quadruple meaning" was at the very heart of Christian life. It provided generations of Christians with the means of attaining and passing on an authentic expression of our Christian heritage and thereby set down the very mystery of Jesus Christ for later generations.

These same themes are considered in a less technical manner in two other works, both translated into English, *Catholicism: Christ and the Common Destiny of Man* (translated in 1961) and *The Splendour of the Church* (translated in 1956).

The first of these studies, in considering the "social aspects of dogma" from the point of view of tradition, once again invokes the testimony of the great Doctors of the Church: Irenaeus, Augustine, Origen, Gregory of Nysse. It is an explanation of the catholic character of both the Church's teaching and her conception of history, and it devotes especial attention to the problem of the person-society relationship.

Realizing that many outside the faith are often grievously mistaken about the essence of Catholicism, Père de Lubac asks himself if this is not to be interpreted as an indication of a pressing need from within the Church to come to a better understanding of that faith by which her members live, "for it is in the intimate knowledge of this mysterious *Catholica* that the fundamental explanation of the 'social' repercussions of Christianity in the temporal order is to be found." His purpose, far from being a desire to write a treatise on the Church or to attempt a systematic, doctrinal treatment of the Mystical Body, is "simply to bring out clearly certain ideas that are inherent in our faith: ideas so simple that they do not always attract attention, but at the same time so fundamental that there is some risk of our not finding time to ponder them."

What he has set out to do in *The Splendour of the Church* is

191

"to meditate, in the light of faith, on certain aspects of the mystery of the Church, as an attempt to work myself into the very heart of that mystery." His theological contemplation, here as elsewhere, is nourished by a prodigious scriptural and patristic erudition, and his meditation reflects a surprisingly curious and lucid mind, profoundly traditional, seeking an intelligence of the faith which is as simple as that of a child and animated by a filial tenderness for the Church, his Mother. He sees her "in all her royal majesty and heavenly splendor, at the very heart of earthly reality, right at the very core of all the confusion and all the mischances which are, inevitably, in her mission to man. Not only as she is ideally, but as she appears in history, and particularly as she appears to us at present."

We say that we believe *in* God whereas we do not believe *in* the Church; we believe *the Church*. She is both the object of faith and the first to believe, and her mystery, though "flooded with light from one side, is nonetheless obscured by the fact that she is both divine and human," and the divine, to reach us, must pass through what is human. The fundamental duality of aspects is written into the very word Church, "which may be taken either actively (*convocatio*) or passively (*congregatio*)." These two aspects, though irreducible, are nonetheless very closely connected for "there are no children without a mother; no people without leaders; no acquired sanctity without a sanctifying power and a labor of sanctification; no effective union in divine life without a passing on of that life; no 'communion of saints' without a communication of holy things. And similarly, no constituted assembly without a constitution which includes a hierarchy; no established community (*Gemeinschaft*) without a society (*Gesellschaft*) in which and by means of which it is established." Thus it is within the Mystical Body that the duality of aspects of this complex reality we call the Church is to be distinguished.

RELIGIOUS PHILOSOPHY

Works of a theological nature have not kept Henri de Lubac

from reflecting, along with his times, on the eternal problem of God as it is debated in our present-day society. He has directed his attention to this very problem in a series of works that might be grouped under the rubric "Religious Philosophy," and that include the discussion of the thought of a Proudhon: *The Un-Marxian Socialist: A Study of Proudhon* (translated in 1948), a Nietzsche, a Feuerbach, a Marx, and an Auguste Comte: *The Drama of Atheist Humanism* (translated in 1949), as well as studies which express the reactions of the faith when confronted with the grave problems of man and his times: *Paradoxes* (translated in 1948), *Further Paradoxes* (translated in 1958), and *Affrontements mystiques* (1950).

In his study of Proudhon, Père de Lubac has followed the advice of Sainte-Beuve: "The account of the mind can be read in a man's letters; that is the place to look for it." By adding a careful study of his notebooks as well, he has permitted Proudhon to act as his own commentator and to relate the story of his life.

On several different occasions over the past half century, attempts have been made "to establish or revive a Proudhon tradition which would enable French Socialism to make a stand against Marxism . . . but the 'Proudhon era' never came." As a result Proudhon, "despised by professional philosophers and ignored by economists and sociologists," is not well known. He was a strong, violent, and provoking opponent of the Catholic Faith in the early 1900's, and Père de Lubac's study is neither a historical analysis of his thought nor an attempt at his rehabilitation, but rather a thoughtful and thought-provoking presentation of his attitude towards Christianity. Inasmuch as it is very well documented on the philosophical controversies that raged on the Continent in the mid-nineteenth century, it is, in a real sense, far more than a study of Proudhon.

But if Proudhon bears witness to the awakening and the subsequent revolt of the lower classes, he also bears witness "with a dreadful bias and yet so frequently with clear-seeing eyes" to the Catholicism of his day. Preoccupied with God throughout

193

his lifetime, as is evident from his writings, he somehow found the means of "shaking us up and making us put our house in order" despite his pessimism and the fury of his attacks; "turning us aside from our earthly cares he succeeded in making us reflect with him unceasingly upon eternal problems."

Père de Lubac's study of Proudhon is, however, but the introductory chapter to his *The Drama of Atheist Humanism*. In this study of the thought of Nietzsche, Feuerbach, Marx, and Auguste Comte he asks himself how it came about that Christianity, a force meant to free mankind from the forces of nature and history, appeared at a given moment of time as an obstacle against that very liberation. God was seen as an illusion hindering mankind from realizing his full potential, and yet by asserting that he did not exist or that he was irrelevant or absent or dead, these men accomplished the very opposite of what they set out to do. The world of Comte, Marx, and Nietzsche is a world where the human person, far from being liberated by society, is crushed by it. The doctrine of atheistic humanism merely underlines the evidence that there can be no true humanism which is not rooted in the "au-delà de l'homme." It took a Kierkegaard and a Dostoevski to see that atheism actually imprisoned man and that the universe it projected, despite its appearance of truth and its inexorable logic, turned men into what one theologian has referred to as "two-dimensional pasteboard figures."

In *Affrontements mystiques,* a series of four brief essays centered around the question of the relationship between the temporal and the eternal and "the tension which exists between the pursuit of the *unum necessarium* and the desire for 'incarnation,' " Père de Lubac confronts the Marxist and the Christian idea of man and presents a penetrating analysis of Nietzsche's tragedy prior to exposing his personal testimony in "The Light of Christ."

Paradoxes and *Further Paradoxes* group together a certain number of thoughts concerning the different problems posed by the intellectual apostolate in the modern day and present the attitude that a Christian should have with respect to his times. Arranged in such a way as to foster reflection, they highlight the richness of contemporary thought, to which Père de Lubac shows himself to be perfectly open, and the essential transcendence of Christianity: two requirements seen as complimentary.

Finally, in *Sur les chemins de Dieu* (translated in 1960 under the title *The Discovery of God*), he groups together a number of modern and traditional texts relative to the problem of God. The brief quotations are focused on the origin of the notion of God, the proofs of his existence, the knowledge we have of him and the need we have to seek him out if we are to understand his mystery.

HISTORY OF RELIGIONS

Under the rubric "History of Religions," Père de Lubac, while treating only incidentally of other major expressions of Asian spirituality such as Hinduism, Taoism, and Confucianism, has published three important studies on Buddhism. This preference for the religion of Sakhyamuni dates back to 1930 when he was assigned to teach the "special course" in the History of Religions at the Catholic Theological Faculty of Lyons.

His choice, as he states in *Aspects of Buddhism* (translated in 1953), was dictated by the fact that, with the exception of the Judeo-Christian revelation, Buddhism is without any doubt the most vast and most complex spiritual fact of human history. Still another factor entering into his choice was the realization that at the end of the nineteenth century the essence of Buddhist thought had made an important and permanent impact on the mainstream of European thought. It was at that time that the beginnings of a rivalry between Christ and Buddha, between Michelet's "second Christ at the end of the world," Renan's "atheistic Christ," and the Christ of the gospels made itself felt. Romano Guardini was able to write in 1937 that no one had yet

elucidated the Christian significance of Buddhism; such a statement would have been impossible some fifteen years later when
Aspects of Buddhism, the final chapters and the vigorous conclusion of *La Recontre du Bouddhisme et de l'Occident* (1952),
and *Amida* (1954), the continuation of *Aspects of Buddhism,*
filled that very gap.

The second mentioned study presents the results of a minute
and painstakingly exhaustive investigation of Buddhism as it is
seen from the West. This historical presentation of the Christian
response to Buddhist spirituality treats of the periods prior to
and following the "scientific discovery" initiated by the eminent
Orientalists of the mid-eighteenth century. During the first period
the Christian response was far too negative, and for two centuries Buddhism was, with rare exception, severely condemned
as being "that monstrous religion," "that abominable sect."

During the second period, on the contrary, when Christian
apologists of the nineteenth century looked upon Buddhism as
"the most striking example of the primitive revelation," the
response was far too receptive. In his balanced consideration,
Père de Lubac, while pointing out that Buddhism and Catholicism are "entirely different in essence" and that it would be a
serious mistake to account for these differences by considering
them as "merely the results of differences in point of view,"
nonetheless underlines the danger in unduly criticizing him who,
"perhaps more than any other man who has ever lived, grasped
the problem of human destiny and led a whole *pars purificans*
towards good, for which Christians, too, can be grateful." As he
makes so clear in *Amida,* Christianity, "after having reopened
the Christian parenthesis," is effectively capable of including
and assuming Buddhism with no danger whatever of harming
her integrity.

Unlike *La Recontre du Buddhism at de l'Occident,* which
treats, as its title indicates, of the meeting between Buddhism
and the Christian West over the past twenty centuries, *Amida*
and *Aspects of Buddhism* attempt a more intrinsic confrontation.
Following different avenues of approach of a moral, cultural, and

symbolic order, they penetrate to the very essence of Buddhism and, by means of a comparison with the most fundamental traits of Christianity, they set side by side two structures of thought, two attitudes in face of the problem of man and the universe.

TEILHARD DE CHARDIN

No presentation, however summary, of the works of Henri de Lubac would be complete without at least a brief consideration of the studies he has devoted to his close friend and fellow Jesuit, Teilhard de Chardin.

The two men first met in Paris in 1921, when Père de Lubac returned to France at the completion of his studies in philosophy on the Isle of Jersey, and despite a difference in age of some fifteen years and Teilhard's frequent and lengthy trips abroad, their friendship remained strong until the latter's death in New York City on Easter Sunday, 1956.

The very titles of Père de Lubac's studies manifest a preoccupation with Teilhard's spiritual thought and if, as is the case in *La Pensée religieuse du Père Pierre Teilhard de Chardin* (1962), he also treats of Teilhard's method and the principal categories of his philosophical thought, it is because Teilhard's interior life was so closely linked with the way he approached and understood his faith. Apologetics, dogma, mystical theology all play an important role in his thinking, but it was his spiritual doctrine, as *The Divine Milieu* makes so clear, that was both the center of his thought and the source of his reflection.

Teilhard de Chardin: The Man and His Meaning (1965) is, in a real sense, the spiritual biography of Teilhard and Père de Lubac, making abundant use of Teilhard's writings, his letters, and his spiritual diaries and retreat notebooks, is once again more concerned with his spiritual message than with his scientific work. As in his earlier study, he leaves no doubt as to the emptiness of the charges of pantheism brought against Teilhard, and he goes on to explain in detail his apologetical method.

Teilhard Missionnaire et Apologiste (1966) is the develop-

197

ment of two conferences delivered in Rome during the Vatican
Council II. In this brief study, which evokes a comparison
between Teilhard and St. Paul and sketches the former's thought
concerning God, the immortal soul, and his vision of Christianity,
Père de Lubac shows that whether as missionary or apologist,
Teilhard was first and foremost the faithful son of the unique
Church of Christ, the unique Savior.

These studies, as well as his *Blondel et Teilhard de Chardin:
Correspondance commentée* (1965), his prefaces to several
other volumes of Teilhard's letters, and the fact that he under-
took to prepare for publication the numerous works of Yves de
Montcheuil and August Valensin, both fellow Jesuits, would
seem sufficient to refute the charge that his "preoccupation with
the Church Fathers" has resulted in a sort of "repudiation of
the Christian thought of later generations."

Some years ago, on the occasion of his fiftieth anniversary in
religious life, colleagues, friends, and former students of Henri
de Lubac gathered together to offer him the now traditional
"mélanges," a three-volume work destined to express their admiration and their gratitude for his contribution to theological
thought over the past forty years. The title chosen, *L'Homme
devant Dieu (Mélanges offerts au Père Henri de Lubac)*, was
selected as the expression of the fundamental inspiration of
his life's work—"the affirmation, the knowledge, and the seeking of God"—and more than one in attendance that day in 1963
thought back to those hauntingly beautiful pages of *Meditation
on the Church* and his profound and moving description of the
vir ecclesiasticus, the "man of the Church."

"Whether we like it or not," he wrote, "there are many non-
essential things which change according to time and place. But
without blinding himself to the plain fact of this diversity, the
man of the Church will make it his business to see also the continuity which exists at an even deeper level of reality. . . . But
for all that he will always give special attention to certain facts
and periods of particular importance; the age of the first martyrs,

the rise of monasticism, the main stages in the formation of dogma, the work of the great saints and Doctors, the big spiritual revivals, and so on. He will take into account the history of missionary expansion, in its main outlines at least, and he will not forget the ancient tradition of eastern Christianity, the 'basic stratum,' the massive main trunk from which we all spring. If he is himself a scholar, he will put to the best use he can the method of his own particular discipline, though he will never lose sight of the fact that Catholic tradition does not open the whole of its secret even to an exhaustive enquiry, and that it becomes fully intelligible only to him who keeps in the line of its axis and studies it from the inside as one who lives by the faith of the Church."

In these few lines Père de Lubac has, unconsciously perhaps, succeeded in sketching his own portrait. He has stated his purpose, identified his sources, explained his method, and established his goal. For he, too, is this "man of the Church" who has "rooted himself in her soil"; he, too, has "formed himself in her likeness and made himself one with her experience." With an Origen and an Irenaeus as companions he has "gone back in spirit to the age of the newborn Church, when the echo of the Apostles' preaching was still audible, Christ's blood still warm, and faith burned with a living flame in the heart of the believer." He, too, is on intimate terms with those who, in the Church before him, prayed to Christ and lived, worked, thought, and suffered for him, "for such men are fathers of his soul." By keeping their company he has "recognized in his spiritual mother the Church of the Fathers."

He, too, has put himself "at the service of the great community," always ready "to give any man a reason for the hope that is in him," for he has "welcomed and made his own, at depth, the preoccupation with truth." Henri de Lubac is truly "a man of the Church!"

Bibliography (up to 1967)

MARTIN BUBER

Works Cited in the Text

Buber, Martin. *Die Stunde und die Erkenntnis, Reden und Aufsätze, 1933–1935*. Translation by Hans Joachim Schoeps. Berlin: Schocken Verlag, 1936.

Buber, Martin. *Israel and the World: Essays in a Time of Crisis*. New York: Schocken Books, 1948.

Buber, Martin. *Between Man and Man*. Boston: Beacon Press, 1955.

Buber, Martin. *I and Thou*, 2nd ed. Translation by Ronald Gregor Smith. New York: Charles Scribner's Sons, 1958.

Friedman, Maurice. " 'I-Thou' and 'I-It.' " *A Handbook of Christian Theology*. Living Age Books, no. 18. New York: Meridian Books, Inc., 1958.

Works by Martin Buber (Selected)

Mamre, Essays in Religion. Translated by Greta Hort. Melbourne and London: Melbourne University Press and Oxford University Press, 1946.

Hasidism. New York: The Philosophical Library, 1948.

Israel and the World. New York: Schocken Books, Inc., 1948.

Israel and the World, Essays in a Time of Crisis. New York: Schocken Books, 1948.

Tales of Hasidim, 2 vols. New York: Schocken Books, 1948. (First volume, early masters; second, later masters.)

At the Turning. Three Addresses on Judaism. New York: Farrar, Straus and Young, 1952.

For the Sake of Heaven. Translated from the German by Ludwig Lewisohn. Philadelphia: The Jewish Publication Society, 1945. Second edition with new foreword, New York: Harper and Brothers, 1953.

Good and Evil. New York: Charles Scribner's Sons, 1953.

Good and Evil. Magnolia, Mass.: Peter Smith, Publisher.

The Legend of the Baal-Shem. Translated by Maurice S. Friedman. New York: Harper and Brothers. London: East and West Library, 1955.

Writings. Selected, edited, and introduced by Will Herberg. New York: Meridian Books, 1956.

Eclipse of God. Torchbooks, TB12. New York: Harper and Row, 1957.

Pointing the Way. Translated by Maurice S. Friedman. Torchbooks, TB103. New York: Harper and Row, 1957.

I and Thou, 2nd ed. New York: Charles Scribner's Sons, 1958.

Moses: The Revelation and the Covenant. Torchbooks, TB27. New York: Harper and Row, 1958.

Paths in Utopia. Boston: Beacon Press, 1958 (1949).

Writings, ed. Will Herberg. Magnolia, Mass.: Peter Smith, Publisher, 1958.

Prophetic Faith. Torchbooks, TB73. New York: Harper and Row, 1960.

Prophetic Faith. Magnolia, Mass.: Peter Smith, Publisher.

Two Types of Faith. Torchbooks, TB75. New York: Harper and Row, 1961.

Tales of Rabbi Nachman. Translated by Maurice S. Friedman. Bloomington: Indiana University Press, 1962.

Ten Rungs. New York: Schocken Books, 1962.

Between Man and Man. New York: Macmillan, 1965.

JOHN COURTNEY MURRAY, S.J.

Works Cited in the Text

"St. Robert Bellarmine on the Indirect Power." *Theological Studies* 9 (December 1948) 419–535.

"Contemporary Orientations of Catholic Thought on Church and State in the Light of History." *Theological Studies* 10 (June 1949) 177–234.

"Governmental Repression of Heresy." *Proceedings of the Third Annual Meeting of the Catholic Theological Society of America* 3 (June 1949 [1948]) 26–98.

"The Problem of State Religion." *Theological Studies* 12 (June 1951) 155–178.

"Leo XIII: Separation of Church and State." *Theological Studies* 14 (June 1953) 145–214.

"This Matter of Religious Freedom." *America* 112 (January 1695) 40–43.

"The Issue of Development of Doctrine." Seven pages (unpublished manuscript for Vatican Council II).

Bibliography

Books (as Sole Author)

We Hold These Truths: Catholic Reflections on the American Proposition. New York: Sheed and Ward, 1960.

The Problem of Religious Freedom. Westminister: The Newman Press, 1965. This essay originally was a background paper for Vatican Council II; it was first published in *Theological Studies* 25 (December 1964) 503–575.

Books (as Editor and Essayist)

Freedom and Man. New York: P. J. Kenedy & Sons, 1965.

Religious Liberty: An End and a Beginning, The Declaration on Religious Freedom: An Ecumenical Discussion. New York: The Macmillan Company, 1966.

Books (as Contributing Essayist) [*Selected*]

"On the Structure of the Church-State Problem." *The Catholic Church in World Affairs,* eds. W. Gurian and M. A. Fitzsimons. Notre Dame: University of Notre Dame Press, 1954.

"America's Four Conspiracies." *Religion in America,* ed. John Cogley. New York: Meridan Books, Inc., 1958.

"Natural Law and Public Consensus." *Natural Law and Modern Society.* New York: The World Publishing Company, 1962, 1963.

"Key Themes in the Encyclical" (an analysis of *Pacem in terris*). New York: America Press, 1963.

"Introduction" and explanatory footnotes to Vatican Council II's document on religious freedom. *The Documents of Vatican II,* eds. Walter M. Abbott and Joseph Gallagher. New York: Guild Press; America Press; Association Press, 1966.

Essays (Selected)

"Christian Co-operation." *Theological Studies* 3 (September 1942) 413–431.

"Intercredal Co-operation: Some Further Views." *Theological Studies* 4 (March 1943) 100–111.

"Intercredal Co-operation: Its Theory and Organization." *Theological Studies* 4 (June 1943) 257–283.

"Freedom of Religion: I. The Ethical Problem." *Theological Studies* 6 (June 1945) 229–286.

"Separation of Church and State." *America* 76 (December 7, 1946) 261–263.

"Separation of Church and State: True and False Concepts," *America* 77 (February 15, 1947) 541–545.

"The Court Upholds Religious Freedom." *America* 77 (March 8, 1947) 628–630.

"Religious Liberty: The Concern of All." *America* 78 (February 3, 1948) 513–516.

"Dr. Morrison and the First Amendment: I." *America* 78 (March 6, 1948) 627–629.

"Dr. Morrison and the First Amendment: II." *America* 78 (March 20, 1948) 283–286.

"St. Robert Bellarmine on the Indirect Power." *Theological Studies* 9 (December 1948) 491–535.

"Contemporary Orientations of Catholic Thought on Church and State in the Light of History." *Theological Studies* 10 (June 1949) 177–234.

"Governmental Repression of Heresy." *Proceedings of the Third*

Annual Meeting of the Catholic Theological Society of America 3 (June 1949 [1948]) 26–98.

"On Religious Freedom." *Theological Studies* 10 (September 1949) 409–432.

"Law or Prepossessions?" *Law and Contemporary Problems* 14 (Winter 1949) 23–43.

"The Problem of State Religion." *Theological Studies* 12 (June 1951) 155–178; also published as "The Problem of 'The Religion of the State,' Part I." *American Ecclesiastical Review* 124 (May 1951) 327–352.

"For the Freedom and Transcendence of the Church." *American Ecclesiastical Review* 126 (January 1952) 28–49.

"The Church and Totalitarian Democracy." *Theological Studies* 13 (December 1952) 525–563.

"Leo XIII on Church and State: The General Structure of the Controversy." *Theological Studies* 14 (March 1953) 1–30.

"Leo XIII: Separation of Church and State." *Theological Studies* 14 (June 1953) 145–214.

"Leo XIII: Two Concepts of Government." *Theological Studies* 14 (December 1953) 551–567.

"Leo XIII: Government and the Order of Culture." *Theological Studies* 15 (March 1954) 1–33.

"The Problem of Pluralism in America." *Thought* 29 (Summer 1954) 165–208.

"A Theologian's Tribute." *America* 108 (June 15, 1963) 854–855.

"The Church and the Council." *America* 109 (October 19, 1963) 451–453.

"On Religious Liberty." *America* 109 (November 30, 1963) 704–706.

"The Problem of Religious Freedom." *Theological Studies* 25 (December 1964) 503–575; also published as a book by the same title.

"This Matter of Religious Freedom." *America* 113 (January 9, 1965) 40–43.

"The Declaration on Religious Freedom" (address delivered at the International Theological Conference, University of Notre Dame, March 20–26, 1966). *Vatican II, An Interfaith Appraisal,* ed. John H. Miller, C.S.C. Notre Dame: University of Notre Dame Press, 1966. Pages 565–585.

BIBLIOGRAPHY

"The Declaration on Religious Freedom: Its Deeper Significance."
America 114 (April 23, 1966) 592–593.

Unpublished Materials (Selected)
"The Issue of Development of Doctrine" (Vatican II background paper).
"Remarks on the Schema on Religious Freedom" (Vatican II background paper).
"On the Method and Principles of the Schema" (Vatican II background paper on *De Libertate Religiosa*).

JOSEF HROMADKA

Bibliography

Books (in German)
Evangelium für Atheisten. Berlin: Käthe Vogt Verlag, 1958.
Sprung über die Mauer. Berlin: Käthe Vogt Verlag, 1961.
Das Evangelium auf dem Wege zum Menschen. Berlin (East): Evangelische Verlagsanstalt, 1961.
Auf der Schwelle eines Dialogs zwischen Christen und Marxisten. Frankfurt/Main: Stimme Verlag, 1965

Books (in English)
Doom and Resurrection (out of print). Richmond, Va.: Madrus House, 1945. Translation of *Sprung uber . . . ,* with recent appendix.
The Church and Theology in Today's Troubled Times. Prague, 1956.
Theology Between Yesterday and Tomorrow. Philadelphia: Westminster Press, 1957.

Essays (in English)
"The Church in Czechoslovakia Faces the Present Turmoil." *The American Czechoslovak Friendship Bulletin* 1, no. 2 (Autumn 1942).
"Russia and the West." *The Fortnightly* (January 1944).
"The Soviet Enigma." *Christianity and Crisis* (January 24, 1944).
"Jesus Christ and the Present Distress." *Theology Today* (April 1945).

"Changing Europe and the Christian Faith." *Theology Today* (April 1946).

"One Year Later: Theological Reflections on the Present Situation." *Theology Today* (April 1947).

"Between Yesterday and Tomorrow." *Theology Today* (July 1948).

"Our Responsibility in the Postwar World." *The Church and International Disorder.* Amsterdam Assembly Series, World Council of Churches, vol. IV. New York: Harper Bros., 1948.

"The Church of the Reformation Faces Today's Challenges." *Theology Today* (January 1950).

"A Voice from the Other Side." *Christianity and Crisis* (March 1951).

"Social and Cultural Factors in our Division." *Theology Today* (January 1953).

"Gospel for Atheists." *Risk* 1, no. 1 (Spring 1965). Published by the Youth Department of the World Council of Churches, Geneva, Switzerland. Translation of *Evangelium für.* . . .

"On the Threshold of a Dialogue." *A Monthly Letter About Evangelism* 1, 2, 3. Published by the Department on Studies in Evangelism, World Council of Churches, 1965. Translation of *Auf der Schwelle.* . . .

Other Contributions

"Von der Reformation zum Morgen." *Von der Reformation zum Morgen.* Leipzig: Köhler und Amelang, 1959. Pages 293–393.

Communio Viatorum. Theological journal published in English, French, and German in Prague, Czechoslovakia (*Jungmannova* 9), edited by Hromadka. See editorials *passim,* especially: 2, nos. 2, 3 (Summer 1959), issue published in honor of Hromadka which contains excerpts from his work previously unpublished; 8, nos. 2, 3 (Summer 1965) on "Roman Catholics."

BERNARD HÄRING

Works Cited in the Text

Das Heilige und das Gute. Munchen: E. Wewel Verlag, 1950. Pages 271, 272.

Macht und Ohnmacht der Religion. Salzburg: O. Müller Verlag, 1956. Pages 63, 71, 72, 74.

The Johannine Council. New York: Herder and Herder, 1963.
Pages 17, 19, 107, 109, 142.
Marriage in the Modern World. Westminster: The Newman Press,
1965. Page 5.
A Sacramental Spirituality. New York: Sheed and Ward, 1965.
Pages 6, 110, 111–112, 183.
Theology in Transition, ed. E. O'Brien. New York: Herder and
Herder, 1965. Pages 240–241.
The Liberty of the Children of God. Westminster: The Newman
Press, 1966. Pages 15, 16, 104.
This Time of Salvation. New York: Herder and Herder, 1966. Pages
33, 41, 42, 48.

Bibliography

Books (in German)

*Das Heilige und das Gute. Religion und Sittlichkeit in ihrem
gegenseitigen Bezug.* München: E. Wewel Verlag, 1950. [*HG*]
*Das Gesetz Christi. Moraltheologie dargestellt für Priester und
Laien,* 3bd. Freiburg: E. Wewel Verlag, 1954–1961. [*GC*]
Soziologie der Familie. Die Familie und ihre Umwelt. Salzburg: O.
Müller, 1954. [*SF*]
Der Christ und die Obrigkeit. Augsburg: Winfried-Werk Verlag,
1956. [*CO*]
Macht und Ohnmacht der Religion. Religionssoziologie als Anruf.
Salzburg: O. Müller, 1956. [*MOR*]
Christ in einer neuen Welt. Lebensgestaltung aus dem Glauben.
Freiburg: E. Wewel Verlag, 1959. [*CW*]
Ehe in dieser Zeit. Salzburg: O. Müller, 1960. [*FdZ*]
Gabe und Auftrag der Sacramente. Salzburg: O. Müller, 1962.
[*GAS*]
Das Konzil im Zeichen der Einheit. Freiburg: Herder, 1963. [*KZE*]
Die Gegenwärtige Heilsstunde. Freiburg: E. Wewel Verlag, 1964.
[*GH*]

Books (in English)

The Sociology of the Family. Cork, Ireland: The Mercier Press,
1959. Translation of *SF*.
The Law of Christ, 3 vol. Westminster, Maryland: The Newman
Press, 1961, 1963, 1967. Translation of *GC*.

The Johannine Council. Witness to Unity. New York: Herder and Herder, 1963. Translation of *KZE.*

Christian Renewal in a Changing World. New York: Desclee Co., 1964. Translation of *CW.*

Marriage in the Modern World. Westminster, Maryland: The Newman Press, 1965. Translation of *EdZ.*

A Sacramental Spirituality. New York: Sheed and Ward, 1965. Translation of *GAS.*

The Liberty of the Children of God. Staten Island, New York: Alba House, 1966. Translation of *CO.*

This Time of Salvation. New York: Herder and Herder, 1966. Translation of the first half of *GH.*

Toward a Christian Moral Theology. Notre Dame: University of Notre Dame Press, 1966.

The Responsible Christian. New York: Herder and Herder, 1967. Translation of the second half of *GH.*

Essays (Selected)

"Alfons von Liguori als Patron der Beichväter und Moraltheologen." *Geist und Leben* 23 (1950) 376–379.

" 'Das Heilige' Rudolf Ottos in der neueren Kritik." *Geist und Leben* 24 (1951) 66–71.

"Moraltheologische Beurteilung der Künstlichen Befruchtung." *Arzt und Christ* 1 (1955) 221–226.

"Autoritätskrise in der Kirche?" *Mitarbeiterin* 7 (1956) 72–75.

"Faule Situationsethik oder toter Legalismus?" *Klerusblatt* 36 (1956) 356–359.

"Private und organisierte Liebestätigkeit." *Caritas* 1 (1956) 249–251.

"Würde und Auftrag des Laien in der Kirche." *Monatsblätter* 69 (1956–1957) 310–317.

"Die gemeinschaftstiftende Kraft der Liturgie." *Liturgisches Jahrbuch* 7 (1957) 205–214.

"Die Neuheit des sittlichen Lebens." *Die Neuheit* 1 (1957) 124–133.

"Die Stellung des Gesetzes in der Moraltheologie." *Moralprobleme im Umbruch der Zeit* 1 (1957) 133–152.

"Demut als Weg der Liebe." *Geist und Leben* 30 (1957) 321–324.

209

"Marxismus als Ersatzreligion." *Theologie und Glaube* 47 (1957) 241–251.

"Der Geist des Technizismus und die Liturgie." *Liturgisches Jahrbuch* 8 (1958) 194–204.

"Liebe und Ehelosigkeit." *Geist und Leben* 31 (1958) 103–106.

"Sacramente und Nächstenliebe 1 Kor 13 und Jo 15:8–17." *Ut Omnes Unum* 22 (1959) 33–42.

"Wege der Nachfolge Christi in der Welt." *Wort und Wahrheit* 14 (1959) 179–189.

"Moraltheologie gestern und heute." *Stimmen der Zeit* 167 (1960) 99–110.

"Sünde und Heiligkeit als Sozialphänomene." *Christ und Welt* 1 (1960) 32–40.

"Tradition und Aupassung in Licht des Geheimnisses der Inkarnation." *Kirche und Überlieferung* 1 (1960) 276–287.

"Liturgisches Frömmigkeit und christliche Vollendung." *Liturgisches Jahrbuch* 11 (1961) 93–103.

"The Christian Message and Apologetics and the Modern Mentality." *Faith and Commitment.* Chicago: Loyola University Press, 1964. Pages 243–252.

"Das Geheimnis der Kirche im Spiegelbilde christlicher Moral." *Gott in Welt.* Festgabe f. K. Rahner, ed. J. B. Metz, 2 Bd. Freiburg, 1964. Pages 186–205.

"Gewissenbildung vom Evangelium her." *Problem der Beichterziehung* 1 (1964) 11–47.

"La Théologie morale et la Sociologie pastorale dans la perspective de l'Histoire du Salut." *Sciences Ecclésiastiques* 16 (1964) 209–224.

EDWARD SCHILLEBEECKX

The quotations of Schillebeeckx's works were translated into English by Father Houdijk. They were taken from the following books:

Maria, moeder van de verlossing. Haarlem, 1955.

"De Bisschoppen van Nederland over het Concilie." *Tijdschrift voor theologie* 1 (1961).

"De zin van het mens-zijn van Jezus, de Christus." *Tijdschrift voor theologie* 2 (1962).

"Dogmatiek van ambt en lekestaat." *Tijdschrift voor theologie* 2 (1962).

Het huwelijk, aardse werkelijkheid en heilsmysterie I. Bilthoven, 1963.

"De natuurwet in verband met de katholieke huwelijksopvatting." *Jaarboek 1961 van het Werkgenootschap van katholieke theologen in Nederland.* Hilversum, 1963.

Het tweede Vaticaans Concilie. The Hague, 1964.

"Openbaring en theologie." *Theologische Peilingen I,* Bilthoven 1964.

"Christus' tegenwoordigheid in de Eucharistie." *Tijdschrift voor theologie* 5 (1965).

"God en mens." *Theologische Peilingen II.* Bilthoven, 1965.

"Ecclesia semper purificanda." *Ex auditu verbi: Feestgave G. C. Berkouwer.* Kampen, 1965.

"De leken in het volk van God." *Godsvolk en leek en ambt* (*do-c dossiers* 7). Hilversum-Antwerp, 1966.

"Wereld en kerk." *Theologische Peilingen III.* Bilthoven, 1966.

Bibliography

Books (in English)

Christ: The Sacrament of the Encounter with God. New York: Sheed and Ward, 1963. Paperback edition, New York: Sheed and Ward, 1963.

The Layman in the Church and Other Essays. New York: Alba House (St. Paul Publications), 1963.

Vatican II: The Struggle of Minds and Other Essays. Dublin: M. H. Gill and Sons, 1963.

Mary, Mother of the Redemption. New York: Sheed and Ward, 1964.

Bernard Cardinal Alfrink. Notre Dame: University of Notre Dame Press, 1965.

Marriage: Human Reality and Saving Mystery. New York: 1966.

Books (as Contributing Essayist)

"Die Heiligung des Namens Gottes durch die Menschenliebe Jesu des Christus." *Gott in Welt* (Festschrift in honor of Karl Rahner), II. Freiburg-Basel-Vienna, 1964. Pages 43–91.

211

"Ecclesia semper purificanda." *Ex Auditu Verbi* (Festschrift in honor of G. C. Berkouwer). Kampen, 1965. Pages 216–232.

JOHN A. T. ROBINSON

Works Cited in Text

Robinson, John A. T. *Honest to God*. London: SCM Press, 1963. Philadelphia: The Westminster Press, 1963.

Edwards, David L., ed. *The Honest to God Debate*. London: SCM Press, 1963. Philadelphia: The Westminster Press, 1963.

Robinson, John A. T. *The New Reformation?* London: SCM Press, 1965. Philadelphia: The Westminster Press, 1965.

McBrien, Richard P. *The Church in the Thought of Bishop John Robinson*. London: SCM Press, 1966.

Works by John A. T. Robinson

Thou Who Art: The Notion of personality and its relation to Christian theology with particular reference to (a) the contemporary "I-Thou" philosophy; (b) the doctrines of the Trinity and the Person of Christ. Cambridge University, 1945 (unpublished dissertation).

In the End, God . . .: A Study of the Christian Doctrine of the Last Things. London: James Clarke, 1950. New edition available in the series *Perspectives in Humanism*, New York: Harper & Row, 1967.

The Body: A Study in Pauline Theology (Studies in Biblical Theology, No. 5). London: SCM Press, 1952.

Jesus and His Coming: The Emergence of a Doctrine. London: SCM Press, 1957.

On Being the Church in the World. London: SCM Press, 1960.

Liturgy Coming to Life. London: Mowbray, 1960. Second edition with new preface, 1963.

Christ Comes In. London: Mowbray, 1960.

Twelve New Testament Studies (Studies in Biblical Theology, no. 34). London: SCM Press, 1962.

Honest to God. London: SCM Press, 1963.

Christian Morals Today. London: SCM Press, 1964.

The New Reformation? London: SCM Press, 1965.

Keeping in Touch with Theology. Pamphlet. London: SCM Press, 1963 (reprinted from *Twentieth Century,* Summer 1963).

The World That God Loves. Pamphlet. London: Church Missionary Society (reprinted: *The Episcopal Overseas Mission Review* 10, no. 3 (1965) 2–7).

Books (as Contributing Essayist)

"The Christian Hope." *Christian Faith and Communist Faith,* ed. D. M. Mackinnon. London: Macmillan, 1953. Pages 209–226.

"Kingdom, Church and Ministry." *The Historic Episcopate in the Fulness of the Church,* ed. K. M. Carey. London: Dacre Press, 1954. Second edition, 1960. Pages 11–12.

"Our Present Position in the Light of the Bible." *Becoming a Christian,* ed. B. Minchin. London: Faith Press, 1954. Pages 48–57.

"The Historicity of the Gospels." *Jesus Christ: History Interpretation and Faith,* ed. R. C. Walton, T. W. Manson, and John A. T. Robinson. London: SPCK, 1956. Pages 45–63.

"The 'Others' of John 4, 38." *Studia Evangelica,* ed. K. Aland, *et al.* Berlin: Akedemie-Verlag, 1959. Pages 510–515. Reprinted in *Twelve New Testament Studies* 61–66.

"The New Look on the Fourth Gospel." *Studia Evangelica,* eds. K. Aland, *et al.* Berlin: Akedemie-Verlag, 1959. Pages 510–515. Reprinted *The Gospels Reconsidered. A Selection of Papers read at the International Congress on The Four Gospels in 1957,* Oxford: Blackwell, 1960. Pages 154–166. Also *Twelve New Testament Studies* 94–106.

"Taking the Lid off the Church's Ministry." *New Ways with the Ministry.* London: Faith Press, 1960. Pages 9–21.

"A New Model of Episcopacy." *Bishops: What They Are and What They Do.* Edited by the Bishop of Llandaff. London: Faith Press, 1961. Pages 125–138.

"Resurrection in the NT." *The Interpreter's Dictionary of the Bible, vol. IV.* New York and Nashville: Abingdon Press, 1962. Pages 43–53.

"The Significance of the Foot-Washing." *Neotestamentica et Patristica: Eine Freundesgabe, Herrn Professor Dr Oscar Cullmann zu seinem 60. Geburtstag überreicht.* Leiden: E. J. Brill, 1962. Pages 144–147.

213

"The Ministry and the Laity." *Layman's Church*. London: Lutterworth Press, 1963. Pages 9–22.

"The Place of the Fourth Gospel." *The Roads Converge: A Contribution to the Question of Christian Reunion,* ed. P. Gardner-Smith. London: Arnold, 1963. Pages 49–74.

"Communicating with the Contemporary Man." *Religion in Television*. London: Independent Television Authority. Pages 27–35.

(As Editor)

The Honest to God Debate, eds. John A. T. Robinson and D. L. Edwards. London: SCM Press, 1963. Pages 228–279.

Reviews

A Review of Oscar Cullmann's *Christ and Time*. *Scottish Journal of Theology* 3 (1950) 86–89.

"The Hard Core of the Gospel: New Thought from Germany." Review of Rudolf Bultmann's *Theology of the New Testament*. *The Church of England Newspaper,* February 27, 1953.

A Review of Oscar Cullmann's *Peter: Disciple, Apostle, Martyr*. *The Church of England Newspaper,* September 7, 1953.

A Review of J. Marsh's *The Fulness of Time*. *Theology* 56 (1953) 107–109.

A Review of *The Biblical Doctrine of Baptism* (Commission on Baptism, Church of Scotland, Edinburgh, 1959). *Scottish Journal of Theology* 13 (1960) 99–102.

Essays

"The Religious Foundation of the University." *The Cambridge Review,* January 20, 1945.

"Agape and Eros." *Theology* 48 (1945) 98–104.

"The Temptations." *Theology* 50 (1947) 43–48 (reprinted in *Twelve New Testament Studies* 53–50).

"Hosea and the Virgin Birth." *Theology* 52 (1949) 373–375.

"Universalism—Is it Heretical?" *Scottish Journal of Theology* 2 (1949) 139–155.

"The House Church and the Parish Church." *Theology* 53 (1950) 283–287 (reprinted: *On Being the Church in the World* 83–95).

"The Social Content of Salvation." *Frontier* (November 1952 [reprinted in *On Being the Church in the World* 23–30]).

"The Theological College in a Changing World." *Theology* 55 (1952) 202–207.

"The One Baptism." *Scottish Journal of Theology* 6 (1953) 257–274 (reprinted in *Twelve New Testament Studies* 158–175).

"Traces of a Liturgical Sequence in I Cor. 16, 20–24." *Journal of Theological Studies* n.s. 4 (1953) 38–41 (reprinted in *Twelve New Testament Studies* 154–157, with the new title "The Earliest Christian Liturgical Sequence?").

"The Gospel and Race." *The Church of England Newspaper,* July 24, 1953 (reprinted in *On Being the Church in the World* 116–120).

"Trusting the Universe": (1) "The Faith of the Scientist"; (2) "The Faith of the Philosopher"; (3) "The Faith of the Christian." *The Church of England Newspaper,* September 17, 24; October 1, 1954.

"The Parable of the Shepherd (John 10, 1–5)." *Zeitschrift für die Neutestamentliche Wissenschaft* 46 (1955) 233–240 (reprinted in *Twelve New Testament Studies* 67–75).

"The Second Coming—Mk. xiv, 62." *The Expository Times* 67 (1955) 336–340.

"The Most Primitive Christology of All?" *Journal of Theological Studies* 7 (1956) 177–189 (reprinted in *Twelve New Testament Studies* 139–153).

"The Parable of the Sheep and the Goats." *New Testament Studies* 2 (1956) 225–237 (reprinted in *Twelve New Testament Studies* 76–93).

"The Baptism of John and the Qumran Community." *Harvard Theological Review* 50 (1957) 175–191 (reprinted in *Twelve New Testament Studies* 11–27).

"Intercommunion and Concelebration." *The Ecumenical Review* 9 (1957) 203–206 (reprinted in *On Being the Church in the World* 96–100).

"Preaching Judgement." *The Preacher's Quarterly* (September and December 1957 [reprinted in *On Being the Church in the World* 135–147]).

"Elijah, John and Jesus." in *New Testament Studies* 4 (1958) 263–281 (reprinted in *Twelve New Testament Studies* 28–52).

"The Teaching of Theology for the Ministry." *Theology* 61 (1958) 486–495.

"Episcopacy and Intercommunion." *Theology* 62 (1959) 402–408 (reprinted in *On Being the Church in the World* 101–109).

"The Destination and Purpose of St. John's Gospel." *New Testament Studies* 6 (1960) 117–131 (reprinted in *Twelve New Testament Studies* 107–125).

"The Destination and Purpose of the Johannine Epistles." *New Testament Studies* 7 (1960–61) 56–65 (reprinted in *Twelve New Testament Studies* 126–138).

"Five Points for Christian Action." *Man and Society* 2 (1962) 13–15.

"The Church of England and Intercommunion." *Prism* 4, no. 3 (1962) 2–15 (reprinted as Prism Pamphlet no. 2, London, 1962).

"The Tercentenary of the Book of Common Prayer." *Parish and People* 36 (Epiphany, 1963) 15–19.

"The Relation of the Prologue to the Gospel of St. John." *New Testament Studies* 9 (1962–1963) 120–129. Reprinted in *The Authorship and Integrity of the New Testament*, London: SPCK, 1965. Pages 61–72.

"On Being a Radical." *The Listener*, February 21, 1963.

"Our Image of God Must Go." *The Observer*, March 17, 1963. Reprinted in *The Observer Revisited*, London: Hodder & Stoughton, 1964. Pages 42–47.

"Der Verpflichtung der Kirche gegenüber dem Menschen der Gegenwart." *Monatschrift für Pastoral Theologie* 52 (1963) 321–328.

"The Great Benefice Barrier." *Prism* 80 (December 1963) 4–13.

"Our Common Reformation." *Catholic Gazette* 55, no. 1 (January 1964) 6–7.

"Theologians of Our Time: C. H. Dodd." *The Expository Times* 75 (1964) 100–102. Reprinted in *Theologians of Our Time*, Edinburgh: T. & T. Clark, 1966.

῾Η ἠθική κρίση καί ἤ ἠθική ἀξίωση, Ἐπόχες (Athens) 18 (October 1964) 3–6.

"Ascendancy." *Andover Newton Quarterly* n.s. 5 (1964) 5–9 (reprinted in *The Pulpit* 36, no. 5 (1965) 4–6; also with the title "The Ascendancy of Christ," *Pulpit Digest* 45, no. 321 (1965) 45–48).

"Rocking the Radical Boat Too." *Prism* 95 (March 1965) 6–10.

"Can a Truly Contemporary Person *Not* be an Atheist?" *The Sunday Times,* March 14, 1965 (reprinted in *The New Reformation?* 106–122).

"Can Anglicanism Survive? Death and Resurrection." *New Statesman,* April 9, 1965.

"Living with Sex." *The Observer,* June 13, 1965.

"1957–1965: The Watershed Years." *Prism* 101 (September 1965).

"God Dwelling Incognito." *New Christian,* October 7, 1965.

"Bearing the Reality of Christman." *New Christian,* December 16, 1965.

BERNARD LONERGAN

Works Cited in the Text

Theological Studies, vol. 7, 1946 (from "The Concept of *Verbum . . .*").

Theological Studies, vol. 8, 1947 (from "The Concept of *Verbum . . .*").

Theological Studies, vol. 2, 1941 (from "St. Thomas' Thought on *Gratia Operans*"). N.B. Only one line was quoted from this volume.

Sciences Ecclésiastiques, vol. 13, 1961.

Spirit as Inquiry. Studies in Honor of Bernard Lonergan. Chicago, 1964. Published by *Continuum,* Saint Xavier College. N.B. The copyright for the article quoted is held by Father Lonergan himself.

Lonergan, Bernard. *Insight. A Study of Human Understanding.* London: Longmans, Green & Co., 1957.

Vers le dogme de l'Assomption. Montreal: La Corporation des Editions Fides. Also Notre Dame: Fides Publishers, Inc.

De Deo Trino, vols. I and II. Rome: Gregorian University Press, 1964. N.B. Only one line was quoted from vol. II.

Bibliography

Works by Bernard Lonergan (Selected)

"St. Thomas' Thought on *Gratia Operans.*" *Theological Studies* 2 (1941) 289–324; 3 (1942) 69–88, 375–402, 533–578.

"The Form of Inference." *Thought* 18 (1943) 277–292.

"Finality, Love, Marriage." *Theological Studies* 4 (1943) 477–510.

"The Concept of *Verbum* in the Writings of St. Thomas Aquinas." *Theological Studies* 7 (1946) 349–392; 8 (1947) 35–79, 404–444; 10 (1949) 3–40, 359–393.

"The Assumption and Theology." Pages 411–424 in *Vers le dogme de l'Assomption.* Montreal, 1948.

"The Natural Desire to See God." *Proceedings of the Eleventh Annual Meeting of the Jesuit Philosophical Association,* 1949. Pages 31–43.

"A Note on Geometrical Possibility." *The Modern Schoolman* 27 (1949–1950) 124–138.

"Le rôle de l'université catholique dans le monde moderne." *Relations* 11 (1951) 263–265.

"Theology and Understanding." *Gregorianum* 35 (1954) 630–648.

"Isomorphism of Thomist and Scientific Thought." Pages 119–127 in *Sapientia Aquinatis.* Rome, 1955.

De constitutione Christi ontologica et psychologica. Rome: Gregorian University Press, 1956.

Insight. A Study of Human Understanding. London: Longmans, Green & Co., 1957.

"*Insight.* Preface to a Discussion." *Proceedings of the American Catholic Philosophical Association* 32 (1958) 71–81.

"Christ as Subject: A Reply." *Gregorian* 40 (1959) 242–270.

"Openness and Religious Experience." Pages 460–462 in *Il Problema dell'esperienza religiosa.* Brescia, 1961.

Intelligenza. Studio sulla comprensione dell'esperienza. Alba, 1961.

"Metaphysics as Horizon." *Gregorianum* 44 (1963) 307–318.

"La Notion de verbe dans les écrits de saint Thomas d'Aquin." *Archives de Philosophie* 26 (1963) 163–203, 570–620; 27 (1964) 238–285; 28 (1965) 206–250, 510–552.

De Deo Trino, 2 vols. Rome: Gregorian University Press, 1964.

"Cognitional Structure." *Continuum* 2 (1964) 530–542.

"*Existenz* and *Aggiornamento.*" *Focus* 2 (1965) 5–14.

"Subject and Soul." *Philippine Studies* 13 (1965) 576–585.

"The Role of the Catholic University in the Modern World." *Continuum* 4 (1966) 278–282.

JOHN HICK

Works Cited in the Text

Faith and Knowledge: A Modern Introduction to the Problems of Religious Knowledge. Ithaca, New York: Cornell University Press, 1957.

Faith and the Philosophers, ed. John Hick. (Product of a two-day conference held at Princeton Theological Seminary, December 1962.) New York: St. Martin's Press, 1964.

Philosophy of Religion. (*Foundations of Philosophy Series,* eds. Elizabeth and Monroe Beardsley.) Englewood Cliffs, N. J.: Prentice-Hall, Inc., 1963.

"Theology and Verification." *Theology Today* 17 (April 1960) 12–31.

Personal letter from John Harwood Hick, Lecturer in the Philosophy of Religion, Cambridge University, Cambridge, England, May 14, 1966.

Bibliography

Books (as Sole Author)

Faith and Knowledge: A Modern Introduction to the Problems of Religious Knowledge. Ithaca, New York: Cornell University Press, 1957.

Philosophy of Religion. (*Foundations of Philosophy Series,* eds. Elizabeth and Monroe Beardsley.) Englewood Cliffs, N. J.: Prentice-Hall, Inc., 1963.

Evil and the God of Love. London: Macmillan, Ltd., 1965. London: Harper and Row, 1966. Second edition, New York: Cornell University Press, 1966.

Books (as Editor)

Classical and Contemporary Readings in the Philosophy of Religion. Englewood Cliffs, N. J.: Prentice-Hall, Inc., 1964.

The Existence of God. New York: The Macmillan Co., 1964.

Faith and the Philosophers. (Product of a two-day conference held at Princeton Theological Seminary, December 1962.) New York: St. Martin's Press, 1964.

219

Books (as Co-editor)

The Many Faced Argument, eds. John Hick and A. C. McGill. New York: Macmillan & Co., 1967. (Old and new writings on the Ontological Argument.)

Books (as a Contributing Essayist)

"The Structure of the War Problem." *Studies in Christian Social Commitment,* ed. John Ferguson. London: Independent Press, 1954.

"Meaning and Truth in Theology." *Religious Experience and Truth,* ed. Sidney Hook. New York: New York University Press, 1961.

Essays (Selected)

"The Nature of Religious Faith." *Proceedings of the Eleventh International Congress of Philosophy,* vol. XI, Brussels, 1953.

"The Christology of D. M. Baillie." *Scottish Journal of Theology* (March 1958).

"Design and Designer." *Saturday Review* 41 (September 6, 1958) 39.

"The Systematic Theology of Paul Tillich." *Scottish Journal of Theology* (September 1959).

"Belief and Life: the Fundamental Nature of the Christian Ethic." *Encounter* (Fall 1959).

"Theology and Verification." *Theology Today* 17 (April 1960) 12–31.

"God as Necessary Being." *Journal of Philosophy,* 57 (November 10, 1960) 725–734.

"Is Religion an American Heresy?" *Theology Today* (April 1961).

"Necessary Being." *Scottish Journal of Theology* (December 1961).

"Courteous Query for Bennett and Ramsey." *Theology Today* 18 (January 1962) 503–505.

"Existence Question." *Christian Century* 79 (February 2, 1962) 166.

"A Philosopher Criticises Theology." *The London Quarterly* (April 1962).

"What Characterises Religious Language?" *Journal for the Scientific Study of Religion* (Fall 1962).

"To Believe or Not to Believe." *Saturday Review* 48 (February 6, 1965) 39–40.

ABRAHAM JOSHUA HESCHEL

Works Cited in the Text

God in Search of Man.
Man is not Alone.
Man's Quest for God.
The Insecurity of Freedom.
"No Religion is an Island."

Books

God in Search of Man: A Philosophy of Judaism. New York: Farrar,
Straus, and Cudahy, 1933. Philadelphia: The Jewish Publication
Society of America, 1956. Paperback edition, New York:
Meridian Books; Philadelphia: The Jewish Publication Society
of America, 1959. (Together the above two volumes represent
the main exposition of Heschel's philosophy of religion.)

The Earth Is the Lord's: The Inner Life of the Jew in East Europe.
New York: Henry Schuman, 1950.

Man Is Not Alone: A Philosophy of Religion. New York: Farrar,
Straus, and Young, Inc. Philadelphia: The Jewish Publication
Society of America, 1951.

Man's Quest for God: Studies in Prayer and Symbolism. New York:
Charles Scribner's Sons, 1954. Paperback edition, New York:
Charles Scribner's Sons, 1966.

The Prophets. New York and Evanston: Harper and Row. Philadelphia: The Jewish Publication Society of America, 1962.

The Theology of Ancient Judaism (Torah min ha-shamayim be-
ispaklaryah shel ha-dorot [in Hebrew]). London and New
York: Soncino Press. Vol. I, 1962; II, 1965.

The Sabbath: Its Meaning for Modern Man. New York: Farrar,
Straus, and Young, 1963. (A paperback edition of *The Earth
is the Lord's* and *The Sabbath* [two works in one volume] was
published in Cleveland and New York: Meridian Books [World
Publishing Co.]. Philadelphia: The Jewish Publication Society
of America, 1963.)

*Between God and Man: An Interpretation of Judaism from the
Writings of Abraham J. Heschel,* ed. Fritz A. Rothschild. New
York: The Free Press (The Macmillan Co.), 1965. A paper-

back edition. (An anthology of Heschel's writings containing a full bibliography up to 1965 and an introductory essay by the editor.)

Who Is Man? Stanford, California: Stanford University Press, 1965.

The Insecurity of Freedom: Essays on Human Existence. New York: Farrar, Straus, and Giroux, 1965.

Essays

"No Religion is an Island" (inaugural address given at Union Theological Seminary, New York). *Union Seminary Quarterly Review* 21, 2, part 1 (January 1966) 117–134.

HENRI DE LUBAC

Bibliography

Books (in French)

Le Fondement théologique des missions. Paris: Editions du Seuil, 1946.

Surnaturel, études historiques. Paris: Aubier-Montaigne, 1946.

De la Connaissance de Dieu. Paris: Editions du Témoignage Chrétien, 1941. Revised, 1945; second revised edition, 1948.

Corpus Mysticum. L'Eucharistie et l'Eglise au Moyen Age. Paris: Aubier, 1944. Second revised edition, 1949.

Affrontements mystiques. Paris: Editions du Témoignage Chrétien, 1950.

Histoire et Esprit. L'Intelligence de l'Ecriture d'après Origène. Paris: Aubier-Montaigne, 1950.

La Rencontre du Bouddhisme et de l'Occident. Paris: Aubier-Montaigne, 1952.

Amida. Aspects du Bouddhisme II. Paris: Editions du Seuil, 1955.

Exégèse médiévale. Les quatre sens de l'Ecriture. Paris: Aubier-Montaigne. Volumes I, II, 1959; III, 1960; IV, 1964.

La Pensée religieuse du Père Teilhard de Chardin. Paris: Aubier-Montaigne, 1962.

Augustinisme et théologie moderne. Paris: Aubier-Montaigne, 1965.

Le Mystère du Surnaturel. Paris: Aubier-Montaigne, 1965.

Teilhard, Missionnaire et Apologiste. Toulouse: Editions Prière & Vie, 1966.

Books (in English)

Paradoxes. Montreal: Fides Publishers, 1948.

The Un-Marxian Socialist. A Study of Proudhon. London and New York: Sheed and Ward, 1948.

The Drama of Atheist Humanism. London: Sheed and Ward, 1949. Cleveland and New York: Meridian Books, The World Publishing Company, 1963.

Aspects of Buddhism. London and New York: Sheed and Ward, 1953.

The Splendour of the Church. London and New York: Sheed and Ward, 1956. Glen Rock, N. J.: Deus Books, Paulist Press.

Further Paradoxes. London: Longmans, Green. Westminster: The Newman Press, 1958.

The Discovery of God. New York: Kenedy, 1960. London and New York: Darton, Longman, Todd, 1960.

Catholicism. Christ and the Common Destiny of Man. London: Burns and Oates, 1961.

The Faith of Teilhard de Chardin. London: Burns and Oates, 1965.

Teilhard de Chardin. The Man and His Meaning. New York: Hawthorn Books, 1965. (This book is identical in all but the title with *The Faith of Teilhard de Chardin*.)

Works Edited by Henri de Lubac

Blondel et Teilhard de Chardin, Correspondance commentée. Paris: Beauchesne, 1965.

Correspondance annotée de Maurice Blondel et Auguste Valensin, 3 vols. Paris: Aubier, 1965.

The posthumous works of Yves de Montcheuil, s.j. (7 vol.); of Auguste Valensin, s.j. (10 vol.).

Works Introduced and Annotated by Henri de Lubac

Pierre Teilhard de Chardin, Lettres d'Hastings et de Paris, 1908–1914. Paris: Aubier, 1965.

Pierre Teilhard de Chardin, Lettres à Léontine Zanta. Paris: Desclée de Brouwer, 1965.

Pierre Teilhard de Chardin, Ecrits du temps de la guerre (1916–1919). Paris: Grasset, 1965.

Pierre Teilhard de Chardin, Letters from Egypt, 1905–1908. New York: Herder, 1965.

(Note: The number of articles, prefaces, introductions, etc., prohibits an exhaustive list. A complete bibliography of Henri de Lubac's works is provided by Edgar Haulotte, S.J., at the conclusion of the third volume of *L'Homme devant Dieu*. Paris: Aubier, 1963. Pages 347–356.)